# Designing the Purposeful Organization

How to inspire business performance beyond boundaries

Clive Wilson

KoganPage

LONDON  PHILADELPHIA  NEW DELHI

First published in Great Britain and the United States in 2015 by Kogan Page Limited

Reprinted 2015

| | | |
|---|---|---|
| 2nd Floor, 45 Gee Street | 1518 Walnut Street, Suite 1100 | 4737/23 Ansari Road |
| London EC1V 3RS | Philadelphia PA 19102 | Daryaganj |
| United Kingdom | USA | New Delhi 110002 |
| www.koganpage.com | | India |

© Clive Wilson, 2015

ISBN      978 0 7494 7220 7
E-ISBN   978 0 7494 7221 4

---

**British Library Cataloguing-in-Publication Data**

A CIP record for this book is available from the British Library.

---

**Library of Congress Cataloging-in-Publication Data**

Wilson, Clive (Economist)
   Designing the purposeful organization : how to inspire business performance beyond boundaries / Clive Wilson. – 1st Edition.
      pages cm
      ISBN 978-0-7494-7220-7 (pbk.) – ISBN 978-0-7494-7221-4 (eISBN)
1. Organizational effectiveness.   2. Employee motivation.   3. Leadership.   I. Title.
   HD58.9.W557 2015
   658.3′14–dc23

                                                                                           2014039530

---

Typeset by Graphicraft Limited, Hong Kong
Print production managed by Jellyfish
Printed and bound by CPI Group (UK) Ltd, Croydon, CR0 4YY

# CONTENTS

## 09    A call to action    223

## Postscript: Signing off with work to do    227

# LIST OF FIGURES

# ACKNOWLEDGEMENTS

I could not have written this book without the experiences of over 40 years in the workplace, divided literally at the turn of the century between 27 years in corporate life and the more recent block in consulting. I have worked (as we all have) with remarkable people who have taught me and continue to teach me all I know. I really feel we have written this together.

In particular I'd like to say thank you and acknowledge the following people:

David Evans has contributed the extra reading at the end of each chapter. David is an avid reader and book reviewer as well as a consultant–facilitator with a wealth of experience in employee engagement. I trust that his tasters will stimulate deeper learning for you.

Co-directors Gary Edwards, Simon Tarver and Warwick Abbott contributed ideas for the activities. These guys have been facilitating engagement with leaders and teams for about a hundred years between the three of them. I am in awe and in debt.

My other co-directors, Sarah Cave, Martin Carver, Russell Evans and Tomas Hancil have reviewed drafts and given me many case studies, ideas and encouragement.

Our team in Malawi, led by Christophe Horvath and Masankho Banda, always inspire me with their music and by the work they do to serve change agents and social entrepreneurs in Africa. I first saw Masankho deliver the heart-shaped activity described on page 5 with a group of leaders under a tree in a village clearing in 2013 while Christophe strummed his guitar gently in the background. Unforgettable!

Our chairman (until he retired from our board in May 2014) and founder, John Campbell, invited me into the Primeast family and into this journey. John's compassion for the business world and for humanity in general has raised the bar for me time and time again.

Colleagues and clients, too many to mention, feature in the case studies and are the source of my knowledge. They have also read drafts and encouraged me to write this book. You know who you are and I hope you enjoy your personal copy.

Last but not least, my wife Frances, my five wonderful children, Jenny, Paul, David, Helen and Chris, and my mum, Margaret, all encourage me and provide welcome and necessary diversions from the world of work, each in their own unique ways.

# FOREWORD

I'm honoured to be writing the foreword to such a well-researched, simply written and practically applicable book by a colleague I respect as a coach, consultant and mentor. The topic of purposeful organizations is both timeless and timely. We find ourselves in a dynamic world, in which clarity of purpose has great value – for individuals, teams and organizations. Among the onslaught of demands on organizations, leaders, and employees to continue to improve effectiveness and efficiency, there are just as many management guides on how to meet those targets. For those of us charged with leading changing organizations or partnering with leaders to make strategic change, the guidance and insight of Clive's book provide a roadmap that brings together a meaningful framework, grounded in research and backed by applied models and readily applicable tools and questions to use today. Most importantly, his approach respects the fact that organizational systems comprise humans, and builds from the fundamentals: motivation, behaviour, reinforcement and inspiration.

I've had the opportunity to partner with Clive and his Primeast colleagues on a variety of organization effectiveness and organizational learning projects and collaborations. Each partnership resulted in positive organizational change as well as professional development and increased understanding for me as a practitioner. To have this level of engagement and collaboration has been instrumental for my career and the organizations I have worked in. As I finished my PhD in Industrial and Organizational Psychology at Rice University (focused on the effects of actual and perceived diversity on team functioning) I went to work for NASA just at the time of the tragic Columbia Shuttle accident. I spent those early years of my career on organizational and individual rebuilding – repairing and improving individuals, teams and the organization after a preventable error that cost the lives of seven talented and treasured crew members. Working within the organization during 'Return to Flight' and the subsequent strategic mission changes was foundational to my professional journey. With a continued interested in global organizations, I moved to ExxonMobil and spent several years working as part of their organizational effectiveness centre of expertise, and designing an integrated approach to learning. Many of the same patterns that had surfaced at NASA also emerged at ExxonMobil, reinforcing for me the importance of looking at organizations as systems while emphasizing the human science to drive strategic change. I am now working in an aerospace and international defence company, and here the importance of creating a purposeful organization is even more critical. The bringing together of stakeholder perspectives to generate a shared purpose and vision that will drive collective action and alignment throughout the organization is vital to both the industry's viability and the success of the company. Having worked in different industries, different cultures, different organizations, I know how important it is to find organizational clarity, harness synergies and create purpose.

In the opening chapter, Clive lays out the foundational definition and value generated by having a purposeful organization. As he says, 'Purpose is the force that keeps all of life growing, creating and thriving. When life steps out of line with purpose, or fails to adapt to changing contexts, unintended outcomes result. In the worst cases life declines rapidly and ultimately dies. So it is with organizations.' In addition to offering evidence of the value of purpose to organizational performance, he outlines the tenets, provides examples and gives a framework for developing a purpose. The guidance on how to help an organization get to the 'why' of its existence and be able to synergize the perspectives of multiple stakeholder views into an integrated purpose is inspirational.

From the foundation of purpose, the remaining chapters each focus on a critical element that aligns the organization to its purpose. Chapter 2 centres on organization vision, that compelling picture of the future we can each hold in our mind's eye. While each of us have probably written and been subjected to more organization vision statements than we can remember (which is telling about their power), the approach Clive describes connects vision to the day-to-day necessity for leaders to 'tell the story' in a range of ways that connect throughout the organization. The connection to cognitive science and neurolinguistic programming provides the foundation for understanding how important language choice and divergent approach are to driving alignment between individuals in an organization. Whereas I tend to choose language that is visual and want to provide a picture of what things will look like in the future, you may prefer to connect to what they will *feel* like or *sound* like when we are successful. Having worked with western scientists and engineers throughout my career, I have found they are apt to emphasise the facts and be less inclined to give the same attention to approaches based on instincts or feelings which other cultures, individuals and customers may value. As the chapter emphasizes, it is the integration of 'head, heart, gut' approaches, personally demonstrated by leaders owning and communicating the vision, that drives the powerful alignment throughout the organization.

Chapter 3, addressing engagement, is a natural extension of the focus on vision. Engagement is where purpose and vision get personal. It's human-to-human commitment. It is that connection, that engagement, that transforms purpose and vision intentions into individual actions that move the organization forward. Clive proposes four simple questions in the opening lines that frame the essence of engagement from an employee's perspective: *Who am I? What is happening? How can I serve? What is my commitment?* Answering these questions for all employees is the crux of organizational engagement. To that end Clive provides both the research basis for the value of engagement to organizational performance (including Gallup findings, learning organization models and discretionary effort findings) and a wonderful parallel to cellular biology which reinforces the natural desire of humans to engage. Through applied models that describe the various components of a learning organization, there are clear and practical examples, templates and guidance for how to work with leaders to create structured and repeated engagement that will drive organization performance.

Moving from engagement and the human commitment to organization purpose and vision, Clive focuses on the rational and logical elements of the organization: structure. This is one of the favourite tools of leaders in scientific organizations trying to make change – move the boxes on the organization chart, change the wiring diagram, put a new process in place to manage errors of the past. The insight provided in this chapter provides a compelling rationale for continued structural change and a methodological approach for identifying and making changes that align with the purpose and vision. The ten principles provided are an excellent framework to drive change in organization structure. Additionally, specific guidance provided to design within the matrixed organizations, team structures and individual networks is excellent in getting to the 'simplicity' that is paramount to effective organization structures.

Building from the other elements, Chapter 5 focuses on character. For me this is one of the most intriguing and potentially powerful elements of designing a purposeful organization. Character is behaviour – it's what we see, what people do, what gets rewarded. It's the manifestation, aligned or not aligned, of the values the organization professes to embody. We've each had the experience of being the new person and can see the anthropological signs that show everyone what is important, what the values are, what is considered normal behaviour. I started in an organization that is known for the famous Apollo-era quote 'Failure is not an option' (NASA) just after a catastrophic accident. It was interesting to be a part of this organization as it reconciled the unfortunate events with the long-standing belief that we can solve the hardest problems. As I entered ExxonMobil, the emphasis on operational excellence was evident – a focus on error detection and elimination was clear in their public signage, organizational metrics and leadership team discussions. I knew instantly in both organizations that there were values, norms, expectations reflected in the demonstrated behaviours and symbols displayed. Clive provides an overview of a variety of models and research, such as GlobeSmart, Barrett Values Center and Human Synergistics, which provide a foundation for assessing and aligning the character to purpose. However, the power of this chapter lies in the personal story of his leadership journey and his realization of how important character is to organizational success. From the leader–learner perspective, we gain practical insights, case examples and additional diagnostics that provide a roadmap for aligning character to purpose.

Linked tightly with the preceding elements is a focus on results. The adage I hear frequently in my current organization is 'you get what you measure'. There are obvious and non-obvious components to this statement, which are teased out in this chapter. The obvious, not always reliably executed approach to results is to set measurement targets with the creation of a vision. The specifics of that vision should provide direction in determining measures of success and tracking what's important. Clive articulates a multi-step process to use to establish and track results, leveraging such frameworks as Balanced Scorecard. What is not as obvious – and Clive clearly brings it forward – is the need for dialogue and interpretation of results relative to future strategy. I realize the simplicity of this statement, but it bears reflection. Results are factual; analysis and interpretation prompts decisions, direction and choice. The power lies in aligning results with purpose.

Chapter 7 focuses on success and we begin to come full circle and make a strong reconnection to the opening discussion of purpose. The duality of success – both an outcome and a sense – reminds us again of the human experience that must be considered as critical to organizational success. As Clive points out, 'success... encapsulates the whole experience and the accompanying feeling we get when we achieve something purposeful'. The guidance in this chapter is applicable to our individual lives, our family lives and our work lives. I remember a simple exercise one of my early managers did with the team that demonstrated his respect for all of us. He asked us to describe a success we had had and to share it with the team. As I listened to my colleagues from around the world, I saw similarities and differences in our definitions. Clive reinforces this perspective and encourages each of us, as organizational designers and leaders, to be clearer about our own definitions of success and increase our understanding and appreciation of others'. It's difficult to help others connect to purpose and celebrate success if we have not managed that ourselves or if we are judgmental in our views. The principles and resources provided form a robust framework to honour individual definitions by engaging with them and influencing a shared sense of success through purposeful leader, structure and process work.

Chapter 8 delves into the critical topic of talent. I appreciate the honest, positive and grounded approach that Clive takes to demystifying many of the recent management trends focused on talent which have not maximized the connection between talent and organizational purpose. Rebalancing your approach to recognize the value of competence and talent is a positive step toward an inclusive, purposeful approach to organizations. Specifically, the focus on strengths, as evidenced by the extensive findings of the Gallup organization, reinforces how important it is to take a different approach to talent in our organizations. I've had repeated powerful changes occur with teams and organizations by simply switching the language from a gap recovery focus to a strength-leveraging orientation. The seemingly simple frame of 'recognize, value, develop, use' is one that each of us should examine and consider applying to the talent in our organizations.

In the final chapter Clive encourages and challenges each of us as change agents in our families, our communities, our teams and our organizations to consider the value and impact that living and working purposefully could have. These connections make the themes and practices provided in this book applicable to a wide variety of organizational, team and community opportunities. As an organizational effectiveness practitioner I'll share this book and frequently pull it off the shelf to access its tools, links and reflection exercises. The importance of the topic and the strong theoretical and research underpinnings paired with practical resources, case examples and references make this book a go-to reference for organizational designers.

In closing, it's been my honour to share a few pages with you and provide an intro to Clive's great work. This book is a direct reflection of the calibre of expertise, insight and intensity that he and the Primeast team bring to their professional work. They are colleagues and friends that I hold in the highest esteem and I admire the positive impact that they are able to generate with organizations, teams, and leaders. I look forward to seeing the next instalment from this team that brings this capability to all of us so that we can take it forward and drive purpose, impact and value in our own organizations and teams.

Kelly Goff

*Global Organizational Effectiveness Director at Raytheon*

# Introduction: Setting the scene

## What a remarkable world

We live in a very different world to the one we inherited from our parents and grandparents. Take stock for a moment to consider how we can travel almost anywhere in the world in less than a day. We've even been to the moon and sent unmanned rockets far off into space to explore other planets. We can communicate 24/7 with people from all over the world in an instant. The goods we buy come from a truly international marketplace. Modern medicine has learnt how to cure many of the diseases that used to kill us and even to replace those parts of our bodies that no longer work. It seems we are capable of solving almost any problem we encounter.

### *Work in progress*

Nevertheless, there is more to do. Our technology continues to advance, providing boundless opportunity for a better world. We still have much to learn about how to live with greater respect for our planet, its people, its life forms and its resources. We are developing new energy sources that could ultimately power our society for as long as we have a planet that supports life. We are still learning how to live in peace with our fellow humans and how we can all avail ourselves of the benefits of a modern world.

In short, there is a great adventure to be had with plenty of work for every-one to do. We're learning all the time about how best to organize ourselves to do it and the workplace is where most of this plays out. This workplace has become increasingly global and increasingly complex, making the job of those in organization development (OD) more and more pertinent.

This book is primarily aimed at people who serve in OD and the leaders and human resource (HR) professionals they work alongside. Collectively

I shall frequently and affectionately refer to this wider group of professionals as the *organizational architects*. I realize this isn't a term in the organization lexicon but it aptly describes the collective and collaborative work the members of this group undertake as they explore and craft a workplace that truly serves the purpose of their organizations. My hope is that these people (you) will discover in this text a blueprint that is translatable for all strategies, one that will align everyone to the strategic purpose, and eliminate the blockages and blockers that inhibit performance. If you have an interest in making your organization more *purposeful* from any perspective, it is my pleasure to be 'speaking' with you.

## The purpose-driven organization

The necessary focus for all organizations these days is performance. This is often interpreted as delivering *results*. However, at the heart of this book is a profound but controversial belief that an over-focus on results is misguided and can create systemic barriers to achieving performance. As we will show in Chapter 6, it's not that results don't matter. They absolutely do. But if they become all-consuming, they will tear the heart and soul from the organization and actually damage the performance they were intended to enhance in the first place. People will become disenchanted, disillusioned, uninspired and will become victims of a results-driven mentality, potential saboteurs or (preferably) leave for more meaningful and rewarding work elsewhere.

Let us make a significant distinction. Results measure our progress to a better future. But they are not a better future in themselves. In fact, even the vision of a better future isn't what it's all about as this will morph and shift in our busy world as our context changes. The thing that really matters is our purpose – our fundamental reason for doing what we do.

So we should be wary when we hear people talk about being 'results-driven' or using macho phrases such as 'show me the numbers'. I wish I had a pound for every time I've heard these phrases used and abused in organizations.

In Chapter 1, I will affirm that for organizations to be successful, they *must* be *purpose-driven*. That is to say, they must establish compelling and inspiring reasons for their existence from the perspectives of all their stakeholders, harmonize and synergize these reasons and place those reasons at the very heart of the organization.

The challenge for the organizational architect is to systematically create the blueprint for an organization that consciously connects everything to purpose. The products of doing this are measurable results and, importantly, a felt sense of success.

## The eight conditions for a purposeful organization

The good news is that this isn't as daunting as it seems. My colleagues at Primeast have been consulting in the fields of leadership, organization effectiveness, culture change and teamwork since 1987. We have systematically and repeatedly helped our clients align the following eight *conditions* (with purpose being the crucial and conscious focus):

- purpose;
- vision;
- engagement;
- structure;
- character;
- results;
- success; and
- talent.

From this experience and the associated client successes, we have collectively concluded that the job of the organizational architect is to 'systematically establish these conditions in such a way that the purpose of the organization can be delivered effectively and efficiently'.

Everything else is a subset or reframing of one of these eight conditions. This book is therefore devoted to exploring these conditions systematically, one per chapter for the next eight chapters, in such a way that you, the organizational architect, will be better informed and equipped to design purposeful organizations that will inspire business performance beyond boundaries.

Which brings me to the subtitle of this book. Before we embark on our journey through the eight conditions, let us first delve a bit deeper into it in order to shine a big spotlight on why this subject is so important. This subtitle wasn't chosen lightly. Let's unpick it one piece at a time: *How to inspire business performance beyond boundaries*.

## *Inspire*

This book is about performance through inspiration. It isn't about cracking the whip or being ruthless. It isn't about working harder or even smarter, though either behaviour could well result. People become inspired when their very breath, their life, is aligned to something that is engaging and meaningful to them. The only thing an organization or one of its teams has that can do this is its purpose. Even the vision of a better future or the personal example of an amazing leader is really a manifestation of purpose. Somehow we have to touch the hearts of our people at a deep level if we are to truly tap into their awesome potential.

## *Business performance*

When we think of business performance we naturally think of objectives delivered or results achieved against targets. Yes, these things matter. They are the basis of the contract between employer and employee and between customer and provider. If targets and their associated key performance indicators are well constructed (as we will explore further in Chapter 6) they will guide line-of-sight performance throughout the organization in a systematic way. They will also help to keep the organization in sync and progressing collaboratively at a well-understood and manageable rate that all subsets of the organization can contribute to and keep pace with.

However, purposeful performance is even more powerful. While not taking their eyes off agreed and measurable performance criteria, purposeful individuals will literally have every cell in their body tuned to their most compelling purpose. This will inspire incredible creativity that wasn't even thought of when the KPIs (key performance indicators) were set but always in such a way that is mindful of the collective good of the organization and its stakeholders.

## *Beyond boundaries*

The whole concept of *performance beyond boundaries* is massive. Please don't mistake it for a fancy catch-phrase. It is a paradigm shift worthy of significant attention. The truth is that we inadvertently place many boundaries around the performance of our people. As we journey through this book, we'll take stock of some of them and this will challenge you to think of a few more. In addition, I offer below as a taster a couple of boundaries:

our limiting beliefs and our vitality. These are just to warm you up to the whole idea of performance beyond boundaries.

Being conscious of the many boundaries we create around performance, we can systematically design an organization with minimal boundaries which will allow inspiration derived from being purposeful to leverage exceptional performance.

## The boundaries of limiting beliefs

We are born as people with amazing potential, much of which will never be realized. From that moment we embark on our life's journey. Along the way, we receive so many, often well-meaning, messages from those we share our life with, programming us to believe we are less capable than we are. These programmes become coded into consciousness and are heart-felt.

### Opening activity: The boundaries of limiting beliefs

To illustrate this point, take a large sheet of paper. Draw a big heart on it and quickly write some words and short phrases to represent what you were told by teachers, parents, siblings, friends and others that may have reduced your confidence.

These 'who on earth do you think you are?' questions and statements have severely limited our performance. On top of this, most of us have many other limiting beliefs because of our life experiences or simply a lack of direct experience of other people's achievements that seem miraculous in comparison to our experiential norms.

The sad thing is that, having had this done to us as we were growing up, we unwittingly continue to do it to each other in the workplace.

## The boundary of our vitality

We perform at our best when we are alive and well. This may sound obvious but, if so, why do so many organizations go to extreme lengths to make their people 'sick'? Weirdly, it is often some of their best people who are the most vulnerable. They could well be the same ones that the company relies on and who work late into the evening more often than is good for them. Organizations that care about performance care about the people who deliver it and especially about their health and vitality.

# Demolishing the boundaries

We will explore many more boundaries to performance as we progress through this book. The aim is to be increasingly tuned in to the boundaries we are placing around performance in our own organizations and to take progressive steps to break them down.

Breaking down boundaries is well and good and definitely something we should seek to do. However, there is another compelling and elegantly simple way of *inspiring performance beyond boundaries* and that is to leverage the *power of purpose.* In doing so we truly engage with the energy of each individual and the context they operate in.

In my work (especially the coaching I do) and in life in general, I have discovered that when people have a strong sense of who they are, of their interconnection with others and of the context in which they find themselves, an energetic reaction occurs. I have also discovered through the work of scientists and thought leaders, such as Gregg Braden, the US author and pioneer in bridging science and spirituality, that this phenomenon can be explained through quantum physics. Contexts and connections cause feelings to arise for the individual which in turn hold vital data on how they can be of the greatest service.

As organizational architects we have the privileged opportunity to put in place the conditions for meaningful engagement. This is the fertile ground from which people can grow their sense of self, connect meaningfully with the strengths and ambitions of those around them and work out how to serve the organization in the most effective way. This drives commitment to actions that represent ever-increasing levels of performance. These actions include the purposeful demolition of the boundaries that limit what people do in the world of work.

# The style of this book

My colleagues at Primeast are experiential learning professionals and have supported me with activities such as the 'heart-shaped' drawing activity on page 5 (thank you, Masankho). They have also given me case studies, book reviews and reflections within the main narrative to ensure there is something for people with a range of learning preferences. Note that some of the case studies will name the organizations and people involved, while some remain anonymous to preserve confidentiality. In some cases, the case studies will be identified as hypothetical – but please rest assured that they are based on my or my colleagues' experiences.

You may also find that some of the 'activities' seem rather tangential. This is intentional, designed to awaken your creativity and stimulate thinking. I'm immensely grateful for the support of my colleagues in preparing both the case studies and the activities, and I trust you will find their contributions as useful as I do.

So, on with the journey.

# The power of a compelling purpose

barriers primary purpose
context-driven
COMPELLING EVIDENCE stakeholder-charters
power the anchor
line-of-sight craft PURPOSEFUL SERVICE
granularity
purposeful partnerships

*He who has a why to live for can bear almost any how.* **FRIEDRICH NIETZSCHE**

# Why are we here?

Arguably, everything in life has its purpose. Purpose is the force that keeps all of life growing, creating and thriving. When life steps out of line with purpose, or fails to adapt to changing contexts, unintended outcomes result. In the worst cases life declines rapidly and ultimately dies. So it is with organizations. Those that are purposeful have the energy to create and grow, to overcome seemingly insurmountable problems. Organizations that lose their way fragment, become chaotic and may end up as prey for predators.

---

### Activity: where did they all go and why?

Think of the household names of just a decade or so ago that are no longer with us, write their names on a sheet of paper, then make brief notes on what happened to them and why. Conduct some simple research on the internet if this helps.

To what extent was it to do with their purpose (eg a lack of purpose, an unclear purpose, an uninspiring purpose or purpose being somehow out of sync with stakeholder needs or the marketplace)?

---

A stated purpose serves to inspire and focus an organization's efforts and those of the teams and people that make up its workforce. As we shall see shortly, the power of purpose to motivate, focus energy and enhance performance is compelling. But we need to be careful. A stated purpose will also create boundaries, some of which may be helpful and some may be severely limiting.

In this opening chapter, I want to demonstrate that purpose is the most important focus for anyone in organizational development (who, to repeat, I may refer to from time to time as *organizational architects*). I shall present compelling evidence in favour of being purposeful, and examine the boundaries created by purpose or its absence. I shall explore the very nature of purpose and how it changes according to context and perspective. I shall discuss how these views can be harmonized and an inspiring primary purpose created. I shall look at the multitude of purposes that exist in an organization and how these need to be aligned to the primary purpose, taking all stakeholder perspectives into account. Finally, I take the power of purpose to a multi-organizational level by exploring purposeful partnerships before leaving you with 10 key questions to act upon as well as further reading should this be required.

Purpose is the fundamental focus of this book and thus takes pride of place in this opening chapter. The remainder of the book deals with the other seven *conditions for organizational success* (*vision, engagement, structure, character, results, success* and *talent*) which should be regarded as subservient to the organization's purpose. This mindset is key to designing an organization that is successful, sustainable, meaningful and (of course) purposeful. I trust you will find in these eight conditions for designing a purposeful organization a formula you can apply as strategists and also one that will be compelling to leaders throughout your organization. After all, they're the ones that can make this a reality.

But before we embark, I'd like to engage you in another activity that will shine a spotlight on the power of purpose.

---

### Activity: The root of my admiration

Make a note of the organization you admire the most (other than the one you work for). At headline level what is it that you admire the most about this organization? Without reference to any material, how would you describe the purpose of this organization?

Now do a little high-level research. Type the name of your chosen organization into your browser, followed by the word 'purpose'. If this search doesn't provide something informative, try similar words such as 'mission' or 'reason for being'. Then summarize the results of your search.

What conclusions can you draw about the power of this organization's purpose, making connections or otherwise to what it is you admire about them?

If you were the CEO or other leader of this organization, what would you do next?

Hold these thoughts as you continue reading this chapter.

# The evidence in favour of being purposeful: The 'Golden Thread'

In December of 2010, the Chartered Institute of Personnel and Development (CIPD) in the United Kingdom conducted a thorough study to find out whether a shared sense of purpose was useful to organizations. The survey report carries the intriguing title *Shared Purpose: The golden thread?* Note that, in common with other commentators, the research team uses the word 'golden' in association with purpose. This reflects their belief that a shared sense of *purpose* is the true identity of the organization and should be the 'golden thread' that connects all aspects of strategy. The research team surveyed over 2,000 working respondents at all levels and across three organization groups: private sector (n=1,498), public sector (n=412) and the voluntary sector (n=103).

The survey examined the effects of shared purpose on employee satisfaction, engagement and sustained performance. In the private sector, the primary perceived purpose was to do with making money and creating value for customers, whereas in the public and voluntary sectors the focus was more on benefiting society and creating shared value. However, there are some important lessons to be learnt from the survey, especially for the private sector. These lessons are reflected in the remainder of this chapter.

In a nutshell, employees, who are the ones who have to do the work, are shown to be motivated less by profit and more by being of service to customers or society. And while there is a good sense of purpose in most organizations, only about a quarter of these believe that there is a deep sense of purpose that pervades the whole organization. For the majority, the sharing of purpose stops short of the whole organization.

For organizations whose main purpose is to add value to customers, 61 per cent of respondents agreed that 'by focusing on customers, in the long run we are benefiting ourselves'; 35 per cent found their organization's customer-focused approach to be positively 'stimulating and encouraging' and 32 per cent agreed that 'it makes me want to work harder to make the customers more satisfied'.

Where profit was perceived as the primary purpose a staggering 32 per cent of respondents indicated that they were actually demotivated that their hard work and efforts were going into the pockets of investors and owners. The situation was improved when organizations had balanced the interests of all stakeholder groups, including investors and owners. We will explore ways of doing this in this opening chapter and as we journey through the book.

There is clear evidence that organizations with a sense of purpose outperform those where purpose does not permeate throughout. This outperformance is in terms of employee satisfaction and engagement indicators as well as financial and service delivery.

Another aspect of the report is the link between purpose, values and goals. We will explore these factors specifically in Chapter 5 when we examine *character* and Chapter 6 when we look at *results*. However, building on the 'golden thread' analogy, the premise of this book is that absolutely everything that happens in an organization should be consciously administered in support of its purpose.

For me the formula is simple:

Alignment = strength and focus = energy reinforced consistently = results and success

This report is essential reading for anyone seeking to design a purposeful organization. It is freely available from the CIPD website at **www.cipd.co.uk**.

## Activity: Start with why!

Now take 18 minutes out and watch a short video. You'll find it on the TED Talks website or on YouTube by searching for 'Simon Sinek TED Talks Start with why'. Simon is an author who is best known for popularizing the concept of the 'golden circle' (there's that word *golden* again) which is all about putting purpose (or why) at the centre of strategy (see Figure 1.1 below).

**FIGURE 1.1**   The 'golden circle'

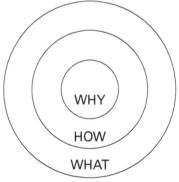

**SOURCE:** © Simon Sinek

When you've watched the video make some notes on the extent to which Simon's philosophy is in tune with the CIPD research above.

Also, make notes about the extent to which your most admired organization seems to be placing their purpose at the core of their operation.

# The power of focus

It's time to say a little bit about boundaries. My proposal is that we should put in place helpful boundaries to focus performance and remove the plethora of boundaries that hamper performance.

## 1 A deliberately constraining strategy

The first important boundary that *purpose* serves is that it is a deliberate constraining strategy. It serves to 'limit performance to a field of attention that is important to the organization and its stakeholders'. In contrast to the many boundaries that dumb down performance, the purpose of our organization is an essential and valuable boundary. It informs all stakeholders about the services the organization will provide and implies also the services it will not provide.

In ratifying the purpose of their organization, I worked with one board of directors who suddenly realized they had been doing work they shouldn't have, work that wasn't truly within their skill-set or brand promise. This work devalued the brand and damaged customer perception. Rather than thinking of purpose as a boundary, it may be helpful to regard it positively as clarifying the strategic focus.

My co-director Warwick Abbott reminds me of how the fences erected around school playgrounds provide a sense of boundary to children that enables them to explore all the way to the perimeter. Without it, most of them would feel vulnerable, concerned about getting lost and would therefore stick close to the school buildings. The minority who strayed would probably wander aimlessly, lose their focus or confidence to know where to go or even what to do when they got there. The risks are obvious.

In the same way, organizations want most of their people to explore widely within the strategic sphere of attention. The aim is to grow a creative understanding of the operation within defined boundaries such as geography, sectors, customer segments, products and services. For those who are required to do pioneering work around the edges, they must be equipped to do so in a manner that adds meaningful value to the core.

## 2 The barrier of an uninspiring purpose

A second and potentially limiting attribute of purpose is that of our language being dull, uninspiring, insincere or lacking credibility. I was recently working at the headquarters of an African revenue authority when I discovered their mission statement majestically framed in their corridors of power. It proudly boasted of how the organization would collect revenue to all the best standards of their profession. I asked the director who was showing me round how inspired she was by the statement and clearly she wasn't. I then asked where the revenues collected went and what they were used for (a *why* question). The director's face lit up as she spoke of road-building programmes, hospitals, education and so on. 'So you're in the business of funding the building of a great nation,' I suggested. She smiled knowingly and got the point. I left feeling convinced that the framed statements would soon be changed.

# Getting to the heart of purpose

As the above example shows, it is too easy to derive a bland purpose. I have experienced it many times. In such circumstances, organizations miss the opportunity to inspire their people to give their discretionary effort to the organization.

You see, we have to ask why we would want to articulate the purpose of our organization at all. On the one hand it absolutely needs to inform what we do and what we don't do. At the same time, if we really want to inspire energy and maximum performance we have to craft our statement in a way that will touch the hearts of the people we most need to motivate. There are actually some great clues to answer the *why?* question in the dictionary.

In the dictionary I use (**www.oxforddictionaries.com**), *purpose* is defined in two distinct ways:

- First, it is a noun: *the reason for which something is done or created or for which something exists* eg:
    - 'the purpose of the meeting is to appoint a trustee'; *or*
    - 'the building is no longer needed for its original purpose'
    - (usually purposes) *'a particular requirement or consideration, typically one that is temporary or restricted in scope or extent:* 'state pensions are considered as earned income for tax purposes'.
- Secondly, it is a 'mass noun': *a person's sense of resolve or determination:* 'there was a new sense of purpose in her step as she set off'.

The 'very reason for existence' description is powerful, as is the piece about 'resolve or determination'. Both aspects provide clues for maximizing performance. As the dictionary suggests, we can easily spot purposeful people. They seem energized, focused and attentive ('with purpose in her step'). At the same time they exude an air of confidence, being less affected by the trivia that gets those who are less purposeful down.

I propose that, as organizational architects, we use *purpose* with the full characteristics of its coupled double meaning:

> The organization's very reason for existence, inspiring resolve and determination from its people.

## Purpose is context-driven

What the dictionary doesn't say is that purpose is context-driven. This is vitally important. For example, when I'm at home cooking a meal for my family, my personal purpose is very different from the one I have at work. And if my carelessness created a fire in the kitchen, a very different purpose would quickly arise for me!

Because, as human beings, we move in numerous contexts, we therefore have numerous purposes – bringing up children; being a partner, friend or colleague; serving our organization and profession; and so on. Some of these purposes will come and go and some may be with us for most of our lives.

Even within the relative constant of our organization, our context may shift. As the market changes, our purpose may change. One of my clients began life making bicycles in the 19th century. The company now makes ducting for nuclear power installations. Another started as a coal merchant and transitioned into international removals and storage as coal went out of fashion.

## Purpose as a strategic anchor

Nevertheless, compared with other aspects of strategy, including the corporate vision, purpose is relatively stable. Its essence may shift a little and, as such, should be kept under strategic review but, for most organizations, the purpose may change little for many years.

This makes *purpose* the most powerful strategic anchor for the organization. It allows everything the organization does to be tested first against the purpose and then against the current vision (more of that in Chapter 2).

## *Purpose is stakeholder-driven*

As well as being context-driven, purpose is stakeholder-driven. In other words, the purpose is dependent on who is observing. For example, customers may see the purpose of the organization being about the provision of excellent services; shareholders about maximizing their investments; governments about growing gross domestic product; staff about earning a wage to provide for their families and having meaningful work to do that inspires them; and communities about providing all the above in such a manner as to maximize positive impact and minimize negative impact, for example on the local environment.

I have supported many business leaders and the best ones had a genuine care for *all* their stakeholder groups, keeping each in a sensible balance with the others. Neglecting one stakeholder at the expense of another puts the organization at risk. We only have to look at the demise this century of the many organizations that placed undue emphasis on shareholder profit, such as many in the banking sector, or directors' bonuses at the expense of the needs of other stakeholders, especially those of the customer.

So in exploring our organization's purpose, we should first take time to properly understand the full range of stakeholder perspectives and capture these in such a way that they can be shared with any party. In doing this we can note the areas of potential conflict and synergy. Exploring these matters with stakeholders is a fantastic opportunity to grow an understanding between them and craft statements everyone can be proud of. The emphasis we place on these statements will reflect the nature and priorities of the leadership. There is no wrong or right in this as balance is clearly important. Note however that this exploration could well produce a lengthy set of statements, attempting to reflect every stakeholder need and inspiring no one.

### Activity: An initial exploration of stakeholder purpose

Make a list of the key stakeholder groups associated with your organization. You might include groups such as owners, investors, leaders, managers, staff, customers, local community, suppliers, politicians. Make the list relevant to your particular context.

For now, think of three particular stakeholder groups that will have different perspectives and where you could easily have a conversation with someone who might have views typical to that group. Make a note of the three groups and your chosen representative.

Now fix a time and place to have an initial chat with these people. Maybe over a cup of tea or a bite to eat. Say that you're doing some high-level research about the focus of the organization as seen from different perspectives. Make it clear that, at this stage, this is an informal process that won't be used for strategic decision-making. When you're with each person, ask them, in whatever way makes sense, how they see the purpose of the organization from their perspective. Don't be satisfied with their initial answer. Drill a bit deeper by asking lots of *why* questions, such as: 'Why do you invest with this organization rather than another?' Or 'What is it about the technology that interests you so much?' Don't stop until you get to the heart of the matter, to the core of their purpose.

Summarize your findings, then ask yourself:

- What can you conclude about this exercise?

- What would be gained by conducting more thorough research into your organization's purpose?

- What would be the best way of going about this?

- And who should you consult with before taking action?

# Establishing our primary purpose

In crafting an inspiring statement about our organization's purpose, it may be helpful to first consider all stakeholder needs and then ask the questions: 'What is our primary reason for existence? What are we fundamentally here to do?' For most organizations the answer is likely to be about providing a specific service or set of services for a particular customer base in a cost-effective way. The reason that this purpose may well be the primary purpose is that all other purposes hang off this one. Without this purpose, there is no employment for our staff and no return on investment to our owners. It is therefore likely to be a statement that all parties can sign on to and be proud of. However, there are exceptions as we shall see with the John Lewis Partnership case study below.

The stakeholder perspectives not included in the statement of primary purpose should not however be discarded. They should be retained, and perhaps usefully articulated in the form of a subordinate stakeholder charter or similar document.

We can also ask: 'Who is it that has to provide this service?' Or more usefully: 'Who must be inspired to provide this service?' The answer will be along the lines of 'our people', meaning our whole workforce including our staff, managers and those service providers who work in partnership with us (and who are often neglected in the organizational development process).

So the *primary* purpose is likely in most cases (but not all) to be a specific variation on: (for our people) 'to provide a (valuable) service to a defined customer base'. Note, however, that it may be possible to make this purpose even more inspiring by asking further *why* questions as Simon Sinek suggests in his video with reference to Apple.

Here are a couple of examples of inspiring purposes that were both cited as great examples in the CIPD *Golden Thread* report. However, both are taken directly from the companies' websites in 2014.

**CASE STUDY 1**    The John Lewis Partnership

This first example is unusual in that the primary, or *ultimate*, purpose is actually the happiness of its members (all those that work there). Bear in mind that the members not only work for the John Lewis Partnership, but have a stake in the business too. Note how the purpose is supported by other principles that acknowledge the needs of the remaining stakeholders too. You may want to take a look at the video *Employee Ownership, A Shared Passion*, on the John Lewis website.

By the way, as I write this chapter, coincidentally BBC News confirmed the following:

*John Lewis staff get 15 per cent annual bonus*

*The 91,000 staff of the John Lewis Partnership will receive an annual bonus worth 15 per cent of their salaries. The bonus is the equivalent to almost eight weeks' pay... .*

**SOURCE: www.bbc.co.uk**, 6 March 2014

*Our principles*
*The John Lewis Partnership's seven principles define how we run our business. They are as relevant today as they were when they were set out by our founder, John Spedan Lewis, in our constitution.*

*Purpose*
*The Partnership's ultimate purpose is the happiness of all its members, through their worthwhile and satisfying employment in a successful business. Because*

the Partnership is owned in trust for its members, they share the responsibilities of ownership as well as its rewards profit, knowledge and power.

The video 'Employee Ownership, A Shared Passion', explains how our employee owned business model operates in practice, and offers insight and advice to anyone wanting to learn more about this sort of model and its benefits.

*Power*
Power in the Partnership is shared between three governing authorities: the Partnership Council, the Partnership Board and the Chairman.

*Profit*
The Partnership aims to make sufficient profit from its trading operations to sustain its commercial vitality, to finance its continued development and to distribute a share of those profits each year to its members, and to enable it to undertake other activities consistent with its ultimate purpose.

*Members*
The Partnership aims to employ people of ability and integrity who are committed to working together and to supporting its Principles. Relationships are based on mutual respect and courtesy, with as much equality between its members as differences of responsibility permit. The Partnership aims to recognize their individual contributions and reward them fairly.

*Customers*
The Partnership aims to deal honestly with its customers and secure their loyalty and trust by providing outstanding choice, value and service.

*Business relationships*
The Partnership aims to conduct all its business relationships with integrity and courtesy and to honour scrupulously every business agreement.

*The community*
The Partnership aims to obey the spirit as well as the letter of the law and to contribute to the wellbeing of the communities where it operates.

**SOURCE: www.johnlewispartnership.co.uk**

## CASE STUDY 2    Google

The purpose of Google is very simple. Note the massive ambition it conveys which must be incredibly inspiring for those involved and yet how well the organization has responded to the challenge. It is identified in its mission statement as follows:

*Google's mission is to organize the world's information and make it universally accessible and useful.*

Interestingly, if you want to discover Google's purpose from the perspective of other stakeholders you have to look a bit deeper on their website. You'll find clues under the banner *Ten things we know to be true.* Note how their owners' perspective is down at No 6: *you can make money without doing evil.*

For this company, purpose is simple but at the same time expansive, allowing for new ways of working, creativity and innovation. I really like the fact that this expansion of purpose is expressed as a set of beliefs. Also, each belief is abbreviated in its title and numbered. I have a hunch that most people in Google can tell you what they are and by number too. Here is the full set of 10 prefaced by a quoted challenge from the company to be held to account. The brief descriptions of these '10 things' are my own interpretations. For the full and latest version simply go to Google online (but of course).

*We first wrote these '10 things' when Google was just a few years old. From time to time we revisit this list to see if it still holds true. We hope it does – and you can hold us to that.*

1   *Focus on the user and all else will follow.*
    Whether it's the homepage or a new browser, Google's focus is on a clear, simple and highly functional user experience.

2   *It's best to do one thing really, really well.*
    Google's focus is summed up in their words *We do search!* This is where their research is focused and the company's aim is to bring the power of search to previously unexplored areas. Don't we know it.

3   *Fast is better than slow.*
    Again, users absolutely know how hard Google has worked to speed up browsing on desktop and hand-held devices. This helps to keep them in market-leader position.

4   *Democracy on the web works.*
    Google operates through the actions of millions of users online, posting links and defining the value of online content so others can benefit. They are also active in open-source software development that taps into the freely given creativity of many programmers.

5   *You don't need to be at your desk to need an answer.*
    Google famously pioneers new technologies to provide mobile services on a global basis. This again capitalizes on open-source software such as the Android mobile platform.

**6**  *You can make money without doing evil.*

As stated above, this is where Google confirms the stakeholder purpose for their owners. I find their honesty and candid openness refreshing. I've included their own words below for this sixth 'thing' for this reason. It also gives you an indication of the narrative you'll find for the other 'things' if you go online.

*Google is a business. The revenue we generate is derived from offering search technology to companies and from the sale of advertising displayed on our site and on other sites across the web. Hundreds of thousands of advertisers worldwide use AdWords to promote their products; hundreds of thousands of publishers take advantage of our AdSense program to deliver ads relevant to their site content. To ensure that we're ultimately serving all our users (whether they are advertisers or not), we have a set of guiding principles for our advertising programs and practices:*

*We don't allow ads to be displayed on our results pages unless they are relevant where they are shown. And we firmly believe that ads can provide useful information if, and only if, they are relevant to what you wish to find – so it's possible that certain searches won't lead to any ads at all.*

*We believe that advertising can be effective without being flashy. We don't accept pop-up advertising, which interferes with your ability to see the content you've requested. We've found that text ads that are relevant to the person reading them draw much higher clickthrough rates than ads appearing randomly. Any advertiser, whether small or large, can take advantage of this highly targeted medium.*

*Advertising on Google is always clearly identified as a 'Sponsored Link', so it does not compromise the integrity of our search results. We never manipulate rankings to put our partners higher in our search results and no one can buy better PageRank. Our users trust our objectivity and no short-term gain could ever justify breaching that trust.*

**7**  *There's always more information out there.*

This expresses Google's obsession with indexing information that wouldn't otherwise be so accessible and searchable. I'm sure we're all grateful for the way phone numbers and addresses just appear on their search pages. But think also of the books, images, videos and news archives that we now take for granted.

**8**  *The need for information crosses all borders.*

Although the business was founded in the USA, it is clearly a major global player with a global purpose. From offices in over 60 countries Google maintains over 180 internet domains and provides search in 130 languages.

**9** *You can be serious without a suit.*

Google's reputation for hard work and fun is impressive. At the one end of the spectrum are lava lamps and rubber balls and at the other is pride in team and personal achievement. They work hard at diversity and culture. True role models for the message I will be sharing in Chapter 6 when we speak about the character of our organization.

**10** *Great just isn't good enough.*

Now here's a company that truly believes in *inspiring performance beyond boundaries.* Google's opening two sentences from this 'thing' sums it all up:

*We see being great at something as a starting point, not an endpoint. We set ourselves goals we know we can't reach yet, because we know that by stretching to meet them we can get further than we expected.*

And finally, towards the end of this 'tenth thing':

*Even if you don't know exactly what you're looking for, finding an answer on the web is our problem, not yours. We try to anticipate needs not yet articulated by our global audience...*

SOURCE: www.google.co.uk

# The wider perspective

Our full set of stakeholder purposes should be in the forefront of leaders' minds as they go about their business. If we don't provide sensible returns to our shareholders, they will not invest and we won't be able to operate. If we neglect the communities we impact, we will find it difficult to operate and attract local employees. We need to have well-defined strategies for stakeholder management and they should be considered each time we review our declared purpose.

## Investing in the craft of purpose

Crafting (I use the word deliberately) the declared purpose of our organization is a real art and worthy of time and energy. We should bear in mind that our espoused purpose will have a significant impact on performance. In corporate life it is probably the most important sentence or paragraph that we will ever write.

If I wanted to define *purpose* for organizational development practitioners, it might read something like this:

> **Purpose:** a short statement that describes the fundamental reason for an organization's very existence saying what it does and who it does it for and expressed in a way that inspires its workforce and its customers. This statement should be supported by a comprehensive stakeholder charter (in one form or another) that describes the wider set of stakeholder purposes and philosophies in words that are meaningful to each stakeholder group and acceptable to (or better still in harmony with) all the other stakeholder groups.

## The power of a stakeholder charter

Giving thought to the organization's purpose with regard to each stakeholder group is both practical and profound. At the practical level, it affords everyone associated with the organization the understanding of how corporate needs are balanced. It reduces the likelihood of tensions arising due to one stakeholder group feeling they are being exploited or favoured at the unreasonable expense of another.

If we look back at the history of industrial relations, it tells a rich story of one stakeholder group feeling unfairly treated in favour of another. We see workers withdrawing their labour when it is under-valued. We see governments taking political action when an enterprise requires too much subsidy. We see business owners 'bailing out' when they can't make reasonable returns. We see pressure groups expressing their anger when an environment or community is being damaged by the undertaking. In short a balance of purpose is important and a good way of doing this is through a stakeholder charter.

## How to draft a stakeholder charter

The best way of drafting a stakeholder charter is through research, investigation and consultation. If we simply asked each group what they expect from the organization, what would delight them and when they might feel let down, the data would be immensely powerful. Failing in this dialogue means working on assumptions that could easily be misguided.

For example, staff might assume that the owners want to make massive returns so they can lead opulent lives. And they might discover that, instead, it is to provide retirement funds, health care for members of their families, investment support to other worthwhile emerging businesses, or trusts for arts, education or famine relief. The fact is, until we ask, we just don't know.

Once we know what's important to our stakeholders, we should usefully capture this succinctly in a stakeholder charter. From each stakeholder purpose, we can define a compelling time horizon and begin to establish a vision for what that stakeholder's world might look like at that time.

**CASE STUDY**   Microsoft – synergy between stakeholder purposes

To identify America's 25 most inspiring companies, Performance Inspired, Inc., a consulting and training firm that helps organizations elevate performance through the science of inspiration, surveyed 4,738 consumers.

Microsoft, the 38-year-old Redmond, WA-based software giant, returned to the No. 1 spot after a two-year hiatus. In 2011 and 2012 Apple landed at the top of the heap – while Microsoft held the No. 3 and No. 5 spots, respectively. But thanks to the company's philanthropic initiatives, passionate employees and stellar leadership, it reclaimed the title of America's Most Inspiring Company this year.

'There is clearly an emphasis within Microsoft to give back,' *Barber says.* 'In speaking with their employees, Bill Gates is often quoted saying, "we have been given much and therefore much is expected of us." What is impressive is that it is not just the Bill and Melinda Gates Foundation worthy of this reputation. The company has donated to over 31,000 nonprofits since 1983 and raised over $1 billion through employee giving. Every Microsoft employee is given the opportunity to have their personal cash contribution matched by the company, dollar for dollar, for up to $12,000. That's impressive.'

*He adds*: 'Many respondents were aware that Microsoft makes huge profits and they actually applauded because it was so obvious to them that Microsoft uses its profit and influence to help make the world a better place.'

*Lori Forte Harnick, general manager of Microsoft Citizenship and Public Affairs, says*: 'We are honored that people feel inspired by Microsoft and our commitment to making the world a better place. We strive to support a culture of giving, and we are proud that so many of our employees donate their time, energy and money to support great causes around the world. With $1 billion raised for nonprofits since 1983, we have our sights set on the future – and how we'll raise our next billion dollars to help make a difference in the lives of many people around the world.'

**SOURCE:** *Forbes*, January 2013

# The granularity of purpose

Working at the highest level, it is relatively simple to provide short statements that sum up the primary purpose of the organization. There is clearly also merit in understanding the purpose of the company from the various stakeholder standpoints. However, it doesn't end there. Without meaning to overwhelm, we should note that there should be a well-understood purpose for every entity in the business and getting those that work in the business to ask purposeful questions is a fantastic way of tuning what we do.

## *Granular purpose and mindfulness*

Understanding purpose in its granularity is a form of mindfulness. About 20 years ago I ran a revenue protection function in the electricity industry. I remember asking about the purpose of a form my staff filled in. No one seemed to know so I sought to find out. I discovered that the form did a tour of several departments before languishing in a file somewhere never to see the light of day again. I assume the data had a use once upon a time but if it did, it had long since been forgotten. So the form 'served no purpose'. Naturally we ceased to use it, saving time and energy with no material loss to the business whatsoever.

People who care about their work ask questions when they don't understand the purpose of something and curiosity often leads to improvement. What excuse do we have for not understanding the purpose of:

- company departments;
- systems and processes;
- company values and behaviours;
- job roles;
- forms;
- meetings;
- projects;
- training courses;
- PR;
- presentations;
- publications.

## *Line-of-sight*

The ultimate aim is for everyone (and everything) in the organization to be connected to the purpose of what they do, at headline level and in the granularity. Importantly they should be able to have *line-of-sight* from what they do to the purpose of the company as a whole. A purposeful organization feels joined up and solid.

---

**CASE STUDY**    Line-of-sight

In about 1990 I had to speak to a group of electricity meter readers about health and safety. We were trying to reduce accidents and also improve sickness absence at the same time. In the opening discussion, we talked with these men and women about their work. When I asked them about the purpose of their jobs, they talked about reading meters. When I asked why they did this, they said it was to collect data. Not content with the answer, I kept asking repeated *whys*. This is the chain of purpose that I revealed with each new *why*:

- to read meters;
- to collect data;
- so that we can determine customer consumption;
- so we can send bills to the customers;
- so we can run the company;
- keep the lights on for our customers; and
- pay for new equipment and the salaries of our staff.

'So,' I concluded, 'without you guys, we wouldn't have any money in the company, no one could do their jobs and nobody would get paid. Pretty crucial, eh? Let's see what we can do to make sure this team stays safe and well.'

---

### Activity: Line-of-sight

Spend an hour or so at the sharp end of your organization's operation. Find something that is done or used that intrigues you. Ask about its purpose. Ask *why* it is important to the organization. Ask *what happens next.* Follow the line-of-sight from this intriguing aspect right through to the declared purpose of the business.

Make some notes on the chain that makes up this line-of-sight. Also, what did you learn and what thoughts did the exercise trigger for you? One question to particularly ask is whether those involved at the sharp end really understood how their work was contributing to the organization's wider purpose.

---

## Purposeful teams

Even the sound of the phrase *purposeful team* is powerful. As we suggested at the beginning the dual dictionary definition for purpose gives leaders a 'double whammy' with which to inspire the listener: a 'reason for being' coupled to a 'sense of resolve or determination'.

In this book we provide all the clues to aligning absolutely everything we do to purpose for a team, an organization, a community, a nation and especially for each one of us.

---

### Activity: Purposeful teams

If you're trying to help a team establish a powerful purpose, this activity will help them determine how important purpose, process and behaviours are.

Subdivide the team into groups of about four people each with a flip chart and four pens: black, blue, red and green. Ask them to think of high-performing teams they admire and brainstorm the attributes of those teams. Get them to fill the flip chart using the black pen.

Then get them to circle all the items to do with *purpose* and *direction* with the red pen. Then the items to do with *process* and *structure* with the blue pen and the items to do with *values* and *behaviours* with the green pen.

Ask them for their conclusions. Most times, the groups will confirm that everything (or almost) has been circled in one of the colours. Some items may be circled more than once. Usually there are most items in green.

Ask them what they conclude. They will usually say that high-performing teams require purpose, process and behaviours and that behaviours are especially important and often not what they're good at.

This is a perfect opportunity to talk with them about purpose and perhaps to deal with behaviour after that.

Note how these items correspond to the eight conditions and the chapters of this book.

## *Purposeful partnerships*

In the text above, we focused on the purpose of a single entity. We have concentrated on companies but it could easily have been a team, a community or a nation. However, some of the most exciting work I have been involved with has been looking at the purpose of partnerships, such as a company together with one of its suppliers. We did this with one of the major energy providers in Europe and its industrial services provider. I found working with 10 managers from each company in one space most inspiring. I think it was the first time they had been given the opportunity for structured dialogue about the purpose of their work together. The event was kicked off with the directors of each business articulating their own perspective and then the rest of the managers working cross-functionally to create a shared sense of purpose.

## *Purposeful reminders*

It's so easy to forget why we're here and yet it can be so simple to remind people. How many factory workers get to see the end-product or better still to speak to an end-user? Where are the photographs that show our products and services being used? What about the thank-you letters from customers? Or the stories of exceptional service. These are all great opportunities to reinforce the purpose of the organization.

## Using purpose in the day-to-day

We can conclude from the above that purpose is pretty important. It is the reference point for all performance responsibility. It keeps us energized, focused and productive. That being the case, could we not make more use of it in our day-to-day lives? There is so much opportunity to reference *purpose* in our conversations. Consider simple throw-away comments such as: 'Wow, that will make so much difference to our customer' or 'That really is taking our service to a new level, let's celebrate the gains you've made'.

Every time we use language like this, we are reinforcing and reminding people of our purpose. Similarly, we can ask purposeful questions of our customer (internal or external) such as 'Was what we did for you last week helpful? Did it help minimize your down time?' Or, 'How are your patients responding to our new medication?' These are all purposeful questions. The truth is, the more we think about our purpose and those of others around us, the more purposeful and focused we become. The key is to keep our language purposeful and encouraging, at the same time taking great care not to be condescending or patronizing.

## It's all about service

Purpose is principally about being of service to others. According to Robert Greenleaf, in his book *Servant Leadership* (2002):

> The servant–leader is servant first. It begins with the natural feeling that one wants to serve, to serve first. Then conscious choice brings one to aspire to lead. The difference manifests itself in the care taken by the servant – first to make sure that other people's needs are being served. The best test, and difficult to administer is: Do those served grow as persons; do they, while being served, become healthier, wise, freer, more autonomous, more likely themselves to become servants? And what effect on the least privileged in society; will they benefit, or at least not be further deprived?

Service is a way of being. In any situation, a sense of purpose will arise which will provide clues as to how we can best serve those around us. In an organization, the aim must be to use a compelling purpose to align the service of everyone into something valuable.

# Looking ahead

In the coming chapters, we will explore how an organization's purpose should drive a *vision* to inspire everyone. We will advocate meaningful *engagement* with stakeholders to take account of their thoughts and actions. We will look at how to *structure* our organization and what it does so that it supports the purpose and enables people to feel empowered and purposeful.

We will show how the *character* of our organization can be a vehicle to deliver our purpose. We will stress that the *results* that get measured should be those that are tracking performance related to our purpose and that we need to attend to what *success* means to everyone because this is a reflection of personal purpose and where it has synergy with the corporate purpose. Finally, to get the best from those involved in delivering the purpose, we need to help them connect their *talents* mindfully to the purpose and vision of what we do collectively.

Here is a simple diagnostic to test the effectiveness of your organization's purpose.

# 10 questions on **purpose**

*To what extent...*

...does your organization have a clear sense of purpose? ☐

...has its purpose been articulated from the perspective of all stakeholders? ☐

...have the various stakeholder purposes been examined collectively to determine areas of conflict and synergy? ☐

...has dialogue and action happened to harmonize stakeholder purposes? ☐

...have harmonized purposes been summarized in a stakeholder charter or similar? ☐

...out of all the purposes, has a primary purpose been established for the organization? ☐

...has care been taken to craft this purpose in the most inspiring way? ☐

...have purposes been established for every subset of the organization: departments, divisions, teams, people and even processes? ☐

...is it easy for people to see a line-of-sight from these sub-purposes to the purpose of the organization?

...have purposes been crafted for key partnerships that the organization is part of?

## Score

| | |
|---|---|
| **0** not at all | **6** reasonably well |
| **2** a little | **8** very well |
| **4** moderately | **10** completely |

What do your scores tell you? Make a note of the implications and actions that spring to mind.

You can find further resources to support your thinking on this topic at **www.primeast.com/purposefulorganisation.**

# Further reading

At the end of this and the other chapters that discuss the eight conditions for a purposeful organization, I have included a brief summary of a further book for recommended reading. These summaries have been provided by my friend and colleague David Evans. In this first one, I love the way author David Marquet describes the leader–leader principle which is very much about getting alignment of purpose and empowering dynamic decision-making.

## Turn the Ship Around! David Marquet

The theme of this book is the change in leadership approach introduced by a US submarine captain in order to get away from the blind obedience that results from a highly directive leadership style, typical of the armed forces. His experience turned a poor-performing unit into a leading performer measured by a number of relevant indicators.

The author's essential tenet is 'Leadership should mean giving control rather than taking control, and creating leaders rather than forging followers', and it is something he terms 'the leader-leader model'. He focuses on three key areas: control, competence and clarity.

The author commences with the practice of directive leadership in the US Navy, which divides the world into two groups: leaders and followers. There is nothing inherently wrong with the leader–follower model ... except that people who are treated as followers tend to behave like followers, with expectations of limited decision-making authority and a diminished incentive to give of their best in terms of intellect, energy and passion. He concluded that competence could not rest solely with the leader but had to run throughout the organization.

David Marquet was determined to change the way things were being done on his ship by divesting control and distributing it to the officers and crew. Control is about making decisions concerning not only how we are going to work but also with what purpose. Doing this meant that some people would be expected to change their perception of their role: from a perceived position of privilege they would have to move to one with accountability, responsibility and increased workload.

One point that Marquet emphasizes is that as the level of control is increasingly divested it becomes ever more important that the team be aligned with the organization's purpose: ambiguous team goals means that devolved decision-making will be blurred.

Divesting control was an important part of developing a leader–leader approach. It was supported by two important 'platforms': competence and clarity.

When Marquet refers to clarity he is raising the issue of organizational purpose: as decision-making authority is pushed further down an organizational hierarchy, it becomes increasingly important that everyone understands what the organization is about. To do this he took the following approaches:

- Take care of your people – encourage personal growth and set personal goals; strive for operational excellence in everything.

- Develop trust – demonstrate your own trust in others and your trustworthiness.

- Leverage your company's heritage and legacy – make use of past successes to inspire the current cohort and develop a sense of pride in the organization for things done and to be done.

- Co-create a set of guiding principles ('this is the way we want to operate around here') – and then use them in everything that gets done (including personal development discussions and decision-making).

- Immediately recognize good behaviours, in the moment, as you observe them – in order to reinforce the desired way things get done around here.
- Begin with the end in mind – know the desired outcomes before embarking.
- Encourage a questioning attitude over blind obedience.

By competence, Marquet is referring to the need for people to be technically competent to make the decisions they make. He found that he could improve technical competence by engendering the following approaches in his team leaders:

- take deliberate action;
- encourage a learning ethos;
- specify goals, not methods;
- 'don't brief – certify';
- continually and consistently repeat comms messages.

Marquet concludes by warning that no two organizations are the same; so, his list of approaches was appropriate for the circumstances he found, not necessarily for everyone else's. However, the key principles of the leader–leader and devolved control concepts remain.

# Clarity of vision

sharing VISION IN LEARNING communication
language modalities clarity
ownership boundaries
focus day-to-day
alignment CASCADING
inspiration

*Life is one big road with lots of signs*
*So when you riding through the ruts*
*Don't complicate your mind*
*Flee from hate, mischief and jealousy*
*Don't bury your thoughts, put your vision to reality*

BOB MARLEY, *WAKE UP AND LIVE!*

# Defining vision

We have spoken about purpose, the fact that we and the organizations we serve have multiple purposes, that these are contextual and can be prone to shift. Having said that, *purpose* is by far the most stable thing around which to design our organization. However, purpose tells us why we're here – but it doesn't tell us where we're going. For that we need a vision.

---

### Activity: What is vision?

Check out the definition of the word *vision* in your favourite dictionary. You will probably notice several definitions for the use of the word as a noun and as a verb. As you explore the definitions you may find some of them obviously fit into an organizational development context. But don't immediately dismiss the others; think expansively about how they might be applied to your operation. Make some notes.

---

I hope that, like me, you found this exercise stimulating. Some of the definitions in my dictionary, such as 'being able to see' are obvious. And I guess 'being able to think about or plan the future' resonated too, especially when coupled to the use of imagination and wisdom. There's also the 'mental image of what the future will or could be' which tells us a little bit about how a vision arises.

Vision is also described as 'seeing something in a dream or trance' which is really important too. On many an occasion, I have been doing something away from my work environment when a vital piece of my future simply appeared as if from nowhere. Many leaders I speak with tell me their vision arises in the most unusual situations such as while walking in nature or driving their cars – and yes they also reference dreams they have had too.

I wonder what you thought about a vision as 'a sight of immense beauty'. Perhaps like me you initially dismissed this as irrelevant to the workplace. But what could be more beautiful than an inspiring image of what our future might be like?

Then there is vision as a verb, a process of 'imagination'. I was actually surprised to discover little reference to 'visionary' as a derivative, despite its prolific use in the subject of leadership.

For me this little exercise taught me something about the immense power of vision to literally see the future in our mind's eye. We do well to remember that most accomplishments in the world of work are first made in the mind before any physical manifestation. As well as using *vision* to describe the big strategic picture, we might also bear in mind that it is equally applicable to the many times people at the sharp end of our operations 'see a better way' of doing something. For it is the cumulative effect of many people discovering better ways that enables our better future to emerge.

In the traditional strategic sense, a vision informs us and others what something will look like at a particular time horizon. For organizations, the time horizon is important. I encourage leaders to focus on a time that has some special meaning, such as just before flotation, but it could equally be the end of the next year, five years' time or, as was the case for one of my clients, just the other side of Christmas. To determine the time horizon, I ask about key events that may be approaching or about how far ahead the leader dares to look. Usually they have a sense of the most powerful horizon. Asking a leader what they can see at that time horizon brings clarity and detail to the journey that lies ahead. As we shall discover, this will also add meaning to others as it is shared and discussed and the views of others integrated.

The ideal vision will reference all aspects of the organization at the intended time horizon, including some sense of the size of operation, geographical reach, technologies, customers, markets, services, products, processes and structures, and equally the people dimensions such as behaviours and the talents people will be bringing to the operation.

Most of all, the vision should be inspiring and have the scope for others to engage with it in such a way that it can grow and motivate those that need to deliver it. And just as all the stakeholder purposes described in the previous chapter need to supplement the primary purpose, a similar approach may be used to condense the vision into a brief inspiring summary that captures the hearts and minds of those involved.

The initial vision of any leader might even be regarded as a hypothesis for testing and may be presented as a possible future that others have the opportunity to challenge and build upon. As more people buy into the vision, the chances are that some aspects will become stronger and less up for debate. However, a good leader will always be open to the thoughts of their followers and a good organization will establish appropriate conditions in which this can take place constructively.

**Activity: Summer holiday**

Think about your next planned family holiday or other event that will involve a number of other people. Spend time with each of the people involved and ask them to imagine the holiday in their mind's eye. Ask them what they see happening and how they feel about it. Ask them what excites them most and to describe it in as much detail as they can.

Make notes on your conversations with them all and then compare their responses:

- To what extent were the descriptions similar?

- In what ways were they different?

- How can you share these visions to enrich the holiday for everyone?

- How can you plan the holiday to take account of these insights?

## What we focus on is what we get

Back to the world of work. The scope and power of organizational visioning is immense. In the previous chapter we identified that each stakeholder group has its own unique purpose. Simply asking what this should look like at a certain time horizon will cause a 'vision' to arise. Try it and see. Ask anyone to name something that's important to them: perhaps their career, their family or life in retirement. Ask them how far ahead they dare look or what time horizon is important to them. Ask them what they *see* (I use this word deliberately). People vary in their abilities to see the future so you may need to support them in some considerable soul-searching and deep exploration. With suitable encouragement, however, the chances are that they will quite quickly begin to *see* something inspiring. This may be practical or aspirational and, whatever the case, it should be important *to them*. The chances are they will *see* something they haven't seen before, especially if you notice that they are clearly excited about something, and ask them to say more. The key is to elicit a deeper journey that engages both logic and emotions.

The vision can be made more compelling by asking more questions such as: 'How do you feel about that?', 'What first steps do you need to take?', 'What does that give you?' or 'What's important for you here?'

Even without a plan, this vision will begin to work its magic. Those who share in the vision will notice things associated with it. Their subconscious will make connections, causing ideas to pop into their heads at convenient times to guide their actions. This is the real power of the law of attraction.

Think of it like this, the more we share our vision, the more others can support our journey. There is every possibility that a corresponding vision will arise for them that has synchronicity with our own. This is how the ripples of a better future spread.

## Activity: Corporate meditation

If you're looking for a reasonably quick group exercise that demonstrates the power of a vision and premonition to a group of leaders, this is a great little exercise to try. I've used variations on this theme in all sorts of environments from business owners to school children. I never cease to be amazed by the results. Perhaps try it first with a small group of people you trust.

Ask for a volunteer who is prepared to share their sense of future with others. Depending on the setting, you may wish to bring them out in front of the audience. Ask them to sit comfortably. Suggest to others in the gathering that they might also close their eyes to join the volunteer on their journey. It's more powerful if they do but it doesn't matter too much if some people decide not to. As facilitator of the process you may also choose to close your eyes.

Take the volunteer through some brief and simple breathing or relaxation sequence of your choice to help them relax and to clear their minds of noise that would impede the vision. Ask them to acknowledge the others in the room and then ask them to let those thoughts fade. Ask them to identify a time horizon that is important in the context of their work. Tell them that this time has arrived and ask them to take us to the heart of the organization and describe it to us. Then ask them to explore this place and just go with the flow, asking questions about what they see, hear, smell, feel and notice generally.

When a suitable time has elapsed, thank them and gently bring them 'back to the room'. After the exercise, be sure to gently coach the volunteer by asking them what they thought of their new insights, whether this was new or previously known and, importantly, what they need to do next. Then make notes on the exercise.

*My own note:*

> *I did this exercise about 10 years ago with participants at a conference for the Confederation of British Industry (CBI). A lady volunteered and 'took us' to the entrance of an impressive headquarters which she described in detail, even down to the glass pyramid above the door. She took us into reception and around the offices, describing what people were doing, the technologies being used and even the views from the windows. There was a railway station visible from one window and woodland through another. After the exercise, I asked her if she had ever been to this place and she confirmed that she hadn't. In fact she had no idea where it was. The amazing thing was that a man in the audience put his hand up and said he knew exactly the place she had described. I suggested the two of them might have a conversation. Sadly I lost touch with the lady, so I can't confirm what future actually emerged for her. I hope she reads this and gets in touch with me again.*

## CASE STUDY   Steve Connolly

Steve Connolly is Chief Operating Officer (COO) at Cape plc, global providers of intelligent solutions for industrial services. I truly believe Steve's success is largely down to the clarity of his vision. I had the good fortune to engage with Steve when he was Cape's UK Onshore Director. He knew then that he was spending far too much time with his managers helping to solve their problems. He had a vision of halving this time by getting his managers to take greater ownership. In this way, he could be more strategic and invest more time with his key customers.

From this insight we were able to explore what his management team needed to look like and how they in turn could give Steve the headroom he needed. This enabled us to work with them to co-create their future and take collective ownership for delivery of the vision. My work with Steve shows that engaging others with one aspect of someone's vision deepens the initial power and enables things to happen. Also, we can note that the sharing of Steve's vision grew a more expansive, relevant and powerful vision in the minds of his managers.

# Where to start?

We can see that the vision of an organization is complex. Visionary leaders have their take on the future and create an initial frame of reference, often at a high level. It's like sketching the outline for a masterpiece. As others engage with the sketch, the dialogue between them adds colour and detail. In reality, no one owns the whole vision and it is always fluid, growing with every conversation. This is probably why many organizations adopt an aspirational vision such as 'to be the best provider of....'. This may be helpful as it focuses minds on a simple statement, but it doesn't create that rich, defining picture of what the operation needs to look like at a given time horizon. And if we don't know our destination in practical terms, how can we plan the journey? More of that later.

The place to start for me is to use the passion of the leader to inspire those on the receiving end to grow their own vision in those aspects of the work that need their attention. In most cases, this will be about the provision of better, more efficient services or products to a growing and satisfied customer base and the conditions necessary to support this.

I once worked with a CEO whose focus was almost entirely on the bottom line. I was preparing him to address his senior management team and, sensing a less than inspiring outcome, I simply asked him what he talked about to prospective customers and the senior people he was trying to recruit to the business. His focus quickly shifted to the technological solutions his business provided to customers and he became quite animated. That, I suggested, should be the primary focus of his address to the management team.

What you focus on is what you get, so when this CEO focused on customer service and engaged his management team in this vision for the future, they too saw opportunities to serve the customer better. This is naturally good for performance, the bottom line and return on investment for the owners of the business. Furthermore it is achievable without demotivating the workforce through an over-focus on profit for business owners. In short, the primary focus should normally be on service first. This enables other purposes to be met in tandem.

# The most inspiring visions

As a facilitator of strategic alignment workshops, I have had the privilege of preparing a platform for many CEOs and MDs to address their people. Sometimes I get to help them craft the sharing of their visions. On one occasion,

I awoke at 3 am before a CEO's opening address with a powerful intuitive insight that what he was about to say would not support the prospect of improving the performance of his business. I wrote some thoughts down and gave them to him before breakfast. With just a simple shift of focus, and while still remaining authentic, he incorporated the suggestions into his own words and passion to inspire his people to be of the greatest service to their customers. There is considerable value in leaders sharing their keynote speeches to stakeholder groups with other people they trust and respect to make sure they achieve maximum impact.

The best visions are usually where leaders tell stories of outstanding service and share a vision for more of the same. Or where they marvel at the technologies they provide and what they could do for mankind. Steve Jobs of Apple was a master at that. Or where they are seeking change in a particular aspect of what their people do to serve others.

## My top 10 visions

In my work, I continue to be impressed by the visions of organizations and of their leaders. Here are 10 headline examples that I have found powerful for a variety of reasons:

- A COO who knew his business would 'struggle to get through the winter' painted a picture for the following March which was about resolving significant challenges and getting a better understanding of the business processes.

- A CEO of a charity that provided housing and employment for people with learning disabilities showed photos of some of the people they had served, smiling in their new homes and jobs, and asked why anyone would not want to see more of the same.

- The HR director of an African revenue authority (mentioned earlier) painted the picture of building an economically more prosperous country with schools, hospitals and roads for the people. And of a country with a growing number of entrepreneurs all contributing to the economy.

- A director (Steve Connolly) who wanted half his time back to grow the business had a vision of self-assured managers working together to run a safe, efficient and customer-focused operation.

- A scientist who had developed a cancer treatment that was about to go into clinical trial firstly shared how he had dedicated much of his life to its development, then described what bringing this drug to market could do for patient care, quality of life and saving life.

- A country director of a global organization that provides learning opportunities for people in regions of tension talked about creating 'magical cultural moments' where people from different cultures learnt or worked together and told some powerful stories of the impact this already had on families and communities.

- A vice-president in a global pharmaceutical company focused on the *how*. She had a powerful belief that if her people focused on *how* they worked together (not just *what* they did), the already good performance of her team could become great.

- An MD of a fabrication company saw 'pride in manufacturing' at the heart of his city's community, with the families of his staff being proud to be associated with a successful company with over a century's heritage.

- A CEO of a West African federal road maintenance agency shared a vision of 'perfect roads'. At first I thought this was going to be 'pie in the sky' until he went on to say exactly what this meant and convinced his management team that it was not only achievable, but the *only* thing that made sense.

- A CEO of a professional services institution saw and emphasized the link between the high standards of professionalism the institute supported and the lives that would be saved as a result in the health service.

**CASE STUDY**   Whole Foods Market

In case you're thinking that a vision has to be succinct in order to be powerful, think again. Whole Food Market Inc, with stores in the USA, Canada and the UK, is a US food supermarket chain specializing in natural and organic foods that first opened in September 1980, and is headquartered in Austin, Texas. Whole Foods Market is a great example of a company with a vision that is openly purposeful on a number of fronts. Its corporate narrative begins with a set of core values which reflects all stakeholder purposes and then unfolds into a vision that can be explored at a high level or deeper if the reader is so interested.

*Core values:*

- *We Sell the Highest Quality Natural and Organic Products Available*

- *We Satisfy, Delight and Nourish Our Customers*

- *We Support Team Member Excellence and Happiness*

- *We Create Wealth Through Profits & Growth*

- *We Serve and Support Our Local and Global Communities*

- *We Practice and Advance Environmental Stewardship*

- *We Create Ongoing Win-Win Partnerships with Our Suppliers*

- *We Promote the Health of Our Stakeholders Through Healthy Eating Education*

Each of these values is further explored on the company website but note how even the headings are carefully crafted to show how the needs of all stakeholder groups are respected and delivered. These values combine purpose with values in an effective way that suits this particular organization.

Now examine the way these *purposeful values* morph into the compelling company vision, described below. The opening summary text is only the tip of the iceberg. Each of the principles beneath it (shown as bullets) is further explained in more detail on the company website and can be examined at deeper levels for those that are interested. Note how this vision is aiming for the realization of a better future. It is inspiring and looks beyond the mechanics of the business into the wider world and the influence this company will have on it.

*Sustainability and Our Future*

*Whole Foods Market's vision of a sustainable future means our children and grandchildren will be living in a world that values human creativity, diversity, and individual choice. Businesses will harness human and material resources without devaluing the integrity of the individual or the planet's ecosystems. Companies, governments, and institutions will be held accountable for their actions. People will better understand that all actions have repercussions and that planning and foresight coupled with hard work and flexibility can overcome almost any problem encountered. It will be a world that values education and a free exchange of ideas by an informed citizenry; where people are encouraged to discover, nurture, and share their life's passions.*

*At Whole Foods Market, we are starting to implement this new vision of the future by changing the way we think about the relationships between our food supply, the environment, and our bodies.*

- *Holistic Thinking in a Conventional World*

- *Actions for a Sustainable World*

- *Healthy Foods and Healthy Products Begin at the Source*

- *Sustainability Beyond Organic Food*

- *Respect For All Forms Of Life*

- *Education and Public Participation*

- *Regulation, Enforcement and Accountability*

- *An Invitation to Join Our Vision*

- *Our 2012 Green Mission Report*

**SOURCE: www.wholefoodsmarket.com**

# Sharing the vision

When leaders share their heartfelt views of the future with those around them, the vision can only grow. As people listen, the spoken word either resonates or causes dissonance for them. If people truly belong to a shared journey, there will be mainly resonance, with additional images being conjured up in their minds. If they do experience dissonance, this should still stimulate conversation through which a better understanding can emerge for everyone. However, it is also worth remembering that if dissonance persists after appropriate dialogue, this might mean that those who find themselves 'out of sync' would be better aligned to another cause.

When I'm facilitating strategic alignment, I like to give a leadership team the opportunity to clarify their leader's vision through questions. But I always like to provide individual reflective space for them to allow a deeper, more personal vision to arise. Using nature as a setting for this is particularly powerful. On one leadership workshop in Malawi, a senior manager was moved to tears. Not only had some compelling insights arisen in his mind's eye, but he also reflected that he hadn't taken time to sit on a hillside and gaze at the distant horizon since he was a boy. People don't forget experiences such as this and it is all part of making the vision powerful and anchoring it in memory.

Once personal visions have become clear, there needs to be time to share. I am always amazed at the degree of synergy when we afford people this opportunity. It's as if they are all viewing something that is truly going to manifest but through slightly different lenses. Leaders often ask what might happen if people have diverse views of the future. The truth is that this seldom happens; after all they've been travelling a shared path for some time already. When it does happen, there is the potential for rich creativity in exploring that diversity to define a better future they could all buy into.

Too often, leadership teams believe that visioning is what they do on a strategic away-day. I like to remind them that this is just one step along the journey. Also, the vision is never 'complete'. Firstly, there will only have been a limited number of people in the workshop together. What about everyone else: managers the next tier down, those on the front line, suppliers, customers and other stakeholders?

## Vision in the day-to-day

Good leaders realize that their job is to bring the vision alive day by day, conversation by conversation, as well as through the corporate brand.

Remember the African revenue authority? Well, imagine the power of having inspiring photographs in the offices and corridors of a country developing infrastructure for its people. Imagine them celebrating the successes of entrepreneurs. Imagine powerful stories in the national news. This is how true visions arise.

In our organizations, every time a manager asks a team member 'what would a better way look like?' or 'how would you like us to deal with this in future?' a vision of a better world is born. Imagine a culture where, instead of arguing, we exchange our future perspectives. What a great way to work and live.

One of my clients attributed the theme of 'right first time' to his vision for the future. He engaged a marketing team to talk to the people in every workspace to ask them what 'right first time' means to them. From these conversations, the creative people in the marketing team produced posters for each workspace as a constant reminder of a vision that has begun to grow for the people there.

## Be inspired but don't get carried away

I always get excited when I get a new insight into a potential future. Just ask anyone in our leadership team at Primeast. However, here is a note of caution that I have learnt the hard way. If you are working with vision your-self or supporting leaders to do so, it's good to recognize the process in play. Visioning is essentially a creative process and it is important to distinguish between a firm premonition and one of many possible scenarios. Creativity is great but it should be recognized as such, especially in a group setting. Once the creative process (divergent thinking) has run its course, there needs to be some grounding. This can be done easily in a facilitated group setting. However, if it is you or a leader you are supporting, I encourage an ensuing dialogue where the vision can be challenged or evolved. It is vital that the ground rules for this are made clear. The vision holder is wise to say what support they need. Is it someone who will build on their ideas or someone who will challenge them?

There is also the danger of visionaries getting carried away. For example, getting too excited can easily turn people off, especially if they just can't see the same future. Similarly, it is too easy to overuse the word *vision* and often better to make conversations about the future more natural, especially in the day-to-day. The chances are that the more natural our conversations are about the future, the more compelling they will become.

# The language of vision

Note that the concept of vision is essentially visual so the language we use is likely to be in terms of 'looking ahead', 'what do we see', 'what would it look like', 'imagine a world where...' and so on. As described above, use of im-agery in any way is likely to stimulate and reinforce the vision.

**CASE STUDY**    Tan Tock Seng Hospital – Vision 2016

Asia Ability specializes in creative team events around the Asia Pacific region. On a number of occasions interactive, experiential team events have been fully customized for clients who are communicating a new or revised organizational vision.

Tan Tock Seng Hospital is a large private hospital in Singapore with a very forward-thinking management team. Together, they conducted various idea-generation and-collection initiatives in order to focus in on a three-year vision for the hospital. The launch of this vision was conducted in a spectacular fashion with

120 of the hospital senior management and staff fully engaged in a vision-focused three-hour team event called The Big Picture.

The group was divided into work teams, each of which was responsible for the painting of two artist's canvases with a pre-drawn design outline. Each team had some of the required information for successful execution but part of the information about the colours for their design was held by other teams.

As well as sharing information and supporting other teams, this cross-team collaboration proved particularly successful when the same colour flowed through a number of different team canvases, with one team taking responsibility for mixing that colour and sharing it across the other teams. After two hours of hard team work the teams took a break while the Asia Ability facilitators assembled the final masterpiece behind a black curtain.

With the whole team gathered, the CEO dramatically revealed The Big Picture which had been carefully designed to depict their Vision 2016. Each one of the team members had painted their part of the overall vision picture. The following day it was hung in the hospital as a powerful daily reminder for everyone of the vision and their vital role in creating and living it.

## What if we're not visual?

The science of tuning in to different senses and being conscious of this in our dialogue is known as neurolinguistic programming (NLP). It is a very effective approach to communication, personal development and psychotherapy and was created by Richard Bandler and John Grinder in California in the 1970s (source: Wikipedia).

NLP teaches us that people operate across a range of modalities: visual, auditory and kinaesthetic being the main ones – although I have also heard leaders talk about 'sniffing out a good deal' and 'enjoying the sweet taste of success'!

People have their modal preferences and, while talking vision with people who are visual is easy, we also need to cater for those for whom the visual is a less preferred modality. We can often recognize these people by the language they use. So if we pick up auditory language such as 'that sounds like a plan' or kinaesthetic as in 'the future feels good to me' we might do well to engage in dialogue using the same modality.

## *Leading with head, heart and guts*

Linked to the NLP, these days I am hearing more and more about 'leading with head, heart and guts'. It acknowledges that we do well to listen to intelligence arising from each of these centres. Our heads help us to work out rationally what the future needs to be like. Our hearts desire a better future and produce a powerful emotional stimulus. And we know in our guts (intuitively) what course of action we should be taking and the risks we need to take and manage.

Again, people tend to have preferential tuning to one of these intelligences. It is helpful and possible to acknowledge and train in all three, serving at least two useful purposes. First, it makes sure we don't miss valuable data. Secondly, it allows us to test data from one intelligence source with data from the other two. In my coaching work I often encourage leaders to explore the future with a different intelligence source to their preferred one. Typically I find many managers lead from their heads and miss massive opportunities to tap into their hearts and guts. So when a leader suggests they can see two possible futures, I might ask which they feel in their guts would be the right one. Or I might ask them which path their heart is telling them to follow. Changing language in this way can either help decision-making (in a convergent way) or open new possibilities (in a divergent way).

In 2006, leadership experts David Dotlich, Peter Cairo and Stephen Rhinesmith, who teach and coach CEOs and executive teams throughout the world, published their book *Head, Heart and Guts*, suggesting that leaders need to be skilled in the use of all three of these intelligence sources. They argue that to be successful in a complex, matrixed, fast-moving world, 'whole' leaders must set strategy, develop trusting relationships with others, and consistently do the right thing based on personal values.

We're all different in how we combine the use of our head, heart and guts. I've tried to be mindful in tracking how I use these intelligences. It may be a generality but I think I tend to operate in the sequence of heart, gut and head, followed by second check of gut and back to heart again. It's a bit like this: on exposure to a stimulus a feeling arises (heart) which I intuitively sense a need to act upon (gut). I mentally work out what I need to do, checking in with my intuition along the way. At the point of commitment my heart must still be in it or I know I shan't deliver.

## Activity: How do your head, heart and guts work together?

Think through a time when you committed to an important action of your own instigation. How did the initiative arise? How did you decide it was important? What determined the action you took? And how did you know it was the right decision? What continued to inspire you to deliver?

Whichever intelligence is drawn upon, it is still worth asking what the future would look like if it was acted upon and capturing this picture in one way or another, especially for the many people who need a picture to move forward.

# Owning the vision

Leaders who own the vision are much more convincing than those who constantly refer to the organization's vision or their boss's view of the future. So in developing a purposeful organization (given that vision is the playing-out of purpose at a particular time horizon), there must be opportunity for each leader or manager to engage with the corporate vision and work out what it means in the context of their own work. The easiest and quickest way of doing this for a group of leaders is in a workshop environment as it brings people together in one shared space. However, it could also happen individually through the stimulus of a progressive performance review. Note my use of the word 'progressive'. Creative visions are unlikely to arise from the punitive criticism of the past which sadly characterizes so many performance review conversations. However, with skill, constructive criticism can be a powerful stimulus for future thinking.

Whichever method is used, it will probably be an organizational development, human resources or communications professional that designs the process to cascade the vision, initially developed by the senior executive team, to other management tiers. The challenge is to give everyone the opportunity to work out what it means to them so they can internalize it and engage with others. This may seem like a tall order for the leaders and managers to deliver but imagine the power of every member of staff having a compelling and deeply personal sense of future to talk about with customers, suppliers, friends and family.

Vision becomes powerful when it is naturally embedded in the stories people tell about their work.

## Contributing to the vision

A learning organization is one where every attempt is made to examine what the organization does, find better ways, continue to improve and consolidate best practice into the 'way things are done' procedurally and behaviourally. So a *purposeful* learning organization is one where this is done consciously to support a well-understood organizational purpose. In such a context this relentless testing and improving of what gets done is bound to affect and contribute to an emerging vision.

There is, however, a danger that learning will not consciously be fed through to those who formally serve as guardians of the vision (usually the executive or strategic planning team). This needs to be managed carefully to keep key people in the loop at an appropriate level of detail.

There is, therefore, clear benefit in establishing a mechanism that allows people to contribute on a day-to-day basis to the vision of the organization. In most cases this will probably be done in teams and fed up the organization through its management infrastructure. But these days technology offers unlimited opportunity for engagement with vision.

Technology giant Microsoft claims that 72 per cent of businesses are deploying social media tools internally to harness information, connect and work together in new ways. It is not hard to envisage how social media can be specifically channelled to share and grow the vision. The key is to explore the vision, see how it plays out around the organization and contribute thinking and discussion. This could be a powerful mechanism for growth of vision. There will be a natural tendency to involve managers and staff but it is certainly also worth considering how to engage other stakeholders, including customers and suppliers.

## Vision in learning

Every time people meet in an organization, there is opportunity to remind them of the vision and consciously engage with it. Good leaders do this automatically and the example that springs to mind is our own MD at Primeast. Russell Evans takes almost every opportunity to reference conversations, thoughts and ideas to our vision. For example, when we were asked to deliver the opening keynote at the American Society for Training and Development (ASTD) conference in Houston in 2012, he immediately and explicitly connected it to our growth plans to extend our service to oil and gas clients, support our US delivery team and share some of our latest thinking. This was a conscious threefold reinforcement of our company vision and he didn't use the word vision once.

Learning events are special times to connect with vision. Too often, learning seems to take place in a context that is separate from the needs of the organization. Coincidentally, often these programmes also assume that people know very little about the subject they have come to learn. Good learning events honour the people in the room, acknowledging that collectively they may know more about the subject being discussed than the subject matter expert. They also position the learning in the context of the purpose and vision for the business and reference the learning to the vision consistently. In this way, they not only make the learning relevant, they also help to support the strategic alignment of the organization. Finally, I believe that the best learning (in the context of any subject) allows people to apply their learning to the resolution of the most important and relevant challenges that need to be overcome in the delivery of the organization's vision. Each learner should leave the learning workshop with a new explicit commitment that will support the more efficient delivery of the vision together with some sense of the value this will add.

## Learning topics that will specifically support vision

From the above thinking, I propose that, for absolutely any topic, learning can be linked to the vision and focused to support its delivery. For example, good health and safety training will clearly support the delivery of a safe and healthy workplace which is a key part of the vision for many organizations. But there are some topics and learning events that are more directly related to strengthening the vision and especially leaders' capacity to engage others with it. Here are a few examples.

### 1 The annual conference

Many organizations have an annual conference of some kind. Typically these events provide the leaders with an opportunity to celebrate the successes of the past and the heroes that contributed to it, reinforce the company purpose and inspire people with their latest vision. The best ones not only cascade the vision, they offer real engagement with it so that everyone, including the leaders themselves, emerges more visionary and more inspired.

### 2 Strategic alignment events

Unless everyone in the organization gets to attend the annual conference, there needs to be a way of further sharing and engaging with the vision. This is best done in a systematic way so that leaders at all levels get to engage with their teams right down to the sharp end of the organization. In my experience, this is also a great opportunity to combine the alignment process with learning and development and cultural change.

## 3 Strategic leadership programmes

Strategic leadership is a key skill for any leader, manager or supervisor. Of course it plays out differently at different levels in an organization, but every leader needs to be equipped to understand the nature of purpose and vision generally and specific to the organization. They need to be able to see the future from the perspective of all stakeholders and through the lenses of different scenarios as discussed earlier. They also need to know how to engage others in events such as those described above and in the day-to-day. Strategic leadership is often learnt in a separate space to strategic planning and scenario planning but it should be remembered that a leader's job is also to provide both direction and structure to those they lead and therefore planning tools are very much part of the strategic leader's toolkit.

## 4 Presenting, persuading, influencing and inspiring

Anyone who needs to inspire others in the future of the organization (which to me includes at least every leader, manager, supervisor and internal service provider) needs to be equipped with these key communication skills. The precise needs will vary according to the individual and their context.

## 5 Performance appraisal and career development

We touched on performance appraisal briefly when discussing the ownership of vision. Rather than seeing the appraisal as a correction process, it might better be regarded as a meeting of minds to provide a shared understanding of what should happen in the coming period. The manager has a real opportunity to engage with the employee and ask them where they would like to be in a year's time or indeed any point in the future. There is a clear link here to career development and it is recognized that many organizations have separate processes for this such as independent career coaching. The point is that development settings such as these are perfect opportunities to facilitate a convergence of perspectives (vision from different viewpoints) – those of the organization, the manager and the employee.

## 6 Leadership development

Leadership development takes many forms and most organizations run multiple programmes for leaders at various levels and for the future leaders of the organization. In the best examples, this suite of programmes will be joined up in such a manner that makes sense without too much duplication of content between programmes. That said, I can't imagine any leadership development programme that doesn't teach the art of visioning and offer opportunity to engage with the vision of the organization in an appropriate and relevant way. Given that leadership development is likely to be a key feature of the organization's learning agenda, consideration should be given to how it can support strategic alignment. It could easily save time and effort rolling out the vision through other media.

A few years ago, one of my clients came with a shopping list for culture change, leadership development and change management. We conveniently agreed a way to do all three in an integrated manner, under the guise of leadership development, with the company vision at the heart of the programme.

## 7 Relationship building

Leadership happens always in the context of relationships. There are the explicit relationships between the formal roles of leader and subordinates and there is also a complex and reciprocal leadership that plays out as people work together in pursuit of a better future. In the latter, one person may take a leadership role in one set of circumstances and happily be the follower of someone else when the circumstances shift. For this to work well, the quality of relationships is a critical factor. It will determine how easily people will co-operate to share and deliver the vision. In fact, conscious and persistent collaboration regarding a desired future can be a very powerful stimulus to improving workplace relationships.

I once worked with the senior leadership team of an institute that served the medical profession. Their job was to facilitate professionalism in such a way that related directly to saving lives. Relationships were not good in this team but the way we facilitated an improvement was not to tackle the relationship issues head on. Instead we engaged around purpose and vision, raising the importance of their work far higher than some of the personal differences that had previously got in the way.

## 8 Masterclasses

I have seen a growing trend recently in masterclasses for leaders and managers but they still seem to represent a very small proportion of the learning offering of most organizations. Masterclasses expose leaders and managers to the latest thinking in subjects that will challenge and develop them. As an example, relating to vision, how many leaders in your organization get exposure to a professional futurologist? Every time I hear from an inspiring futurologist my mind becomes full of ideas for the future of the work we do. I feel compelled to share these insights with colleagues.

As with all learning, it is wise to make sure there is opportunity during or after the class to make sense of the learning, share insights with others and make appropriate commitments to transfer the learning to the workplace. We'll say more about this in the next chapter as we explore how learning can work in the context of a learning ecosystem.

# Aligning perspectives

There is no right or wrong way to align the perspectives of individuals to one shared sense of future, but the ideal outcome is where all stakeholders of the organization have a real sense of the organization's future that is aligned to the corporate strategic direction. This does not mean everyone will see it the same way. This is impossible. Everyone should be able to articulate what the future means to them and this should be aligned to the shared and espoused strategic direction. We call this line-of-sight (to both purpose and vision). Also, people should appreciate and respect the views of others, especially those from other stakeholder groups. It is worth considering what opportunities there might be for customers, suppliers, shareholders, leaders, staff and community representatives (in varying ways and combinations) to exchange ideas for the future in a constructive manner.

An unwritten line in every manager or leader's job description should be to provide opportunity for their people to share future perspectives. Organizational development professionals can encourage and facilitate this engagement, whether day-to-day, or at workshops or through printed or online media. The stronger the shared sense of future, the more purposefully aligned people will be and the more chance there will be to leverage and align high performance. In this respect, it is really important that communications consultants, trainers, facilitators and coaches have a good understanding of the corporate purpose and vision in order to make sure the focus is kept aligned in all interventions.

## The vision facilitator's toolkit

Facilitating the development and sharing of vision is one of the most satisfying jobs I get to do. Over the years, I have drawn on an array of tools and modalities. Here are just a few of them which can and should be used independently or concurrently to suit the context.

# 1 Visionary interviewing

Before exposing a leader to any workshop or other event where they will present or discuss their vision, I like to spend time with them in an interview. Sometimes the organization will record these interviews on video for use later. If this is going to happen, I still like to have a warm-up chat to agree the ground we might cover.

In interviews of this nature, questions and prompts will probably bounce back and forth between purpose and vision and may cover the perspectives of different stakeholder groups. I consciously try to make sure the interview is balanced and inspiring. The leader may have a tendency to focus on one aspect of the business, such as the finances, but I try and steer them onto the most inspiring topics. In our opening chapter we spoke about the primary purpose of the organization and said it was probably about a group of people providing a set of services to a customer, ultimately serving a useful purpose for humanity. This is likely to be a great focus for the vision interview. As the interview progresses, there will often be merit in enquiring about *how* services will be delivered at important time horizons. This was particularly important for one vice-president in a pharmaceutical company who made the *how* of the future the majority of her conversation. This was deliberate as she was trying to influence more productive behaviours going forward.

# 2 Scene-setting at events

Facilitating vision work is often done in the context of conferences, workshops and learning events. Setting the scene is a critical tool. Choosing an inspiring venue is essential. I encourage the leader to welcome people and set the tone of the event and later, when I ask them to share their vision, I set the scene carefully. Usually leaders like to stand and become quite animated. However, I've also used fireside chats to good effect. At one of my most memorable events I acquired an old leather armchair, stately and relaxed at the same time. The CEO, who would normally stand and present, relaxed in the chair and shared a few thoughts and photos on a big screen. His presentation moved his people to tears. I have learnt that when hearts are engaged in this way, distractions begin to fade away, creating a trance-like calmness in the room from which the facilitator can launch the rest of the learning programme.

At another workshop, it was important to present a shared vision from the senior team. Here I conducted 'thinking rounds' with the team in advance of the workshop. In the first round, each member of the team got to say what they saw at a 2019 horizon. In the second round they commented on what was powerful in what they had just heard. Later in the day they were joined by managers from the next tier. Having had the thinking rounds as warm-up, I was now able to stage a panel interview with the whole senior team in front of their managers. Both exercises were video-recorded for future leadership needs, including training, recruitment and induction.

The key is to set things up in a manner that is congruent and authentic for those involved. The style of delivery needs to reflect their personal character and values with due respect for the audience and its needs.

## 3 Reflective space

Earlier we spoke of using the outdoors, especially places with a view, to create reflective space for vision work. I've used hillsides, lakesides, parks, rooftops and balconies. The key thing is to be creative and use whatever is available in a manner that suits the characters of those involved and which will serve to inspire them.

## 4 Active space

There are many ways to give people the opportunity to share the vision that has arisen in their mind's eye following engagement with their leader. The most common one is to get people to write insights onto separate sticky-notes and post them to a wall. This makes it easy to cluster the notes to form an affinity diagram. In small groups, this may be replaced by dialogue in the form of thinking rounds or similar. Consideration should be given to blending energy and learning styles. Active engagement of the group doing something physical together in this way works well after the reflective space described above.

## 5 Anchoring in art

Once a shared vision emerges and becomes clear, it is great to anchor it through some combination of words and art. Tan Tock Seng Hospital, mentioned earlier, is a good example. The art could be posters, collages, sculptures, music or drama. It all depends on the available time and the appetite of the group.

## 6 Storytelling

This is a much under-valued tool for visioning work and for leadership in general. As well as being a multi-dimensional image, a vision can become a story. In difficult change scenarios, I encourage the leader to make sense of the past and present in a way that doesn't alienate those involved in the journey so far. Even if the organization is in a bad situation, the leader's job is to present compelling evidence to explain the past and present and then inspire them with a believable promise of a better future. Learning the skill of storytelling can be a fun and inspiring activity and is invaluable for equipping leaders to align their people's efforts to the job in hand.

## 7 Eight optical lenses for exploring possible futures

I love the idea of looking at the future through different lenses. This always gives us deeper insights from which a strategy can evolve. There is no limit to the variety of lenses we can 'wear' but here are my eight favourites to begin with:

- stakeholder lenses (one for each stakeholder group);
- personal lens (for any individual);
- preferred future lens (the future we want);
- expected future lens (the future we expect);
- the surprise lens (the future we least expect);
- the carry-on-regardless lens (if we don't change);
- the doom lens (the worst case scenarios);
- the utopia lens (the best we can imagine).

Imagine the fun people at any level of the organization could have in groups looking through these different lenses. Maybe they could even invent some of their own. There is of course the usual health warning with any creative exercise that stimulates vision. Care must be taken to determine the scope and permission for people to determine their own futures. If the scope is limited, people could become excited about possibilities one minute and feel shackled and disempowered the next.

# Capturing vision at the workplace

We tend to be good at this when we do it at formal workshops. But what about the power of vision that simply arises in people's minds as they live their lives? At the very personal level, I use a notes app on my smartphone to capture every single insight I get for the future. I suppose the work I do has trained in me a deep awareness of the power of vision and intuition. So if a thought for the future arises, I always ask myself when this will happen. I then make a corresponding note alongside other notes for that year. If there is something I can do immediately to create a chain of events leading to the visualized event, I either do it straight away or make a note to do it on a particular day. This action could be as simple as sharing the idea with someone else.

---

### Activity: Capturing the vision

Think about how you get insights about future scenarios. How do you record and explore them? Make some notes.

---

**MINI CASE STUDY**    Work of art – creating a visual reminder of the scope of operations

---

A family-run care service asked all of its stakeholders including carers, service providers and those receiving care to complete four-inch square tapestries depicting the work of the service. These were all sewn together to form a massive blanket that hangs proudly in the hallway of their day centre.

---

As our vision arises we begin to see the power in what we have created and continue to create. The stronger our vision is and the more widely we use it, the more it serves our purpose. I'd like to move on to discuss a few ways our vision might be used.

## Cascading the vision

This is probably one of the most obvious uses of the organization's vision. In the traditional sense, what often happens is that the vision is agreed by the board members and it is then cascaded down through the organization. Clearly it is good to share the vision but the manner of doing this can be much improved with engagement at each level.

So, in a traditional hierarchy, the vision at the top level can be shared at the next level down. It is important to remember that each department, division or function will be more affected by some aspects of the vision than others and that for these aspects they will have much to add to the picture shared 'from above'. Good leaders will recognize this and adjust their account of the vision to suit the audience. It should be remembered that in any one account, it is impossible to share the whole vision because it is (*a*) probably too big and (*b*) probably a bit unclear around the edges. So the leader will probably provide an overview of the big picture, drawing attention to those parts they believe will be of most interest to those they are in dialogue with. It is good to acknowledge that those on the receiving end will have ideas of their own, about any aspect of the vision as told and especially about the future of the particular work they are involved with.

This is where real engagement is powerful. After a leader has shared their version of the vision, it is good to provide opportunity for their audience to engage with it (see Figure 2.1). Some people may need some time to reflect

**FIGURE 2.1**    Cascading the vision

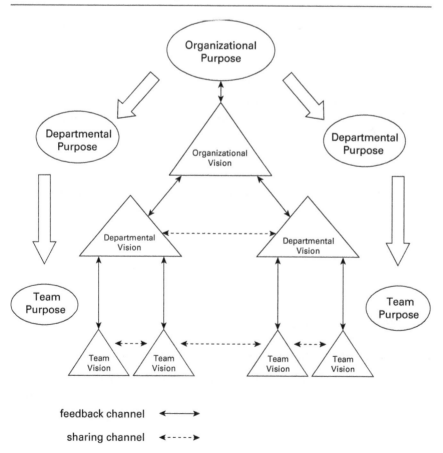

alone and others will want to discuss their thoughts in small groups. The facilitator may want to provide space for both and to use the various techniques as described above to share emerging perspectives, giving people a chance to explore synergy and difference within the dialogue.

## Internal communications, marketing and public relations

We've already touched briefly on the power of storytelling by the leader but this can be vastly supplemented by corporate storytelling in words and images. There may be merit in getting a team of professionals on the job. Or if that isn't practical, a team of enthusiastic volunteers from the workplace who take responsibility for making it happen. They can always be supported by professionals as appropriate.

Unleash your team of journalists on every event where vision is being shared, co-created, worked upon or delivered. Capture what is said in words, photos and videos. Use this to create great stories and other content. One of our clients is planning a workshop where the future is being discussed and shared. They've already booked cameramen, photographers and journalists. The workshop will culminate in people saying what the future means to them in teams and as individuals. They will discuss the strengths they bring to this vision and make commitments (aligning their strengths to the vision). Each commitment will be a reason for one of the journalists to later come knocking at their doors asking for evidence, updates, stories and more pictures. The more these stories get reported, the more the vision gets a life of its own. It also makes managerial follow-up on promises easier as the journalists will already be promoting and paving the way.

Most organizations' communications teams will have a strategy that guides the stories they tell. Clearly the organization's purpose, vision and associated success stories are crucial.

## Being mindful of the boundaries of vision

While acknowledging the inspiration a vision can bring, it is important to remember that a vision can also be limiting especially if we don't refresh it. A clear and compelling vision provides us with a real picture in our mind's eye of what the future might hold. It can be used to galvanize the efforts of a whole team, organization or even a nation. However, the vision is never as powerful as the purpose that lies behind it. The great thing about keeping a vision alive, co-creating it with those around us, is that it will grow as our world develops around us.

We do well to remember that the dreams we have today are sufficient to set us in motion towards a better future. But we should also always remember that tomorrow will bring new dreams that should continue to steer our journey.

To close this chapter, test the effectiveness of your own organization's vision.

# 10 questions on **vision**

*To what extent...*

...does your organization have a clear and compelling vision that reflects its purpose as seen by all key stakeholder groups?

...have key stakeholders had the chance to discuss and contribute to the organization's vision?

...have all leaders, managers and supervisors had the opportunity to discuss this vision and work out what it means in the context of the work for which they are responsible?

...have leaders had the opportunity to test and develop the organization's vision by looking at it through a range of creative and stakeholder lenses?

...is the organization's vision tested and refreshed as appropriate on a regular basis and when there is a significant shift in the organization's context?

...have all staff, in their teams, had the chance to engage with the future of the work they do, how it supports the organization's purpose and vision and how they can support its delivery?

...are visual reminders used to reinforce the vision and how it plays out in the organization's workspaces (physical and virtual)?

...is the vision of the organization referred to as a reference point at key strategic, problem solving and learning events?

...have people at all levels had the chance to explore the synergy between their talents, their careers and the future of the organization?

...is there a day-to-day mechanism for anyone to contribute visionary thoughts into the strategic planning process of the organization?

## Score

| | |
|---|---|
| **0** not at all | **6** reasonably well |
| **2** a little | **8** very well |
| **4** moderately | **10** completely |

What do your scores tell you? Make notes about the implications and actions that spring to mind below.

You can find further resources to support your thinking on this topic at **www.primeast.com/purposefulorganisation**.

# Further reading

David's book recommendation for this chapter on vision is a compelling read. I like the way Billy Beane has a vision about the use of results or data on talent to drive a winning performance. It neatly combines the threads from a number of chapters of this book.

## *Moneyball: The art of winning an unfair game,* Michael Lewis

The story of Billy Beane and the unlikely rise of the Oakland A's baseball team under his coaching auspices may seem like an unusual book recommendation in this business environment. However, this best-selling book not only encapsulates the power of visionary thinking; it also demonstrates in simple and encapsulating terms the effectiveness of using relevant metrics, deploying human talent optimally and developing a compelling team structure and character.

It was the success of mavericks like Billy Beane – alongside the development of data-management tools and ever-increasing computer capacity – that has led to the now-everyday use of sporting statistics. Back in the 1980s and 1990s, the use of metrics to select and develop teams was almost unheard of. Beane had the vision and conviction to use data to do this, with extraordinary results.

This is a fascinating, exciting and heart-warming account of how one man and his carefully selected colleagues upset the odds; and many of the doyens of an established 'industry'. The lessons contained within are applicable to all organizations and they involve thinking the unthinkable and the art of the possible.

# Engaging to create a learning ecosystem

*You've got a song you're singing from your gut, you want that audience to feel it in their gut. And you've got to make them think that you're one of them sitting out there with them too. They've got to be able to relate to what you're doing.* JOHNNY CASH

## A declaration

Sing the right song, in tune and with passion. Help others to sing with you in perfect harmony in their hearts and minds and out loud.

**Activity 1: Dan Pink's video on 'Drive: the surprising truth about what motivates us'**

Before you launch into this third chapter, I invite you to take some time out. Grab your tablet, computer or smartphone and check out this RSA Animate video by Dan Pink based on research done at the Massachusetts Institute of Technology (MIT) on motivation. Just type the above title in the YouTube search field and you'll be there in a second.

Make a few notes about what you learnt on the subject of engagement.

**Activity 2: The engagement mind-map**

Alternatively, if you prefer to do something more hands-on, try this yourself or, better still, with someone you know.

Think of something you really enjoy doing or really care about. Take a sheet of paper, the larger the better. Write the title of this 'something' in the centre. Now create a mind-map by thinking of all the things you do to engage with this topic. Perhaps you read books, go to events, talk with friends, practise and so on.

Now begin to trace these activities and events back towards their source. Who introduced you to them? Who or what encouraged you to attend that event? Who bought you that book? Be as creative as you can in exploring connections and recording them on your map.

Now make notes on the conclusions you can draw from this exercise, especially about the complexity of engagement.

# Evidence that engagement makes good business sense

## *Engaging for success*

Here in the UK, as the global economic recession began in 2008, our then Secretary of State for Business, Innovation and Skills, Lord Mandelson, commissioned a report, *Engaging for Success*, to find out whether engagement strategies could impact performance in our workplaces. (The report can be downloaded from tinyurl.com/nz6mbks.)

As you might guess, the findings were a loud yes. As Tim Besley, leading economist and member of the Monetary Policy Committee put it, 'There is an increasing understanding that people are the source of productive gain, which can give you competitive advantage.'

The report concludes that positive engagement strategies do impact performance significantly. Not only that, but the effect on the lives of those at work is described as 'transformational'.

## Gallup study on employee engagement

Now let's go to the USA. Further evidence for engagement is found in the Gallup report on *Employee Engagement*, subtitled *What's your engagement ratio?*

Gallup's employee engagement work is based on more than 30 years of in-depth research involving more than 17 million employees. This research has appeared in many business and scientific publications, including the *Journal of Applied Psychology* and the *Harvard Business Review* and in its best-selling books *First, Break All the Rules* (Buckingham and Coffman, 1999) and the sequel *12: The Elements of Great Managing* (Wagner, 2007).

The 12 core elements that the Gallup research identifies as those best predicting employee and workgroup performance are as follows:

1 I know what is expected of me at work.

2 I have the materials and equipment I need to do my work right.

3 At work, I have the opportunity to do what I do best every day.

4 In the last seven days, I have received recognition or praise for doing good work.

5 My supervisor, or someone at work, seems to care about me as a person.

6 There is someone at work who encourages my development.

7 At work, my opinions seem to count.

8 The mission or purpose of my organization makes me feel my job is important.

9 My associates or fellow employees are committed to doing quality work.

**10**  I have a best friend at work.

**11**  In the last six months, someone at work has talked to me about my progress.

**12**  This last year, I have had opportunities at work to learn and grow.

As for the conclusions, I quote Gallup:

> Research shows that engaged employees are more productive employees. They are more profitable, more customer-focused, safer, and more likely to withstand temptations to leave the organization. In the best organizations, employee engagement transcends a human resources initiative – it is the way they do business. Employee engagement is a strategic approach supported by tactics for driving improvement and organizational change. The best performing companies know that developing an employee engagement strategy and linking it to the achievement of corporate goals will help them win in the marketplace.

Gallup has found that world-class organizations have twice the proportion of engaged people than the average. Disengagement hits the bottom line significantly, costing $300 billion in US lost productivity alone. Earnings per share are 3.9 times higher in organizations with world-class engagement than in those with lower levels of engagement.

You can find the full report at the Gallup website: **www.gallup.com**.

So engagement really, really matters. Yet, despite evidence on the value of engagement, my experience is that when organizations claim to focus on engagement, too often they do little more than conduct an employee engagement (or opinion) survey. Yes, this is a form of engagement but it is only the beginning of the journey. A well-constructed survey will give lots of clues as to how engagement could be better. The hard part is making the change. To put it another way, is the engagement purposeful, do people learn as a consequence, and is the ensuing learning applied in a constructive and sustainable way? We'll pick up on this cycle of *engage – learn – apply – sustain* (which we call ELAS) later in this chapter.

Another thing to remember is that 'employees' is just one stakeholder group among many for a typical organization. We drew attention to this in the opening chapter when we acknowledged that the purpose of an organization will be seen differently through different stakeholder lenses. So the challenge is to make sure there is *purposeful* engagement within and between **all** stakeholder groups.

---

### Activity: Testing engagement first-hand

Next time you visit a commercial premises, such as a shop, a restaurant or an office, spend a little time with one of the front-line staff. Ask the shop assistant, waiter or receptionist what sort of a day they are having. Follow the energy or your intuition to find out more about their workplace. How long have they been there? Do they like it? What's it like to work there? What are the company's plans for the future? Perhaps enquire how they get together with other staff at team meetings or annual get-togethers. You might even throw in some of the questions suggested by Gallup above. Then make some notes on the following:

- What did you learn about how engaged they are?

- What ideas did this give you for your own workplace?

## CASE STUDY    What's in it for me?

A few years ago I had the privilege to interview Octavius Black, founder and CEO of Mind Gym. We were discussing the subject of talent liberation. Octavius is an amazing storyteller and I'll never forget the story he told me of how he developed coaching skills with supervisors working for the Royal Mail in the UK. In dialogue with his client he deduced that the supervisors were not likely to be terribly receptive to coaching their colleagues but highly receptive to helping their children and other family members with homework and life skills generally. So the intervention they did was explicitly aimed at helping the 'posties' with coaching in their families, with the added benefit that it might also be useful in the work context.

Watch the interview now on YouTube by searching for 'Octavius Black philosophy on talent'.

There are important lessons in this simple case study when it comes to engaging people in the purpose and vision of the business. Certainly it will be easy if the direction is inspiring as discussed in Chapters 1 and 2. But it will be significantly more powerful if there is a win–win for those involved. The win could be a practical win such as is the case for many managers I work with who feel under pressure to do more and more with less and less time. Helping them engage their teams has the significant benefit of giving them headroom to be more strategic and play to their personal strengths. The other classic win is the alignment of personal ambition with those of the organization. The more synergy that can be found between what the organization wants and what individuals want, the more likelihood there will be of improved performance.

# Engagement lessons from the natural world

I'd now like to give you a short break from the workplace for a few minutes and offer you a brief science lesson. My hope is to explain why engagement is essential and to suggest that we can learn a great deal from the natural world in terms of how to design and embed sustainable engagement practices in our organizations.

In almost 30 years of service, Primeast has become convinced that there is something natural and compelling about the way successful organizations grow in support of serving the perceived purposes of their stakeholders. About 10 years ago, this natural growth insight was intuitively reflected in the Primeast brand with imagery taken from examples of growth in alignment with the Fibonacci progression. (The Fibonacci sequence is a mathematical progression where each number after the first two is the sum of the previous two: 0, 1, 1, 2, 3, 5, 8, 13, 21 etc.) An example is the nautilus shell on the front cover of this book. Since that time we have learnt more about the way life develops and organisms grow. We have discovered that there are critical patterns that play out in single-cell organisms that are reflected in more complex life forms such as humans and further reflected when these complex life forms group together to form communities, whether these be teams, organizations, communities or humanity.

The term for the way things play out in similar ways at different levels is 'self-similarity' and the mathematics behind self-similarity is 'fractal geometry'. A fractal is a self-similar repeating pattern in which, no matter how much the observer zooms in or out, the patterns they see will be similar. There are thousands of inspiring fractal image examples on the internet.

So, life is indeed fractal in nature and, if we understand how single cells work and what happens when they group together, we can be usefully well-informed to make teams and organizations effective and efficient.

In exploring the lessons we can learn from cells, I have been fascinated by the work of scientist Bruce H Lipton PhD (**www.brucelipton.com**). In his books *The Biology of Belief* (2005a) and *Spontaneous Evolution* (Nith Bhaerman, 2011), and his audio book *The Wisdom of Your Cells* (20056), Dr Lipton describes the lessons he has drawn from his work as a stem cell scientist. These lessons are crucial for understanding the behaviour of humans and communities of humans. Much of what follows is derived from the work of Dr Lipton and others, for which I am most grateful and inspired.

There are some key ingredients about cell life that correspond directly to the chapter headings of this book. This is absolutely no coincidence.

1  Cells serve a *purpose*. Primarily this purpose is the growth, reproduction and enjoyment of life itself. As cells have divided, this purpose has increased to include co-operation with other cells to enable multi-cellular life to thrive.

2  Cells have a sense of future. They have the capacity to learn what will support growth and act in support of this better future. With the evolution of consciousness, humans and communities of humans are able to truly see this future in the form of *vision*.

3  Cells *engage* with their environment and with other cells. This is a critical insight. Every living cell has receptors and actors that provide two-way communication. They perceive information and act according to this information using the programmes in their DNA as a prescription to their behaviour which can be modified as their perception of the environment changes. This insight is a key ingredient in the development of the efficient learning ecosystem we will discuss below. Note that when cells learn something useful for their future wellbeing, they don't waste it; it is stored in both the DNA of the cell and, at human level also, in our subconscious mind. Purposeful organizations do the same by consciously learning, retaining and deploying valuable insights. In other words, they don't waste learning or constantly reinvent the wheel.

4  Cells form *structures* to support their collective evolution. They also master processes and behaviours that enable them to work together. These key processes and behaviours determine the *character* of the cells and their clusters (such as in a particular organ) and are recorded in the cell DNA to support efficient reproduction, including cell succession (to conveniently borrow a term from our people-management lexicon).

5  When cells are unable to perform their functions, they die and are adequately replaced by other cells that can do the work in hand at

least as well, if not better. In this respect, it might be considered that cells monitor progress and act according to the quality of *results* and *success* factors in order that life can thrive. Note the similarities with organizations where people come and go but the organization thrives as long as its functions are monitored and sustained through 'new blood'.

6  Finally, as multi-celled organisms have evolved, they have learnt to share duties in a way that supports life on a greater scale and complexity. Cells in our brains play to their 'brain' strengths while those in our livers play out a very different role. This is despite the fact that scientists can now grow both liver and brain cells from the same stem cells. The similarities with how organizations can best manage *talent* are striking and vitally important in designing a purposeful organization.

Note how the above features of cells (life at its most basic level) are reflected in the wider content of this book which I have proposed as a blueprint for designing a purposeful organization. Note also how the features can be extrapolated into complex organisms and communities of organisms.

This is why the eight *conditions* discussed in this book so conveniently describe, and can therefore test the elements of, a healthy living entity at any level (the principles of fractal design). In the work of organizational design we are particularly interested in helping individuals, teams and organizations to thrive productively in support of shared purposes.

## Cells naturally learn and evolve

Note that in our initial description of cell life, there was more than a hint of learning and evolution. Cells are designed to evolve. In other words, they learn how, through engagement with their context, they can improve their associated structures, processes and behaviours.

At the most generic level, cells are engaged in continuous improvement with the singular purpose of enabling life to thrive. With multi-cellular organisms, because life's duties have been shared, so too have the purposes of individual life forms. So a particular life form will have a particular purpose which is a subset of 'enabling life to thrive'. And, in the same way that many similar cells come together as the organizations we call organs, we humans also form organizations to serve a particular purpose in the service of our species.

Within our organizations, as they grow in size and complexity, so their functions divide and form teams of an increasingly specialist nature. Such is the fractal nature of life and the teams, organizations and communities we are all part of.

# Cue the 'learning organization'

So, clearly, evolution is all about learning. And with billions of years of experience to draw on it would be remiss of us not to learn from life itself when we facilitate learning in our organizations.

Not surprisingly, organizations that learn effectively are nowadays known as *learning organizations*. My colleagues and I have great respect for the work of thought leaders such as Peter Senge and others who have described the features of a learning organization. In particular we encourage our clients to align their learning at every level with the purpose of the organization.

At the corporate level, this means having a culture of enthusiastic learning and a desire to be critical of process and behaviour in order to find the best way to undertake work. It means steadfastly recording the best way to do things and embedding this in our corporate DNA (taking a convenient term from cellular biology) through knowledge management and cultural management. Unlike less evolved organizations, these organizations comprise people who are happy to have their ideas scrutinized without taking personal offence.

The way this cycle of learning and evolution plays out is described in the SECI model in Figure 3.1, articulated by Nonaka *et al.*

- **Socialization:** Practices (processes and behaviours) that are socialized in the way things are done are learnt on the job.

- **Externalization:** These practices are described in writing or verbally, which creates learning in both the describing and the sharing.

- **Combination:** As practices are shared, critically compared and integrated, further learning evolves and a best practice (at that time) results.

- **Internalization:** When the best practice is taught to all who need to know and embedded into operations, the learning cycle is complete. However, it should be noted that learning doesn't end here. Rather, a new SECI cycle begins to ensure continuous improvement or evolution.

By the way, do you notice the similarity between the spiral of growth in learning in the SECI diagram and the nautilus shell on this book's cover?

**FIGURE 3.1**    The SECI model

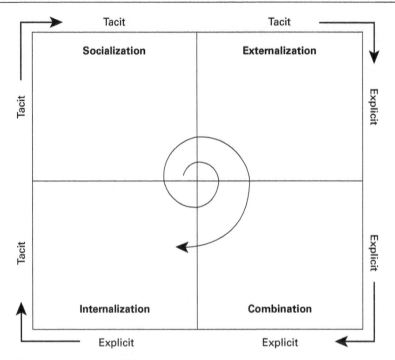

SOURCE: Nonaka and Takeuchi (1995)

This is no coincidence. Life learns and grows in a continuously evolving manner, physically and intelligently.

## A learning ecosystem

The narrative above describes the operation of learning at the corporate level. For an organization, this is the highest level of what could be regarded as a *learning ecosystem*. However, given the fractal nature of life, of which organizations are part, we need to explore lower levels of this learning ecosystem and explore how people learn collectively in organizations. It will be no surprise to discover striking similarities between how organizations learn (SECI) and how individuals learn.

## Learning cycles

Kolb and others describe how people learn from doing something, reflecting on the outcome, drawing conclusions and evolving a theory which can

**FIGURE 3.2**    The learning cycle

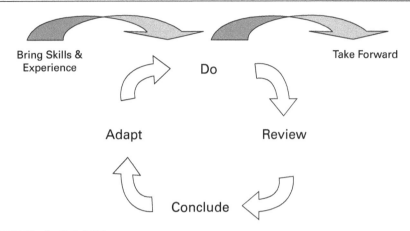

SOURCE: after Kolb (1983)

inform future actions. Note the similarity in concept between this and the SECI cycle from the theory of learning organizations. The strength of SECI is the emphasis on corporate sharing and combining learning; whereas Kolb's personal focus reminds us that learning is always cyclical in nature and that we each have preferences regarding how we like to learn (see Figure 3.2).

## Engage–learn–apply–sustain (ELAS®)

Primeast's own learning framework, ELAS®, developed by Warwick Abbott, describes how the learner must *engage* with the need for learning and then *learn*. Also that the learning must be *applied* and *sustained* (see Figure 3.3). ELAS resonates strongly with both SECI and Kolb. Its strength is that it simply and elegantly roots the driver for learning in the workplace, takes the learner through relevant learning experiences and application and makes sure learning is sustained in an effective manner.

There are other models that similarly emphasize the need for engagement and learning transfer, such as the 6Ds® method favoured by many of our clients and which Primeast supports through associated interventions.

The 6Ds process is defined in the book *The Six Disciplines of Breakthrough Learning* (Wick *et al*, 2010). Will Thalheimer called this 'the most important book in the workplace learning field in the past decade'. Dr Thalheimer is a learning expert, researcher, instructional designer, business strategist, speaker and writer who has worked in the learning-and-performance field since 1985.

**FIGURE 3.3**   The ELAS model

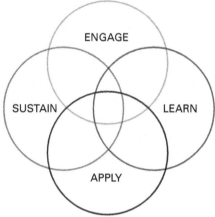

**SOURCE**: © Primeast, 2009

The 6Ds are the six disciplines practised by the most effective learning organizations:

D1: **Define** business outcomes

D2: **Design** the complete experience

D3: **Deliver** for application

D4: **Drive** learning transfer

D5: **Deploy** performance support

D6: **Document** results

# Purposeful engagement in learning

If you believe, as I do, that life is essentially purposeful, then we would naturally conclude that learning should be equally purposeful. *Purposeful learning* is designed consciously to fit the above concepts and to add value in the most efficient way to the organization. In a nutshell, I would suggest that purposeful learning can be described as follows:

> A learning intervention that affirms (within the context of a particular subject or challenge) the strengths of those involved and the real challenges they face now or in the future; that gives the learner the opportunity to experience the need for leaning and equips them with the necessary tools to tackle the challenges that lie ahead. The learning will include the application of the tools in such a way that firm commitments can be made to apply the learning in a productive manner back at work.

In this way we can see that, from the perspective of the organization, learning isn't complete until it is applied, embedded and sustained.

Note also that the learning isn't fully sustained until it is embedded into the DNA of the organization, in other words, it must be embedded in the structures and character of the organization so that in future the new ways are the norm and old ways discarded. In the early days of such an evolution, the change will need to be conscious but, with time and practice, the new way will become subconscious. To put it another way, the learnt behaviour or process, that needed to be consciously applied at first, becomes a subconscious habit that serves well going forward. Think back to when you learnt to drive or ride a bike. At first, it took brain power but later it required very little thought.

## Curriculum interventions and critical event interventions

Note that purposeful learning takes place in one of two contexts (or some hybrid combination of the two). As described above, the learning could be within the context of a particular subject, the mastery of which the organization has deemed necessary to support its growth. Subjects could range from inspirational leadership to managing relationships and conflict. The collection of such subjects makes up the organization's curriculum. Alongside curriculum needs are the needs presented by critical events such as the launch of a new project, the maintenance of a team or the need to solve a particular problem (such as how to win business in a recession or provide service to a new customer group).

The challenge is to make both these types of intervention purposeful, aligning them with the corporate purpose, affirming the strengths and challenges of the learners and always culminating in value-adding commitments. Furthermore, in the spirit of ELAS, learners must be supported to ensure value is delivered and sustained through coaching and follow-up, whether this is resourced internally through line management or by a learning practitioner.

## Purposeful engagement in the day-to-day

While it is great to facilitate engagement at events and interventions such as those mentioned above, there is no substitute for purposeful engagement in the day-to-day. When people are having enthusiastic conversations that support the delivery of the organization's purpose, whether they be leaders, managers or anyone else, progress has been made. But this enthusiastic way of doing things doesn't happen by accident (as we'll see in Chapter 5 when we examine the character of the organization). People first need to be fired up about the purpose and vision and then equipped with the right skills and behaviours.

Skills and behaviours for engagement can be taught and practised and there is a significant opportunity to support the purpose of the organization when this is being done.

## Build on existing strengths

Whether the focus is on presentation skills, giving feedback or engaging leadership, learners will already have some awesome skills and personal strengths. Appreciative enquiry is a great way to draw these out but a simple early reference to the organization's purpose in the opening of a learning event allows the facilitator to anchor the skills being discussed in the context of the purpose. So instead of simply asking what people are already good at, the conversation might go something like this (prompts from the facilitator):

- What is the purpose of your organization?
- How is this supported by the work you do in your team and by you personally?
- What are you already good at in this subject that supports the work you do?
- What are the challenges you face that could be overcome by greater ability in this skill?
- What sort of tools do you think you need? (Let's try some now.)
- How can these tools be applied to your specific challenges?
- What commitments do you need to tackle these challenges back at work?
- What support do you need, and from whom, in order to deliver your commitments?

While every learning event will be different, a skilled and trusted facilitator will take learners through a process such as the one above. Furthermore, the learning event should not happen in isolation... .

## ELAS begins and ends in the workplace

Let's delve deeper into the ELAS model discussed above. Don't be fooled into thinking that *engagement* (E) begins when the learner arrives at the learning event. We would hope that engagement is the natural state of the learner while they're focused on their work and consciously delivering the organization's purpose. Ideally the learner will be actively monitoring the effectiveness of what they do in this context. When they feel there is an opportunity to improve, that should begin a process of inquiry that initiates a learning process. In addition, their manager will be monitoring the effectiveness of all their people individually and collectively. In some cases, a skilled employee will simply identify the learning need and, if it is straightforward, they may tackle it themselves through dialogue with colleagues or manager, reading a book, attending a professional seminar or a thousand alternatives that make up the *learning* (L) phase of ELAS.

Of course, learning only adds value to the learner and their organization when it is *applied* (A). So whether the learning is informal as suggested above or more formal such as attendance on a training programme, the learner needs to consciously make a commitment to apply the learning at the workplace until it becomes their natural *modus operandi* (a habit). We all benefit from encouragement in this respect, whether from the facilitator, a coach, our manager or our colleagues.

Even when the learning is applied, there is a significant danger that there will be a lapse back into old ways. This is less likely in tasks that are continuous or frequent as they become embedded into daily routine. It is more likely that lapses occur when tasks are less frequent, such as a product launch or even a performance appraisal. In such cases *sustaining* (S) the new and better ways may need to be supported by refreshers or built into documentation or other systems.

# Examples of the learning ecosystem (ELAS) at work

Remember what we were saying about the fractal nature of life? Well here is why it's so useful in designing our organization. And also why ELAS is the perfect fractal model for engagement. Consider the following applications of ELAS as a multi-layered framework that is so simple to apply, it could easily become the mantra for the organization. Below we will describe a few examples that represent layers and cuts for ELAS. The truth is that, like fractals, the applications are infinite. Just remember that in the same way that cells *engage* with their context, *learn* better ways, *apply* them and re-code their DNA to *sustain* the improvements, so do we, so do our teams, departments, organizations, partnerships, communities and even (or especially) the human race. Engage, learn, apply and sustain is the simple mantra for effective learning organizations. Here are a few examples of ELAS being played out:

1  An **individual** becomes frustrated with the time she wastes on e-mails. When she arrives at work, her inbox typically has hundreds of messages waiting to be processed. This wouldn't be such a frustration if she weren't so *engaged* and interested in her work. The e-mails just seem to get in the way. She notices a colleague doesn't seem to have the same difficulty so she asks them if they could share a coffee and talk about e-mail efficiency. Coffee comes around and the two colleagues *engage*. The individual *learns* so many techniques to prevent e-mails becoming a burden. She sets up her smartphone to receive and send e-mails on the go. She realizes the folly of using prime office time for e-mails and instead plans to attend to e-mails during down time, while waiting for appointments, on trains and so on. She plans to make better use of junk and spam filters and avoid getting caught in unnecessary e-mail trails. And this is just the start.

   After the coffee the individual *applies* the learning but has difficulty with some of the more technical aspects. Fortunately she had anticipated this and had already arranged to meet her colleague (who has now become her 'e-mail mentor') for a second coffee the following week. Returning to the mentor, she was able to *sustain* improvement by ironing out the problems that could so easily have put her back to square one. She even *learnt* some new techniques, beginning a new cycle of ELAS.

2  A **team** in expansion is forced into working remotely in order to cover the wider geography of their operations. *Engaged* in the work, they notice that communications are not what they used to be when they worked in close proximity. They hire a learning facilitator who specializes in remote team-working who suggests they gather for a team workshop. They agree and meet up. The first thing they do is *re-engage* with their work. The facilitator asks them to share their personal accounts of how the job has changed and take stock of the challenges they now face. They are then asked to share the various ways members of the team keep in touch and support each other.

They are astounded as they *learn* of their colleagues' creativity. The facilitator encourages them to take stock of their methods and together they create a toolbox of best practice. This is mainly from their own dispersed practices plus one or two new tools offered by the facilitator. Equipped with their new tool kit, they *re-engage* with their challenges and work out how to *apply* the tools in order to make their team more effective. The facilitator asks them to make firm commitments and asks what support they will need to *sustain* the benefits. They agree to meet online on a monthly basis to see how they are getting on and to reconvene face-to-face with their facilitator in three months to evaluate their progress and *learn* some more.

3 **A learning programme** was being designed by the training manager of an oil and gas company, who was consciously applying ELAS to the design. Learners were identified through the *engagement* of managers with their teams who interviewed those they thought could benefit from the programme. They took stock of the skills these learners already had and agreed some challenges to take into the learning workshop. On attendance, the learners *re-engaged* with their pre-work and shared their skills and challenges with others. This was already a beneficial *learning* experience. The workshop facilitator added to their expertise by providing further tools and techniques. They used action learning to determine the next steps they could *apply* to their challenges and committed to these by sharing SMART (specific, measurable, achievable, realistic and time-based) actions. The design of the programme made sure that the learning was *sustained* by ongoing support from their manager and by retaining their workshop facilitator as a coach. Part of the manager's role was to also consider new *learning* once the performance had been consolidated.

4 **A problem** arose in an operational delivery team faced with ambitious growth plans. They were concerned about the efficiency of their approach to bidding and winning work. The growth plans had fostered an increase in tendering activity and their concern was that they were spreading their effort too thinly, bidding for lots of projects but actually winning fewer because of a reduction in bid quality. The managers involved took the opportunity to *engage* around this problem, pool their knowledge and *learn* an optimum approach to *apply* and *sustain*.

5 **A new** *acquisition* of a global business was struggling with how it could fit and prosper within the context of its new owners. Their

senior managers came together at a strategic alignment workshop to *engage* with their new future and *learn* what this meant for each member of the team and, from this data, for the team as a collective. They then *engaged* with the journey they needed to take to become better integrated with the parent company. They applied a number of strategic alignment methods that considered their structure, character of operation and team strengths. Within this framework, *learning* arose from within the team which they *applied* through team and personal commitments. The most powerful learning was about the power of brand. This resulted in the acquired business dropping their separate brand and relaunching as a subdivision of the parent company, hence *sustaining* the learning in a permanent way.

6 A **partnership** between an industrial services company and their customer had significant scope for improvement. Following *engagement* through dialogue between the two senior managers, they came together formally in a facilitated workshop. Both of the senior managers presented their vision for the future of the partnership, explaining what, for each them, good partnership looked like. Ten managers from each company *engaged* around this vision, co-creating a shared sense of the future that everyone could buy into. From this *learning* they identified a plan of action for *application* at the site in question and agreed to monitor progress as a partnership team in order to make sure progress was *sustained*.

7 A **company** sought to become a true learning organization. *Engaged* in the challenge, they facilitated *learning* for their managers. They examined the learning organization concept and took part in experiential learning activities that supported the need for such concepts to be embedded in the organization. In *applying* this learning, they implemented a plan to change processes and behaviours in the organization that would *sustain* the benefits as several cycles of ELAS were implemented.

8 A group of **talent managers** from a range of organizations meets quarterly in order to *engage* with the latest challenges in their profession. They share these from their personal perspective and choose one challenge to *engage* with at a deeper level. One member takes the 'hot seat' and becomes the subject of action learning until they can commit to action, *applying* the insights they have *learnt* during the forum. The forum ends with everyone confirming their *learning* from the process at any level. As the group meets quarterly

and keeps in touch as a network, there is plenty of peer review to *sustain* those committing to action.

**9** **National activists** seeking an environmentally sustainable and food-secure country in Africa *engaged* people from all stakeholder groups associated with this desired future. Farmers, politicians, village chiefs, scientists and change agents all met for three days to be part of a Future Search workshop. They *learnt* about the past and present from each other's perspectives and *engaged* to determine common ground for action. This *learning* was *applied* through the formation of a number of projects for which there was 100 per cent consensus. It was the level of consensus derived from the Future Search method that increased the chances of *sustained* progress.

**10** An **African country** is exploring how ELAS can be applied to bring its people out of poverty during its 50th anniversary of independence. The embryonic plan is to *engage* its people through the national newspaper and a national values assessment (NVA) using the methods offered by the Barrett Values Centre. This country has the opportunity for its people to *learn* about what is important to them (values) and to agree what can be *applied* to affect *sustainable* change. There is every possibility that Future Search will be combined with the values methodology to repeat several further cycles of ELAS for each value that the people hold dear.

In connecting the above examples with the essence of previous chapters, I propose that engagement without purpose is meaningless. In an organization, there must be constant engagement aligned to the corporate purpose. Furthermore, this engagement has to be aimed at sustainable improvements. Author and business guru Jim Collins refers to this as 'another push on the flywheel', suggesting that organizations move from *Good to Great* (2001) and become *Built to Last* (2005) (to draw on the titles of his two best-selling books) when they understand their purpose, are engaged with it and make improvements which go with the flow (or with the momentum of the flywheel) and apply learning in an iterative and sustainable way. This requires leaders at all levels to serve the interests of the organization before their own personal interests.

Some of the mini case studies above are hypothetical, although they are all grounded in our own experience and combine facts from various true stories to make a point. And the point is this: effective and purposeful engagement is about people coming together in various groups to really understand what is going on in their context, learn how to be more effective, and apply this learning in a sustainable way.

This cycle of ELAS is truly fractal in nature, meaning that what is effective at the smallest level is likely to reflect best practice at the macro level. So the way cells engage with their environment, learn how to thrive, apply the learning in the way they evolve, and code this in their DNA to make life easier for future generations of cells should tell us something, as should the way cells have come together in their tens of trillions to form us as human beings, specializing, playing to their strengths and building the teams we call organs. Mimicking the natural engagement strategy of cells is the recipe for making our organizations and even our humanity great.

Consciously applying the simple and hugely adaptable ELAS concept to engagement and learning produces a true learning ecosystem, beginning with the individual, how that individual comes together with others as a team, and how that team survives in the world as a thriving organization that is truly a learning organization alive with purposeful people all pulling together to deliver a compelling purpose.

# Overcoming the boundary of current knowledge

We live in an amazing, interconnected world where knowledge is growing fast and is available at the touch of a hyperlink. We can now have a thought and straight away feed it with new knowledge. It is no longer just what we know that gives us competitive edge; it is how rapidly we can learn, apply and consolidate what we continue to learn that will cause our performance to accelerate exponentially. Organizations that fail to invest in learning place massive boundaries around performance.

**CASE STUDY**    Four key questions on engagement to inspire *performance beyond boundaries*

A couple years ago, I was asked to deliver the closing keynote for the European Mentoring and Coaching Council (EMCC) in London. During my presentation I commented on the immense and tangible energy in the conference hall and enquired how many of the delegates had noticed this and how they would describe it. I also asked how many were actively studying energy as it applied to coaching and mentoring. I was astounded to discover that over half the delegates were doing so, with many of them studying specific subjects like consciousness and quantum physics.

The following year, the organizers asked if I would work with my colleagues to stage an experiment in one of the conference workshops. Always enjoying a challenge, we agreed and set out to organize a workshop that would explore energy in coaching. We asked the group of about 40 to divide into groups of six or more. We asked for a volunteer in each group to be coached and for four further members of the group to act as coaches, each taking the volunteer through one of four questions. The questions were:

1 Who are you?
2 What's happening?
3 How can you serve?
4 What is your commitment?

The coaches had about 10 minutes to explore their question in whatever way suited the context before handing the baton to the next coach. During the second round of coaching ('What's happening?'), there were tears in about half the groups. We checked with the groups to affirm that everyone was in a place of safety and wanted to continue. This was so. As they continued, people got a profound sense of purpose from which opportunities to serve naturally arose.

What I believe happened that day is that the volunteers got a real sense of who they are from the deep and sensitive questions posed by their coach. It was like 'turning up the volume' of their personal energy. Then, in this state, they were subsequently and consciously immersed in their context ('What's happening?'). This caused an energetic reaction which they felt in their hearts. Depending on what was happening, this reaction was one of either resonance or dissonance, or to put it another way, of harmony or discord.

I have since learnt that touching people's hearts in this way takes them into a mild state of trance. The way it works is this. They become so absorbed in the conversation that they close off other thoughts, allowing a deeper level of engagement. It is easy to see how, as the other questions progress, people become committed to change.

We took the learning from this experience to Texas in 2012 to the annual conference of the American Society for Training and Development (ASTD) in Houston. In our opening keynote entitled *Inspiring Performance beyond Boundaries*, we shared the four powerful questions described above together with a case study (with the kind permission of one of our clients). This was extremely well received and prompted much more thought among our team. One consequence is that we agreed to use the 'inspiring performance beyond boundaries' theme in the subtitle to this book.

**The thing is this:**

If we can facilitate opportunities for people to really understand who they are and, from this foundation, engage with the purpose of their organization, we can help them to find meaning that will transform their work from a transactional chore to a joyful service, in pursuit of which they will need little coaxing to go the extra mile.

Unless of course they discover that they don't belong and their purpose is elsewhere, in which case we will have helped them to make the right personal and purposeful career choice to find a new path.

To close this chapter, test the effectiveness of engagement in your own organization:

# 10 questions on **engagement**

*To what extent...*

...does your organization facilitate opportunities for engagement within and between all stakeholder groups, so that they may share perspectives, learn and grow together in support of the organization's purpose? ☐

...do people come together to examine the way things are done, criticize processes and behaviours with a view to evolving a shared best practice? ☐

...is attention paid to establishing a positive culture for engagement, so that criticism is welcomed in a spirit of openness and shared learning without blaming or diminishing individuals. ☐

...has the organization established the key skills for the engagement of those involved in its work and formed this into a curriculum of learning that is effectively tuned to its purpose? ☐

...are there opportunities for people to come together at critical times, such as strategic changes, team forming and development, project alignment and problem solving? ☐

...are learning programmes and critical events systematically timetabled and well facilitated so that engagement is translated into commitments to action?

...when people make commitments to action do they then receive managerial support and coaching to ensure action is taken?

...is there systematic follow-up of commitments arising from group engagement to celebrate the gains made and to share associated learning?

...does the organization have suitable systems in place to store knowledge arising from engagement that also facilitates ongoing engagement with and evolution of the knowledge to keep it alive and effective?

...does the organization have a communications strategy that facilitates and supports engagement in alignment with the organization's purpose?

### Score

| | |
|---|---|
| **0** not at all | **6** reasonably well |
| **2** a little | **8** very well |
| **4** moderately | **10** completely |

What do your scores tell you? Note the implications and actions that spring to mind below.

You can find further resources to support your thinking on this topic at **www.primeast.com/purposefulorganisation.**

## Further reading

The David Evans book choice for the end of this chapter on engagement focuses on the discretionary effort that employees will bring to their performance once they are truly engaged with the purpose of the organization and have perceived alignment with their own purpose. It makes a good bridge between the subject of engagement and that of corporate culture which features heavily in Chapter 5 when we examine the concept of *character*.

## *Beyond the Call*, Marc Woods and Steve Coomber

Opening with a statement from the influential Edgar Schein, 'The only thing of real importance that leaders do is to create and manage culture', the authors go on to discuss the concept of discretionary effort (DE). This is something they feel has been under-researched and under-rated amidst all of the interest in organizational commitment and employee engagement of the last 30 years.

The book's aim is to close the DE gap – between what people actually do and what they are potentially prepared and able to do. It is compiled from extensive experience and research and it defines DE as: 'the effort that employees choose to exert in service to themselves, their co-workers, or their employers'. Put another way, it is the extent to which employees are prepared to perform above and beyond their job description – 'beyond the call of duty'.

Different from other constructs, the authors propose that DE comes in two forms: in-role and extra-role. The former relates to 'effort that goes beyond the expected level within one's job description, neither punished nor rewarded'; the latter to 'effort that goes beyond one's job description, neither punished nor rewarded'. Furthermore, research has identified the drivers of both in-role and extra-role DE as internally and externally derived. The research also demonstrates the business benefits of DE by comparing groups of organizations with high DE with those with low DE scores. This showed that DE positively improves performance factors such as absenteeism, performance quality, performance management, commitment and job satisfaction.

The authors select six of the drivers of DE on which to concentrate; implying that these are the most significant or the easiest to influence in seeking to develop a DE-conducive environment. The six are:

1 **Autonomy and empowerment:** Employees with more autonomy are more likely to act freely to benefit others, more likely to expand their role and more likely to perform a greater breadth of tasks. Organizations that enable autonomy and empowerment need to be able to set boundaries, get a balance between freedom and control, and provide appropriate support for empowered employees.

2 **Self-sacrificial leadership:** This is where leaders give up personal interest and gain for the benefit of the collective good. Acting as role models, these leaders motivate and inspire to behave in a similar way. Promoting self-sacrificial leadership requires organizational support in areas such as performance management and reward systems.

3 **Individualized consideration:** This involves understanding and fulfilling the needs of individuals (and is a fundamental element of transformational leadership theory). This becomes more difficult as organizations become larger, multinational and multicultural in nature.

4 **Procedural justice:** This is the way in which employees perceive procedural fairness, decision-making and the way they are treated in organizations. This is strongly linked to team theory and the theory of organizational equity. Delivering this challenges organizations on issues such as openness and transparency and may involve difficult shifts in culture.

5 **Team identification:** The more that individuals feel a sense of identity and unity of purpose with a team, the more likely they are to go beyond the call of duty. This is being challenged in the global and virtual world in which we increasingly operate. Team identification stems from the behaviour and influence of others around the individual.

6 **Trustworthiness:** A social construct which, in the organizational and DE context, refers to our willingness to have confidence in the words and actions of others and ascribe good intentions to others.

The messages in this book are not new. Even though the authors state that DE has been under-valued and under-researched, nonetheless there is a vast body of research and commentary on similar concepts and constructs such as organizational citizenship behaviours (OCB), pro-social behaviour and work engagement. Moreover, myriad leadership books and articles cover the ground laid out in this book. It has an easy-read style and a dialogue that is suffused with apposite examples. It is easy to sense the authors' enthusiasm for the topic and they have clearly enjoyed doing the extensive research which supports the book's theses. Additionally, throughout the book the authors explain psychological and social concepts in plain language and easily understood terms.

# Building structures to deliver

fractals PURPOSEFUL
evolving character
corporate structure talent
engagement
success learning from life
structure for results
visionary

> *Clouds are not spheres, mountains are not cones, coastlines are not circles and bark is not smooth, nor does lightning travel in a straight line.* BENOÎT MANDELBROT

## A proposition

It is the duty of those responsible for organizational development to work with leaders to provide sufficient and appropriate structure, creating clarity, simplicity and efficiency so it becomes possible for everyone to be *on purpose*. The structures we place around the work we do and the lives we lead can serve to empower or enslave. The choice is always ours.

## Activity: How to juggle three balls

Before we get into the body of this chapter, I'd like to ask you if you can juggle with three balls. If you're not sure, have a go. If you still don't have any success, try again. Still no luck? Write down your thoughts on this.

Now go to YouTube and search for 'how to juggle three balls'. You'll get several hits. Find one that attracts you. I quite like the 10-minute video by Brad Moss. He seems like a cool guy and he claims to teach anyone to juggle three balls in 10 minutes. See how you get on and make some more notes.

Oh, and why did I get you to do that? Make notes before you read on.

OK, you probably guessed it. There is a clue in the title of this chapter. Brad, or whoever you chose, gave you some structure, a process, even some dimensions. He told you to imagine a square within which to work. He described the precise action of your wrists. He even showed you what the positioning of your arms would look like from the side as well as the front. He gave you some timings and told you what to focus your attention on.

This little activity proves the point that structure helps us to get things done. It also helps if we have the right structure. Imagine if Brad had given us a two-hour lecture on the fundamentals of juggling hidden in a password-protected website. We would probably have lost the will to live and moved on to something more interesting.

I trust you will find some similarities regarding the need for structure in the purposeful organization as you read on.

# Corporate structure

In this chapter, from a corporate perspective, we use the word *structure* to describe physical structures, systems, processes, plans, policies, accounts, reports, meetings, diaries and e-mail. In fact structure embraces anything that supports, channels and makes sense of the resources, including talent, time, finance and materials that collectively deliver the purposes of our organization.

Linking back to Chapter 3 on engagement, it should be noted that structure gives us a framework within which to learn, as the juggling activity showed. It also gives us a means to embed and sustain the learning through the formalization of new systems and processes.

What we are not talking about here is behaviour, which will be explored in the next chapter as we describe the *character* of our organization. It is our organization's character that determines *how* we process the resources of our organization from a behavioural perspective. It is *structure* that creates order in a complex world regarding *what* we do. However, as we shall see, there even needs to be structure in the way we manage character.

I shall begin with an extension of the biology lesson from earlier chapters to affirm that life is fractal in nature, that humans are complex adaptive systems and so are the organizations in which we operate. Also, that we are only conscious of a small part of what's going on, so what we pay attention to is critical. Being mindful and present enables these factors to inform the decisions we take to improve the structures within our organizations.

Afterwards, from this backcloth, I will take you on a tour of the elements that make up the chapters of this book to explain how we can use structure to create a purposeful organization, complete with a vision that inspires, people who are engaged to deliver it, behaviours that are aligned, results that measure purposeful progress, success for everyone and talents that are deployed so we can play to our strengths.

So hold on, here we go...

# Learning from life

The first thing to realize is that humans are not the first life forms to build structure around what they do in order to thrive. All living entities on the planet, from single cells, through plants and animals to humans, right up through communities and nations to humankind create structure in the form of physical structure, systems and processes in order to thrive. Those that don't no longer exist or are under threat of extinction. Life has been practising the development of structure to survive and thrive for millions of years, so it seems sensible to learn a few key lessons from history.

We are fortunate in so many ways to be living at this time. Scientists have made significant progress in understanding how life forms organize themselves in order to adapt to their environments or indeed to alter their environments to evolve and thrive. Understanding how this happens is the secret to knowing how organizations can do the same.

There are so many lessons we can draw from science to help us design structures to support our organizations. But for now, let's just focus on three important discoveries.

## *Discovery 1: We live in a fractal universe*

We have mentioned fractals in earlier chapters and, as this geometry is especially pertinent to how we structure our organizations, this seems a good time to go a little deeper, first with some brief history.

Benoît Mandelbrot was born in Warsaw in 1924 to a Lithuanian Jewish family. His family moved to Paris in 1936 where they managed to survive the Second World War years. Despite a lack of education as a boy, Mandelbrot turned out to be a brilliant mathematician and was awarded a master's degree in Paris before emigrating to the United States. Here, in 1958, he secured work in research and development with IBM as computer science was developing.

Mandelbrot noticed patterns in seemingly unrelated data, such as variations in the price of cotton, and later made the connection to patterns in nature. In 1982 he wrote *The Fractal Geometry of Nature* in which he noted:

> Clouds are not spheres, mountains are not cones, coastlines are not circles and bark is not smooth, nor does lightning travel in a straight line.

In searching for similarity in such seemingly random patterns, he discovered that they conformed to the formula

$$z \rightarrow z^2 + c$$

In this equation, $z$ and $c$ are complex numbers and the patterns can only be seen when millions of calculations are made on a computer. Don't worry if, like me, the maths stretches the grey matter. The important thing is that fractal theory defines the principle of self-similarity, whereby patterns seen at one level can be seen to repeat infinitely as the observer zooms in or out.

In the design of organizations, this is a vital lesson: if we want our organizations to be naturally efficient, it makes sense to build on the principles that have worked well in the smallest building blocks of life for millions of years.

We can notice, for example, the relative simplicity of small multi-celled creatures compared with the complexity of human beings. In a similar fashion, small organizations might work well with many people being multi-skilled. But they need to adapt as they grow by forming specialist departments in much the same way that evolution gave us specialist organs to conduct specialist functions on behalf of our wider community of cells.

Today, we can access hundreds of examples of fractal patterns easily on the internet. Why not have a brief search on YouTube? We may also begin noticing fractals in nature such as in the way a pine cone or sunflower head organizes as it develops.

---

### Activity: Discover your own fractals

It's time you had a breath of fresh air. Take a walk outside, preferably into the countryside or a garden. See how many fractal patterns you can find.

Before long we start seeing fractals everywhere, even in our organizations. Think about how we deal with management information. An appropriate level of detail is required at board level to understand the performance of the organization as a whole. As we zoom in to departments, then to teams and individuals, the detail becomes clearer but the patterns are similar. At each level there is a breadth of information that gives sufficient clarity without being overwhelming. Think also about how we get people to work together in groups at a conference. When the groups get too large, we break them into smaller sub-groups to make them effective. The individuals contribute to their small groups in a similar way that the groups themselves might contribute to the larger conference.

---

## Discovery 2: Life adapts systematically to its environment

The second scientific fact we need to embrace is that living organisms are complex adaptive systems.

> Complex adaptive systems are special cases of complex systems, often defined as a 'complex macroscopic collection' of relatively 'similar and partially connected micro-structures' – formed in order to adapt to the changing environment, and increase its survivability as a macro-structure.
>
> Gupta and Amish, *Insights from Complexity Theory*

In an age when organizations are increasingly global in reach and subject to rapid change and complexity, the argument for mimicking nature's design becomes compelling. By the way, this doesn't just apply to organizations. In her compelling book *Biomimicry: Innovation inspired by nature* (2003) Janine Benyus describes how lessons from the natural world are increasingly inspiring advances in science, technology and business. She likens this to tapping into 3.8 billion years of research and development with 10 to

30 million compelling case studies. I would strongly recommend watching her TED Talk for a taste that will probably inspire you to get hold of her book.

In his book *Spontaneous Evolution* scientist Bruce Lipton affirms that we humans are complex adaptive systems, with many similarities to the cells in our body. Each one of the 50–100 trillion cells in our bodies perceives information from our environment and systematically recodes the DNA held within it. Cumulatively this forms the evolving programme for our lives. Employees similarly need to evolve the DNA of the organization and the organizational architect might usefully provide a blueprint for the 'nervous system' and behaviours to enable this.

In this way, Lipton acknowledges that we are indeed fractal beings linking systematically to our environment in such a manner that enables us to thrive. The essential lesson regarding the story of mankind that I draw from his amazing work is as follows (my words):

> Single cell creatures came together, initially as separate and similar organisms, in order to thrive. Over time they worked out that, by playing as teams, they could divide their duties and be more efficient. This resulted in humans having the most amazing society of trillions of cells made up of several specialist teams such as brain cells, heart cells, skin cells and so on, all pulling together as a mega-organization to make us what we are.
>
> In true fractal form, what happens at the cell level is also what happens at the human level and also what happens at the level of society. We take in information and resources from our environment and use them efficiently to thrive. The best ways to do this can be coded in our DNA and this programming must evolve over time to take account of our environment.

As Lipton concludes: 'evolution moves forward by increasing community and expanding awareness'. This could so easily be the mantra for the purposeful organization.

## Discovery 3: Our conscious mind is only aware of a small proportion of what is actually going on

Because our cells are highly intelligent at an individual level (remember they were originally capable of living independently), they can function efficiently in teams (organs). In doing so, they are able to thrive with very little conscious awareness. In fact about 99 per cent of what happens to us is controlled by our subconscious mind, leaving our conscious mind to focus on activities that require concentration, usually to do with managing change, paying attention to the most important things or whatever captures our interest.

This is an important lesson. Left alone, our subconscious mind will continue to run our bodies and our lives according to learnt habits. This is exactly the reason people are realizing the benefits of mindfulness, ie being present to their subconscious behaviours so they can consciously reprogramme them to be more helpful. Exactly the same must happen in the workplace or we will corporately fall victim to our collective habits.

Our fractal awareness as organizational architects must be capable of jumping the scale from the cellular level to the human level to the corporate level. We can deduce that the sub-components (eg teams and departments) are very capable of running pretty well on learnt habits (to a point). But we have to make sure there is 'corporate mindfulness'. That is to say that we maintain a watchful eye on what is going on so that key processes can be challenged and improved systematically. This is exactly why we need to become a true learning organization as proposed in the previous chapter on engagement.

It is also why we need to give headroom to key people to stay strategic in so many ways. Staying strategic is to the organization what being mindful (or conscious) is to the individual.

Incidentally, fractal awareness allows us to make use of these insights in a wide range of contexts. Workplaces are not the only organizations that need to be strategic (mindful). The same can be said for our communities, nations and families. Think about the benefit of having family members who are not working flat out on their own 'stuff'. Retired family members or full-time parents have the opportunity to be more mindful about family matters than their busy relatives. They are maybe the ones who can notice unhelpful behaviours and suggest alternative approaches. We do well to value this and in busy families to ask how family mindfulness can otherwise be achieved.

# Fractal geometry: Critical implications for corporate structure

Once we understand the essence of fractal geometry, complex adaptive systems and conscious awareness, we can establish some basic principles, learnt from the natural laws of the universe to make our organizations more efficient:

1 **Scalability and adaptability:** What works at one level may well work in a similar way at a higher or lower level. But be mindful that scale also brings a need to adapt. So in large organizations teams may well

need to behave as individuals do in smaller organizations and as cells do in people.

2  **Devolved growth:** We should structure our organizations to allow individuals and groups of individuals to excel at what they do and in a manner that they can evolve both independently and interdependently.

3  **Create channels for flow:** We should create systems to facilitate the efficient flow of resources including energy, talent, money and materials in support of our corporate purposes.

4  **Interconnection:** We should join up these systems with evolving efficiency being constantly mindful of best practice and next practice.

5  **Evolution:** We should seek to evolve our structures, systems and processes continuously in order to adapt to the changing environment and to thrive.

6  **Redundancy:** Redundant structures, systems and processes should be completely decommissioned.

7  **Consciousness:** At the same time as trusting teams to do their work with minimum interference (confident in the corporate subconscious), there needs to be a conscious awareness to discover where workstreams are not serving the evolving corporate purpose. In these circumstances, we need to consciously reprogramme our operation in order to thrive.

8  **Engagement and headroom:** A key challenge is to encourage the conscious engagement of people at all levels. In large organizations, the people at the top cannot be the only ones who are consciously engaged. If they get sucked into the detail, they will simply become less conscious at their strategic level.

9  **Confidence in our subconscious:** As we learn better ways of doing things, these should be stored in our corporate DNA or knowledge base and reinforced through appropriate corporate learning and development.

10  **Fit for purpose:** Following these principles, we can develop efficient structures, remembering that too much structure can cause bureaucracy, too little gives rise to chaos. It's always about designing the right structures to deliver our purpose and vision.

In the first chapter we named the eight conditions for corporate success (purpose, vision, engagement, structure, character, results, success and talent) and agreed to unpick them in the eight chapters to follow.

Structure absolutely must take account of each of the other seven conditions for success. So let's systematically explore some of these relationships now.

## Purposeful structures (Chapter 1)

My opening chapter described the analysis we should undertake in order to understand the multiple purposes of our organization. Having established and understood these purposes, we should systematically determine the structures we need to put in place in order to deliver them. There should always be a link between purpose and structure.

For example, if we are intent, as most organizations are, on delivering a high-quality service to customers or end-users, we should define what this looks like in order to provide structure for our people. The very act of definition in some kind of standard or service level agreement gives helpful clarity to what we do. Then we need to understand the mechanisms for delivering the service, the training required for those people involved, and the degree of monitoring and adjustment necessary for continuous improvement. All of this structure arises from a simple purpose or intention to deliver excellent service.

If another of our purposes is to provide meaningful work to our people in the context of the service we provide to the customer, then we need to structure what we do accordingly. We need to structure our recruitment processes, questions and other assessments to test for the behaviours we need. This will enable us to recruit people who will enthuse about some aspect of the service we provide and deliver it well. We then need the full range of human resource processes from recruitment, appointment, development, performance management, reward, recognition and so on right through to retirement and beyond to be aligned to this aspect of our purpose.

On the subject of purpose, even the establishment of purpose requires structure. The regular and systematic assessment of our organization's purpose and the ordering of that information in the form of some kind of stakeholder charter as described in Chapter 1 is one example of where structure helps. Simply doing this once is good (and better than many organizations) but doing it on an annual or other regular basis (which shouldn't take long) will ensure that the organization has a structured and continually improving handle on its very reason for existence.

# Visionary structures (Chapter 2)

If we have completed our visioning process well, engaging people at all levels with their futures, it will provide a rich and detailed insight into the structures we need in every part of the organization. Bear in mind here that even the term *visioning process* suggests that we need to provide structure for doing this on a regular and systematic basis. I cannot imagine a successful organization that doesn't formally attend to its vision on at least an annual basis and engage the whole workforce in an appropriate and systematic manner.

We need to put in place structure to deliver our vision *and* have a vision for our structures of the future. Compared to purposes, our evolving vision adds a deeper granularity to what our business needs to look like at specific time horizons and provides valuable clues for the structures we should have. So even simple things like our vision for target markets, products offered, how many people will deliver what we do and where they will be based will tell us a great deal about how to structure the organization. And we will have a vision for the technological advances that will allow us to structure our business differently. What effects did we foresee about total internet connection, home working, video-conferencing and webinars that allowed us to create the corporate structures we have in place today? What technologies do we anticipate and how can we exploit them in the next decade? How will they impact our structures for the years to come?

## *Limitations of top-down structures*

A key thing to remember is that the structures needed in organizations where the vision is widely shared, co-created and aligned are very different from the traditional top-down hierarchy. In the latter, there are serious limitations on the numbers of direct reports a manager can have, simply because the leader will be the source of knowledge, direction and power and therefore a hub. Consequently they will very likely be drawn in to all problem-solving conversations. In the former, when a vision is shared and co-created and a team is empowered in its delivery, the manager one level up does not get so consumed with micro-management or micro-support. This frees them to either manage a greater span of the organization or to engage more productively in strategic or key commercial matters. Taken to its ultimate, this type of organization becomes progressively less like a hierarchy and more akin to the way the cells in our bodies are organized, with senior leaders creating the conditions for the organization to thrive, being consciously aware of change and malfunction and facilitating the reprogramming of systems and processes where necessary. It is not a coincidence that these are the features of what we have come to know as *learning organizations*, the mechanisms for which were discussed in the previous chapter.

One director we know described his less than satisfactory role as being the hub at the centre of a wheel and wanted to 'connect the spokes together more intelligently' so that the limitations of the single hub didn't impede efficient functioning. This insight enabled him to work with his direct reports to co-create the future with increased interdependency throughout the team and greater autonomy for them to deliver.

At Primeast we use the principle of devolved leadership and the concept of circular connection for monthly performance appraisal. Each of our eight directors sets their own performance goals and agrees them briefly with our managing director. From then on, we have (nominally) monthly buddying catch-ups with one of our co-directors to encourage performance and resolve challenges in a coaching manner.

# Structures for engagement (Chapter 3)

In the last chapter we affirmed that the best purpose and vision in the world are worth little until we engage stakeholders and get them to support their delivery. This is unlikely to happen well without some kind of structure. We need effective communications systems that engage with purpose and vision: regular meetings, conferences, forums and workshops; coaching and mentoring time; problem-solving time; time with customers, shareholders, members of the community, business partners, even competitors. None of this will happen effectively without structure, without planning. Engagement must not be left to chance.

When we experience the symptoms of failure with a particular stakeholder group we can usefully explore the structures we have (or don't have) for engagement. By comparing our findings to the engagement methods in more successful stakeholder situations we can tune our methods appropriately.

There are often significant ways we can improve our structures for engagement. We could for example:

- **right-size:** make engagement events smaller or larger scale according to needs;
- **automate:** use more (or less) technology;

- **intimate:** be face-to-face (or video rather than just voice if remote);
- **multi-channel:** use multiple media for important messages;
- **outsource to experts:** use professionals – writers, speakers, marketers, counsellors, mediators, facilitators, mentors, coaches;
- **intensify:** make engagement more or less frequent;
- **inspire:** use inspiring environments and media;
- **be memorable:** use the arts as alternative ways to engage;
- **energize:** vary the methods to energize those involved;
- **reciprocate:** use two-way *engagement* rather than one-way *transmission;*
- **listen:** create the space and the will to listen better and be open to feedback;
- **embed:** engage in the day-to-day as well as at special events;
- **simplify:** make our communication systems simpler, less complicated.

The key thing to remember is that engagement doesn't work well by chance. There has to be a conscious intent for engagement that gets translated into structure for the organization. Engaged and empowered teams get together on a regular and sufficient basis and spend time getting to know each other, sharing and solving problems and generally learning together. They are well-equipped with tools and skills for effective team-working.

## Structures for project team engagement: Living in the matrix

In modern, large organizations, people often work in matrix structures. In the simplest of cases, people belong to a functional hierarchy and are simultaneously deployed into projects. Typically, life in projects is all-consuming with the urgent demands of the task in hand taking up every minute. The problem is that in such circumstances the less urgent but often important needs of the function (and wider organization) get neglected. My colleagues frequently facilitate project teams and functional teams where these matters are of significant concern.

This situation is seriously damaging to the organization and the individual. Organizations suffer when project people are so consumed by the demands of the project that they have no time to engage with their headquarters or functional team. Their potentially valuable contributions to the whole are thereby lost. At the individual level, people lose personal development opportunities and career progression. This in turn further damages the organization because succession isn't provided for and retention is damaged. In short, people leave because there is an absence of development, progression and engagement on a professional or personal level.

When we work with people in matrix organizations, we get them to examine both (or all) cuts of the matrix using the eight conditions defined in this book. In other words, for each team (eg functional and project) they are part of ask the following:

1 **What is the purpose of this team?** How is it aligned to the purpose of the organization and what are the tensions and synergies between this purpose and that of the other teams we are part of?

2 **What is the vision for this team?** How does it fit within the corporate vision and how does it conflict or support the vision of the other teams we are part of?

3 **Is there adequate engagement with members of this team?** How does this compare with engagement in other teams?

4 **Are there adequate structures in place?** Especially if this team is more remote, as is often the case of functional teams compared with site-based projects?

5 **What is the character of this team?** Corporate values will almost certainly translate into different behaviours for different cuts of the matrix. These can usefully be formed into distinctively different team charters.

6 **What are the key results for this team?** And where are the tensions between those of other teams we are involved with?

7 **What does success mean to the members of this team and the team as a whole?** Personal and team success will mean something different for us and our (different) colleagues in the context of the teams we are part of. Have success factors been defined and shared in all the teams we are part of? Has the team defined what success means for the collective?

8 **How are we deploying our talent?** Finally, when we are part of more than one team, we may bring different talents into play in each set of circumstances. Each team we are part of will have a different blend of people, talents and challenges so we have to adapt. Have we had the chance to think about this and articulate how this works? Also, have we had the chance to share this with colleagues in all the teams we are part of?

---

How the matrix works for you

To find out how your organization is being helped or hindered by its matrix
structure, try the following. On a sheet of paper, draw three columns. In the
first column list the eight conditions (from *purpose* down to *talent*). In the
second column, against each of the conditions, and using the questions
above as a guideline, make a note of how this aspect plays out for your
functional teams (eg 'What is the purpose/vision/engagement etc of the
functional team?'). Then in the third column do the same for project teams.

---

## Structures for engagement in 'networks of interdependent service'

An extension of the matrix structure is one where we are part of multiple
teams and relationships that form our working network. I like to think of
these as 'networks of interdependent service'. Welcome to my world.

I am amused by people who say with conviction, 'You can't work for
more than one boss.' In a way they are right and it's maybe to do with the
use of the word 'boss'. If a boss is someone with complete control over us,
then clearly this is true. But if we recognize that we live in a complex world
with complex demands coming from many angles, then I would suggest that
no one has complete control over anyone. As intelligent beings we should
be capable of serving this or any given context with integrity.

Back to my world as an example. I am a member of several teams: the
Primeast board, our management team, our upstream development team
(that looks after the development of our proposition and routes to market
etc). I meet as a part-time member of various client management and project
teams. I also actively represent a number of professional institutions and
meet with others who do the same. I have close partnership relationships
with clients for whom I manage accounts and for others whom I coach
personally. I have a couple of mentors and a coaching supervisor. As a
member of the directors' team at Primeast, I provide support to one of my
co-directors on the delivery of their objectives for the year and receive
similar support from another director. These relationships change each year
and there is absolutely zero sense of hierarchy. Incidentally we also meet
with all our staff as a headquarters team quarterly. The point is that this
is absolutely an evolving interdependent ecosystem. Thriving within this

complexity is exciting, dynamic and challenging all at the same time. It probably wouldn't suit every organization but I bet if you examined your own organization, including its connection to the outside world, you'd see similar evolving complexity.

---

## MINI CASE STUDY    Apple

Just in case you're thinking that a fluid interdependent structure is OK for a comparatively small organization like Primeast, I invite you to consider the example of Apple. I really enjoyed the recorded interview with Steve Jobs at the 2010 D8: All Things Digital conference. Incidentally the 2007 D5 interview with Jobs together with Bill Gates is also stunning and both are available at the time of writing on YouTube. But for the purposes of this case study, take a look at the 2007 interview and make your notes about structure, interdependency and fluidity at Apple.

I like the way Steve Jobs describes Apple as being like a start-up. He claims they have 'zero committees'. Instead, individual people are in charge of aspects of delivery and teams form around them as defined by the needs of the job. Teamwork is modelled at the top of the company and filters down throughout. Note also the devolved sense of purpose in the company and the lack of hierarchical power. Steve jokes about being challenged frequently by his colleagues during his wide and varied team meetings.

---

With these thoughts in mind, let's see if it's possible to bring some structure to such fluid and complex situations. Time for another activity. This time the case study is you.

### Activity: My personal corporate network

Take a sheet of paper, and write the word ME in the centre. Then draw in all your connections to others, beginning with the ones where the connection is most critical. Make it a sort of mind-map in whatever way suits you. Perhaps you could make the thickness of connections represent the degree of their importance. Perhaps circle or otherwise identify teams or groups. Include those who are suppliers, customers or other external partners.

Once you've done this, pick three relationships you'd like to explore further and use the eight conditions for a purposeful organization to investigate what could be done to improve them. So for example, what is the purpose of this relationship? What would it look like at a specified time horizon when working well? How do you engage with this person (how often, where do you meet, for how long, what is the tone of these meetings)? What structures facilitate your relationship (regular meetings, agendas, social media, telephone catch-ups)? What is the character of the relationship (friendly, supportive, challenging, frosty...)? How do you measure the effectiveness of the relationship? And do you know what success means to both (or all) parties? Finally, do you know which of your talents are useful and appreciated in this relationship and the same for the other person?

Are you beginning to see the fractal nature of structure in your organization? In the same way that our organization needs *purpose, vision, engagement, structure, character, results, success* and *talent*, so does every relationship with which we need to engage. So does every meeting within a relationship and even every conversation within a meeting. We can usefully hold these eight conditions in our consciousness as we go about our work and bring them to mind when a relationship or dialogue isn't working.

## Structures to evolve the character of what we do (Chapter 5)

At the risk of stealing too much from the next chapter, suffice to say that in complex systems, behaviour is mega-important. Contrary to popular belief, there are many structures and systems we can use to manage the behaviour of people and thus evolve the character of the organization in a positive way. Some of the most obvious include:

- **Organization charts** that show who reports to whom and potentially about what. Carefully crafted charts will also encourage dialogue between the more formal reporting lines (often the dotted lines). They may also show the major project teams and work groups. At Primeast we don't have a typical organization chart. Instead we have a 'honeycomb' of hexagons representing roles that meet the needs of

**FIGURE 4.1** Honeycomb structure of organizations

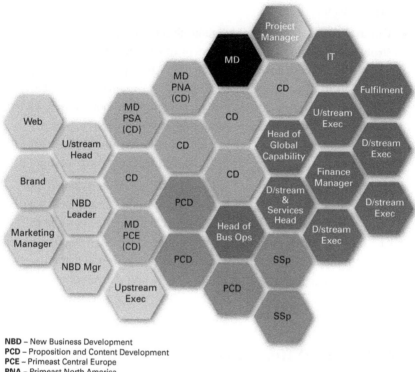

**NBD** – New Business Development
**PCD** – Proposition and Content Development
**PCE** – Primeast Central Europe
**PNA** – Primeast North America
**PSA** – Primeast South Africa
**SSp** – Subject Specialist

**SOURCE:** © Primeast, 2013

our business flows (see Figure 4.1). An individual might have multiple roles (and therefore more than one hexagon) depending on their strengths and fit to the team.

- **Recruitment processes and policies** can bring new people on board who fit the desired values and behaviours of the organization. I recently enjoyed interviewing Liane Hornsey, when she was People Director EMEA (Europe, Middle East and Africa) at Google where she described the Google approach to talent. She said, 'It's very simple. We recruit the best people and develop the hell out of them.' She then went on to describe with passion that 'best' principally meant a behavioural fit to the Google way. Skills can be taught but personality and attitude are much harder to change. This is why more and more organizations are conducting 'culture fit' interviews alongside competence in technical, verbal and numeric reasoning.

- **Personal development strategies** should focus not just on the skills for the job but also on alignment to the purpose, vision and values of the organization.

- **Cultural transformation tools** facilitate the measurement and (from these outputs) the management of organizational culture. More of that later. For now, suffice to say that I was blown away in the 1990s to discover that the culture of an organization can be shown in a single easy-to-read diagram and even more impressed to learn how to define the best culture to deliver the purpose of the same organization on a comparable chart in a manner that enabled a gap analysis and a programme of coaching for transformation.

- **Corporate values** can be defined scientifically, through dialogue or preferably a combination of both. They should be crafted to describe what matters most to the organization. They can then be used to facilitate the development of team charters which align the behaviours of team members to the purpose of the organization and specifically that of the particular team. This cascade is best delivered in a structured way.

## Structures to measure results (Chapter 6)

We will explore more about the nature of results in Chapter 6. Here I just want to stress the need for our measurements systems to be structured in order to (a) measure what's important and (b) be efficient and effective.

What's important should be determined from the purpose and vision of the organization and being efficient is to do with measuring an appropriate level of detail and communicating what is needed for the recipient, nothing more. This chapter's opening thoughts on fractals are useful in this respect. As we zoom in on the management information (as is necessary at the sharp end) we should see more detail and less scope. As we zoom out (in the boardroom) there will be less detail and more scope but the patterns will look familiar.

## Structures for success (Chapter 7)

Success is a much under-discussed phenomenon in organizations. Success is about outcomes and the personal and shared feelings associated with these outcomes. I like to think about success being more oriented to people than results, meaning different things to different people. However, we should not forget the notion of team or corporate success which will be very different from the more left-brain notion of team or corporate results. Of course at the highest level, through the stakeholder audits alluded to in Chapter 1, we will have identified in all probability what success means to stakeholder groups. But within the stakeholder groups, there may be significant variance. For example, one shareholder may simply delight in dividends for personal gain, another may have the interests of a third party in mind, such as the pensioners that depend on a pension fund or a trust that funds noble works in a developing country. Another shareholder may simply delight in knowing they have funded the work of an amazing organization and celebrate each advancement in the product or service offering. Despite this diversity, it is worth trying to get some commonality of what success means to groups and teams. This allows the systematic celebration of success which is a deep and vital reinforcement of purpose.

For our staff, some may be keen to be part of a successful organization because it means continued employment. Others work their socks off because they believe in what they do. And for others it could simply be appreciating the smiles of satisfied customers. We can systematically discover more about our staff's perceptions of success through employee opinion surveys and team audits.

Similarly, systematic customer surveys will tell us what success means to this primary stakeholder group. One of our clients engages our facilitators on a regular basis to run 'voice of the customer' workshops where their managers and customer teams engage to explore the customer's perception of success so operations can be tuned to deliver it.

The point is, we need systems to help us understand what success means and also to provide the right feedback to meet all needs. We also need to structure our work calendar with time to celebrate success at all levels. Remember, every celebration of success is potentially a reinforcement of purpose.

# Structures for talent (Chapter 8)

Far too many organizations have structures that actually sabotage the talent of their people. As we shall see in Chapter 8, if managed badly, performance appraisal, competence frameworks and remedial learning programmes too often focus on what people do badly or, at best, *not well enough*.

We need systems and approaches that recognize, value, develop and use talent in delivering the purposes of the organization. At Primeast, we call this *talent liberation*. As we shall explore later, each word in the phrase *recognize, value, develop* and *use* implies structures and processes we need to put in place so we get the very best our people have to offer aligned to the organization's purposes.

For example (and as a taster), recognizing talent requires the training of managers to spot what they and their people do well. Valuing talent requires a systematic appraisal of the value we add when we are playing to our strengths, and a sharing of this with our team. Developing talents into strengths calls for disciplined career and personal development. And putting talent to effective use should be the key feature of our performance appraisal and management systems.

So, as we can see, with just this small number of examples, there is scope for tuning our people management systems and processes to maximize the contribution of our people.

# Who designs the corporate systems?

The only honest answer is: we all do. This takes quite a bit of understanding. But once we do understand, life becomes simpler. It may be helpful to use the three-legged stool analogy. Imagine a stool with three legs. Here the three legs are the managers (especially the senior team), design experts and everyone else.

Clearly **managers** are responsible for creating the structures that make their organization (or part of it) simple. In the process of doing this, they may well engage people who understand about organization design and they will affirm the responsibility of everyone to organize themselves in such a manner that they can work effectively in the context of the organization and their immediate team.

Within the organization, there is clearly merit in appointing appropriate **design expertise** in anything that adds clarity and structure to the corporate machine. The list is as long as it needs to be and likely to include a mix of accountants, engineers, quality professionals, project managers, planners, risk managers and (of course) organizational development professionals. Notwithstanding the benefits of expertise, care should also be taken to avoid creating further complexity from the integration of too many specialists.

The role of all these people is to put in place structure that facilitates effectiveness. The list of structures is even longer than that of the people whose job it is to put them in place. We are likely to need financial accounts, regular meetings, strategies, plans and contingencies, an organization chart, a set of values, e-mail protocols and so on.

Finally there is the role of **everyone in the organization**. In a dynamic world, everyone must monitor the effectiveness of the structures and processes they work with. They must be encouraged to find ever better ways of doing things. This is consistent with being a true learning organization.

The purpose of stating all this is to remind us that structure is complex. It is different from one organization to another and it changes as the company evolves over time. Typically organizations need more efficient structures and processes as they grow. They can't get away with the more fluid approach that characterizes a new business.

---

### Activity: How organizations evolve?

Go to YouTube (youtu.be/GMEsAO9V8xs) and see what Dr Gerry Faust has to say about how organizations follow a natural life cycle of growth and decline. Make some notes on how this might affect the structure of the organization.

---

In the 'growing up' phase of the life cycle described by Faust, there is a need to evolve the structures and processes that were less relevant during the organization's infancy. Failure to do this is one of the several potential causes of 'early mortality' that Faust describes.

Think about what happens if a tree grows too quickly, perhaps through overwatering. It becomes limp and straggly; it doesn't have the structure to withstand its environment. Think also of the benefits of pruning and feeding.

## Keeping it simple

I'd like to move towards the close of this chapter with a plea for simplicity. Far too many organizations seem to make life in the workplace difficult by making it complicated. In response to this, I offer some 'simple thoughts' (excuse the pun) on four practices that help to keep things simple: *widespread simplicity, reduction, redundancy* and *visibility*.

## 1 Widespread simplicity

Simplicity is a virtue and the creation of it is a craft that can and should be taught to everyone. It is a powerful attitude that serves to keep our systems, processes and other structures as effective as they can be, in order to serve the delivery of our purpose and vision. This applies as much in our personal lives as it does in the workplace.

Having said all that, many of today's organizations are incredibly complex. And it is worth understanding what we mean by *complex*. This is different from *complicated*. Systems become complicated because of their scale, numbers of components and the way they are connected. Nevertheless, complicated systems can still be predictable if we understand them sufficiently.

Systems become complex when they are based on relationships which are variable, in a state of flux and uncertainty. So in today's corporate world involving thousands of human beings, multiple cultures, customers, markets and stakeholders, all with their different and variable behaviours, things are indeed complex (as well as complicated). As discussed earlier, systems like this are referred to as *complex adaptive systems* in that they adapt as the circumstances or variables change. Wherever complex adaptive systems are present it is important to recognize that attention has to be given to more than just the structure of the system. In fact paying too much attention to the structure may be counter-productive. We also need to pay attention to the character of the system, the way its components behave, the principles behind what they do, the way they engage and so on. We will come back to this in the next chapter.

The conclusion I have come to in the work I do with organizations is that the more complex they are, the more attention needs to be given to *behaviour* and to making things *uncomplicated*.

## 2 Reductionism

One way of simplifying things, and making them less complicated is through *reduction*. Most things can be reduced for simplicity. Examples that spring to mind are reducing the numbers of meetings we attend or the numbers of people that attend them. What about reducing the number of people we copy into e-mails and the number of e-mails we receive?

We can even reduce our lexicon. Most projects I've been associated with have processes to manage issues, risks and changes. And yet people also talk about challenges, blockages, hindrances, problems, updates and versions and thus add complication. There is a perfectly good system for managing issues, but when a problem arises, no one knows what to do with it. Why should we conceptually have ten things to manage when three are sufficient? Part of organization design is managing the language and labelling of the business so everyone speaks the same consistent and simple language.

## 3 The redundancy principle

Coupled closely to the simplicity principle is the redundancy principle. This principle states that when an improvement is made, tested, proven and fully adopted, the old way (now redundant) should be scrapped in such a manner that it can't creep back into the corporate way. This is particularly relevant in a growing organization where new ways are being implemented to cope with expansion. Old processes relating to old structures must be dismantled and discarded permanently.

Failing to do this adds complication into the system. In fact it can easily make matters worse than not having the improved system at all. Let's take the example of introducing a new computer-based filing system with document control and the ability to tag files for easy retrieval. This new system means everyone can access it easily and it sounds great. However, as with all these things, if the system has flaws, such as the absence of access for remote working, people will tend to introduce their own work-arounds. The potential for confusion is obvious. Instead of there being one system to look in for documents, there is instead *one more* than was available previously. In other words, an attempt to gain efficiency has resulted in complication through failure of redundancy.

Think how often we do this. Again at a personal level, we open new bank accounts without properly closing the old ones. We buy new gadgets and keep the old ones in an already cluttered attic. We have three places we keep our car keys instead of one. Redundancy is a mindset and a mindset that can be taught and practised as the corporate way.

## 4 The visibility principle

Of course, we can have the best structures, systems and processes in the world but if no one knows they are there or how they work, they are unlikely to serve our purpose. In fact in the absence of visibility, people will simply 'reinvent the wheel' causing further complication. Effective organizations make their systems visible through simple file structures and help guides, induction and training.

In general terms and at a personal level, each day that I manage to do more to streamline my life and work (through tools like simplification, reduction, redundancy and visibility) than I do to add complication, is probably a day well spent.

**CASE STUDY**    Evolving the structure and processes of an organization

One of our clients had two specific aims which they perceived as critically important to their corporate success. One was a company-wide strategic matter and the other related to a critical business development strategy. After much consultation we agreed to work with them to tackle both matters simultaneously.

Having engaged with much of the theory in this book (prior to publication of course), the head of human resources and the chief executive shared an intention to become a learning organization, one that would consciously engage people in sharing and combining the learning associated with any process that was key to delivering the business vision. This was the company-wide strategic matter for attention.

The business development issue was one such key process, essential for delivering the business vision for growth. In collaboration with the client, we agreed to teach the managers associated with the business development process about the key attributes of a learning organization, especially the need to externalize knowledge, combine it, critique it and establish the current best way of doing something. Then we stressed the benefits of creating a spiral of continuous improvement so that the best way could evolve still further. With this learning fresh in their minds we tackled the business development challenge.

The managers worked together in a workshop setting to examine their business development process. They first mapped it on the wall and then asked five critical questions:

1  What is missing from the process that we do but which isn't formalized?

2  What is missing from the process that we should do but don't?

3  What assumptions do we make in implementing this process (eg that it will work for our customers)?

4  What do we like about our process (what works well)?

5  What do we dislike about our process (what doesn't work well)?

The managers used sticky notes to annotate their defined process systematically. They used colours and shapes that corresponded to the five questions above. We also limited them to three sticky notes per manager for each of the five questions. This prevented them dropping into the detail too much.

On completion of this work it became clear what needed to change. We asked the managers to vote according to their priorities for change. There was one key area that demanded urgent attention and a small number of secondary issues. We worked on the key area in the workshop using action learning, allowing one of the managers to commit to action with clarity. Another manager took the other issues away for systematic attention at a later date.

By engaging the managers in the concept of learning organizations and then dealing with a mission-critical specific challenge, the need and advantage for systematic corporate learning in a structured way was reinforced.

Now: how effective is the structure of your own organization?

# 10 questions on **structure**

*To what extent...*

...is regular and ongoing attention given to the structure of the organization at a senior level, supported by appropriate organization design professionals? ☐

...does this attention refer systematically to the purpose and vision of the organization? ☐

...is there adequate empowerment of managers and others at all levels to manage the structures that support their span of operation? ☐

...does everyone in the organization receive appropriate training and support to structure their work environment in such a way as to deliver their purpose and that of the organization in the most efficient manner? ☐

...is there adequate structure in place to measure and manage the character of the organization that is required to deliver the purpose and vision on an ongoing basis? ☐

...are there adequate structures in place to measure the results of the organization, related to the delivery of the vision as it plays out at each level and division of the organization?

...are there sufficient mechanisms to establish what success means to everyone in the organization and to ensure this is monitored, delivered and celebrated?

...are there sufficient mechanisms in place to recognize, value, develop and use the unique talents of everyone involved in delivering the purpose and vision of the organization?

...do the structures, systems and processes in the organization take full account of complexity and, in particular, support matrix and partnership working?

...are structures tuned on an ongoing basis to make them adequately simple, taking every opportunity for reduction, redundancy and visibility?

## Score

| | |
|---|---|
| **0** not at all | **6** reasonably well |
| **2** a little | **8** very well |
| **4** moderately | **10** completely |

What do your scores tell you? Note the implications and actions that spring to mind below.

You can find further resources to support your thinking on this topic at **www.primeast.com/purposefulorganisation.**

## Further reading

We've focused a great deal on complexity, complication and simplicity in this chapter on structure. So I'm very grateful for David's end of chapter recommendation. The title says it all.

## From Complexity to Simplicity,
## Simon Collinson and Melvin Jay

The authors' main thesis is that simplicity in organizations creates wealth; complexity inhibits wealth-creation. In order to show this, the authors first define complexity as:

> the number of components in a system + the variety of relationships among these components + the pace of change of both the components and the relationships.

Complexity in this context is not the same as 'complicated', since the latter merely reflects the size and necessary inter-relatedness of things whereas the former points to ambiguity and unpredictability. Achieving organizational simplicity means that there is the right number of essential components and connections to deliver successful outcomes.

Complexity arises out of strategic, operational and organizational decisions and frameworks. Collinson and Jay demonstrate through case study how different types of unnecessary complexity have stymied some well-known corporate behemoths.

The authors' research into the causes and impacts of complexity conclude that as much as 10.2 per cent of EBITDA is lost by companies that are over-complex, compared to those that appear to be managing their organizations with appropriate levels of complexity.

What becomes clear, as the book's first section concludes, is that the balance of complexity/simplicity is – as much as anything – about knowing what your corporate capabilities are and then playing to them as strengths; bearing down on non-value-added processes and constantly reducing pointless bureaucracy; and maximizing new customer-centric opportunities to develop new revenue streams.

The authors spend around 35 per cent of the main body of the book discussing the impact of people and organizational design on complexity. This is because people – with their multi-various operational relationships – are a great source of complexity. The main people-issues (identified from the research which underpins this book's thesis) relate to unhelpful management behaviours, complex comms and meeting-structures and a poor focus on simplicity.

Organizationally, decisions about divisionalization, centralization, geographic spread, functionality, cultural diversity and management control-spans determine levels of complexity. The authors' research shows that complexity is minimized where organizational structure is focused single-mindedly on delivering the greatest degree of customer-centricity. They offer a good summary of the ways in which organizational complexity can be reduced, using tried and tested methods.

The book also looks at complexity arising from corporate strategy and the pain that is caused by frequent changes in strategic direction. The authors highlight as unduly ineffectual the sheer process of developing/updating annual budgets. They offer some standard approaches to challenging strategic direction and ensuring that the right priorities remain at the forefront of activity.

Also discussed as purveyors of complexity are operational processes, product/product portfolios and external factors.

Researched exhaustively, the book is supported by academically robust findings from desk research of 200 of the Fortune Global 500 companies and a survey of 600 managers from large European organizations.

# Strength of character

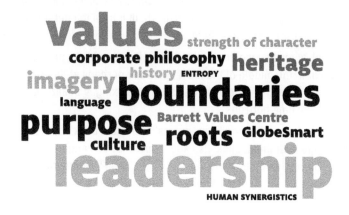

## 05

> *Only one who devotes himself to a cause with his whole strength and soul can be a true master. For this reason mastery demands all of a person.* ALBERT EINSTEIN

### Activity: Mealtime

Before we get stuck in to this chapter, I wonder if I can set you a task?
You have my permission to put it off if you're dying to get on with the read.
But at least think about it.

   I want you to put on a special meal for your family, or for a group of friends
or neighbours. And I want you to put into practice every chapter of the book
so far, including this one, making notes after each of the following tasks:

- First of all, what will the *purpose* of this meal be? No, don't immediately
  jump to the purpose as you see it; think about it from the perspective of
  each guest. Better still, ask them.

- Now, pick some key moments to *visualize*. Perhaps it's as people are
  arriving or in the middle of the main course or perhaps at the end when
  everyone has enjoyed the meal and they're relaxing. Visualize what you
  see at these time horizons.

- What will you do to *engage* your guests? Don't just think about how *you*
  will engage with them, think also about how they will engage with each
  other. Will you have any activities before the meal? Where will people
  sit? Will you change the seating plan between courses so people get to
  spend time with various others? Do you want a particular topic of
  conversation and if so how will you encourage it?

- What *structure* do you need? Arrival at a certain time to eat a while later?
  Seating plans have been touched on. What recipes and drinks will you
  offer? How many courses? Name cards?

OK, I guess you would probably have done most of the thinking up to now
anyway. But as we're starting a new chapter, its time to introduce *character*.
Character is all about the values that people hold dear and how they
manifest as behaviours, so:

- How well do you know the *character* of your guests? Could you guess
  their values, things that are important to them? Perhaps note them below
  under each person's name? How can you play to their values in the
  planning of your meal? Some things may be obvious in terms of food
  choice. But what about the mood of the room, topics of conversation,
  music choice and so on? Make notes on any insights you gain from
  thinking this through? Is it worth doing any subtle research?

Now go back to the purpose of the meal that you described at step one and
check for alignment. Is everything you've decided to do aligned to the purpose?
If it is, this could well be the most purposeful meal you've ever served. Enjoy.

# Roman roots

The way beliefs, values and behaviour play out for an individual determine their *character*. We can also talk about the character of a team or other group of people but when we speak of organizations, geographic regions or countries, we tend to use the word *culture*. Character also works in the corporate setting but we more commonly use *culture* here too. So, in this chapter you will read both terms and please feel free to use them interchangeably as appropriate.

Turning to culture, in a human context the word dates back to Roman times when the phrase *cultura animi* was used to describe the cultivation of the soul. In the 17th century, it became associated with the betterment of individuals principally through education and upbringing. Today we use the term 'culture' to describe the beliefs, values, behaviours, history, language and artefacts of a particular group of people together with a sense of how someone might 'fit in' with that group. We speak of national and ethnic cultures, regional cultures and, of course, corporate culture.

Interestingly, there are critical relationships between beliefs, values, behaviours, history, language and artefacts of any culture and understanding these is important in designing a purposeful organization.

Throughout this chapter we'll be focusing on organizational culture and its impact on purposeful performance. But it would be remiss to do that without first saying a brief word about global and other cultural influences.

# Be 'GlobeSmart'

In an increasingly global world, organizations are discovering, often at great cost, that they cannot expand to or trade with other parts of the world without understanding and managing the cultural differences. At Primeast we are fortunate to work closely with Aperian Global, a company that specializes in helping organizations to manage these factors. In their publication *What is Global Leadership?* (2011), Aperian Global's experts, Ernest Grundling, Terry Hogan and Karen Cvitkovich define 10 key behaviours that characterize great global leaders (in 2003, Grundling wrote *Working GlobeSmart*). They emphasize that many organizations around the world are missing a key point: that global leadership is distinctly different from the leadership skills needed for domestic operations. The global economy requires a new set of leadership skills. Leaders need a global mindset in order to be cross-functional and effective across cultures and nationalities. These skills were not as critical even a decade ago. Readers are provided with detailed descriptions of each behaviour, as well as information on how these behaviours can be applied in the context of leadership development programmes, executive coaching, global teams and leader-led action learning. Aperian Global famously provides a set of *GlobeSmart* tools to predict global cultural challenges and how to manage them. You can read more at tinyurl.com/qg9dtyc.

# Strength of character

Culture is talked about extensively in organizations, especially by leaders and those of us in organizational development. It translates down from the whole organization through departments to teams. We even use the word to describe the behavioural norms of a country or community. One context in which we don't use the word culture is when we're describing ourselves as individuals. Here, we tend to use the word *character* to describe the nature of who we are, a product of our beliefs, values and behaviours. People make judgements about our character based on what they see us doing and hear us saying. These judgements may be accurate and sometimes they are not.

The powerful thing for me is that the word *character* translates in any context. Also, where I have used it to describe the way an organization is, people get it. It is an acceptable word in most circumstances.

Because *character* is often used in the context of an individual, it is a useful word in that it reminds us that what we do as people really matters. Our character will have an effect on those around us and together we shape the character of our organizations. I love the phrase 'strength of character' because character can be powerful in the extreme, in good ways and bad, as we will discuss. It is our strength of character that largely determines the level of our performance as individuals, teams and organizations.

With all this in mind, while I encourage more widespread use of the word *character* in organizational development, I will revert to the word *culture* in this text, especially when referring to culture change methods that are well known.

# The power of culture

The knowledge that corporate culture has a significant effect on performance is not new. Kotter and Heskett's *Corporate Culture and Performance* (1992) was one of the first books I read about the power of culture.

Describing an 11-year study of organizations in the United States, the evidence is compelling. On several counts, those firms with adaptive cultures significantly outperformed those with unadaptive defensive cultures.

Specifically, the studies arrive at the following four conclusions (abbreviated):

- Corporate culture can have a significant effect on a firm's long-term economic performance. Over an 11-year period, firms with cultures emphasizing all key managerial constituencies (customers, stockholders and employees) and constructive leadership at all levels increased revenues by 682 per cent compared to 168 per cent for those that didn't. They also grew their workforces by 282 vs 36 per cent; stock prices by 901 vs 74 per cent and net incomes by 756 vs a mere 1 per cent.

- Corporate culture will probably be an even more important factor in determining success or failure for firms in the future, this being linked to a greater need to manage culture as the rate of change increases.

- Corporate cultures that inhibit strong long-term financial performance are not rare; they develop easily, even in firms full of reasonable and intelligent people.

- Although tough to change, corporate culture can be made more performance-enhancing. But this is complex, takes time and leadership guided by a realistic vision of what kinds of cultures enhance performance.

---

**CASE STUDY**   Culture change in the electricity industry
(how I got into all this)

---

In the 1990s I managed a number of change programmes in the UK electricity industry. One programme was associated with the introduction of competition in electricity metering. We had to make it possible for customers to buy their electricity from any UK company and to put in place systems enabling the associated data collection and metering systems to produce a timely and accurate bill. At its height, this programme comprised over 20 projects and I was proud of how our project teams were getting everything to knit together. The work was of national importance and, not surprisingly, our programme was subject to external audit. The auditors were thorough and we were delighted to secure a favourable audit report for our work. Favourable that was in all but one category: 'culture change'.

After the natural initial disappointment, I was intrigued. I knew nothing about this topic and was determined to understand more, for the good of the programme *and* to satisfy my curiosity. I made some enquiries with the auditors and was referred to a team of specialist consultants. We decided to spend a few days together. One of my team joined me for a weekend retreat, in Buxton, UK, where we met with two specialists in culture change.

The consultants enquired what I knew about culture change. I thought the answer was 'very little' but they focused on a time, earlier in my career, when I had managed our company's factory for refurbishing electricity meters. They asked me what I had done there and I told them a story of factory renovation, management team restructuring, team building, renaming rooms and introducing women into the management team for the first time in its history. The consultants said that the work I had undertaken to change the way this factory operated included a significant element of culture change. They also pointed out that I had gone about this work, like many managers, intuitively.

In the two-day retreat, I learnt that culture had a significant effect on performance, to the extent that it often made the difference between failure and outstanding success. I also discovered that culture, far from being nondescript and hard to pin down, was in fact very measurable. Not only can culture be measured in its current state, it can also be measured in the form it needs to be in order to deliver the purpose of the organization.

As programme manager, I was so excited that I handed the reins of the programme to my assistant manager and set off to the United States to learn more.

## Human Synergistics: Diagnosing culture by examining style

I visited Detroit, headquarters of Human Synergistics, founded by Dr J Clayton Lafferty, who is described on the website as:

> A pioneer in the psychology of achievement and human effectiveness, Lafferty founded Human Synergistics in 1971 to provide organizations and consultants with research-based materials for individual, leadership, and team development. Lafferty's background in clinical psychology, both practical and theoretical, and his knowledge of organizations and leadership in ancient and modern cultures, provided him with a broad and unique perspective for addressing the problems facing contemporary businesses, managers, and society in general.
>
> Source: tinyurl.com/kr6umkd.

J Clayton Lafferty sadly died in 1997, just before my trip to Detroit. Nevertheless I enjoyed a week with the Human Synergistics team, learning their methods. I returned to the UK and used their diagnostics to measure the culture we had in the electricity metering operation. We also examined the one we needed to support the new systems and ways of working and finally we measured the styles of managers and other key people involved in the operation. Subsequently I coached each one of these people in ways to shift their style in support of the intended culture. They were all very receptive and I was impressed by the power of the new methods I had learnt.

When the programme was complete, I had a short spell as a management development adviser in the electricity industry before taking my new-found skills, first into my own private practice, and ultimately into Primeast where I've enjoyed my consultancy career since 2002.

I have come to appreciate the quality of the culture change methods and diagnostics provided by Human Synergistics. They have been used extensively around the world for about half a century now. The diagnostic chart (Figure 5.1) is referred to as a 'circumplex' and is completed by undertaking a series of surveys of the organization in question from a number of different organizational and personal perspectives. Results are plotted by block, shading the 12 segments from the centre.

As well as having been tested by some of the world's most successful organizations, the diagnostics have a further advantage, in my view, in that the data collected by Human Synergistics have been used effectively to norm the measurement tools so that different results such as current culture, ideal culture and leadership style can be directly compared in a meaningful way. For me, this power becomes most pronounced when I'm coaching a leader in their style with the agreed aim of supporting a wider change in culture that has been diagnosed and agreed by their colleagues. Sitting in the coaching space with the leader, I remind them of the current cultural norms they had been involved in identifying and show them the associated circumplex. I then hold a second circumplex showing the target cultural norms they had defined with their colleagues. Once they're in the right space, I show them two further charts illustrating their personal style as seen by themselves and then their style as seen by their colleagues.

This progressive revealing of data has to be done in a sensitive way, which is why Human Synergistics will only allow the tools to be used by accredited practitioners. When the leader can see these four circumplexes on the table in front of them, it becomes quickly apparent how they could commit to

**FIGURE 5.1**    The circumplex

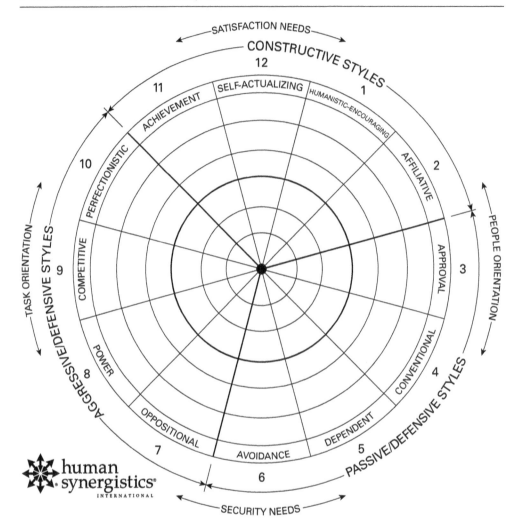

Research and development by Robert A Cooke PhD and J Clayton Lafferty PhD.

personal change to move the culture in a positive direction. I'm keen to emphasize that this is not about creating cloned leaders that all perfectly match the target culture. It's about everyone consciously modifying their behaviour (or character) in a positive and progressive manner that still values their uniqueness.

I've looked at many other diagnostics for culture change in almost 20 years as a practitioner and there are some interesting methods available. The only other one that I would personally hold alongside Human

Synergistics as a world-class tool that measures corporate culture and displays the data in a compelling manner is that offered by Richard Barrett and his colleagues at the Barrett Values Centre.

## Barrett Values Centre: Diagnosing culture by examining values

During the late 1990s and especially since joining the team at Primeast, I've probably spent more time on strategic alignment with a strong focus on culture change than anything else. As well as using the Human Synergistics methods, we have deployed other techniques. One such method that has impressed me significantly is the Cultural Transformation Tools (CTT) designed and offered by the Barrett Values Centre, the organization established by Richard Barrett.

Richard is an author, speaker and social commentator on the evolution of human values in business and society. He is the Founder and Chairman of the Barrett Values Centre and an internationally recognized thought leader on values, culture and leadership. He is the creator of CTT currently being used in over 90 countries to support more than 6,000 organizations and leaders in their transformational journeys. He is a Fellow of the World Business Academy, and Former Values Coordinator at the World Bank (source: **www.valuescentre.com/richard_barrett**).

I trained in the CTT methods under the guidance of Primeast's founder and chairman, John Campbell. Through Primeast, we have applied CTT to cultural challenges in organizations, and communities. As I write, we are exploring opportunities to embark on programmes that will measure the national cultures of two countries, one in Europe and the other in Africa.

The thing I love about CTT is that it identifies the values a population sees, the ones they personally hold dear and the ones they would like to see for the future. Not only that, it allocates the values to Barrett's framework depicting seven levels of consciousness ranging from *survival* at the base to *service* at the top (see Figure 5.2). Those involved in the associated change quickly understand how the living of these values massively affects the felt culture and effectiveness of those involved working together.

Practitioners will have their own views on the relative merits of culture change tools such as those offered by Human Synergistics, Barrett Values Centre and others. My personal view is that these two methods are world-class and provide useful data to help people understand what's happening in their world. Human Synergistics principally uses the language of *style* and Barrett focuses on the language of *values*. Each is valid and one may be more appropriate than the other in a particular context. Choice is important

## FIGURE 5.2  Seven levels of consciousness

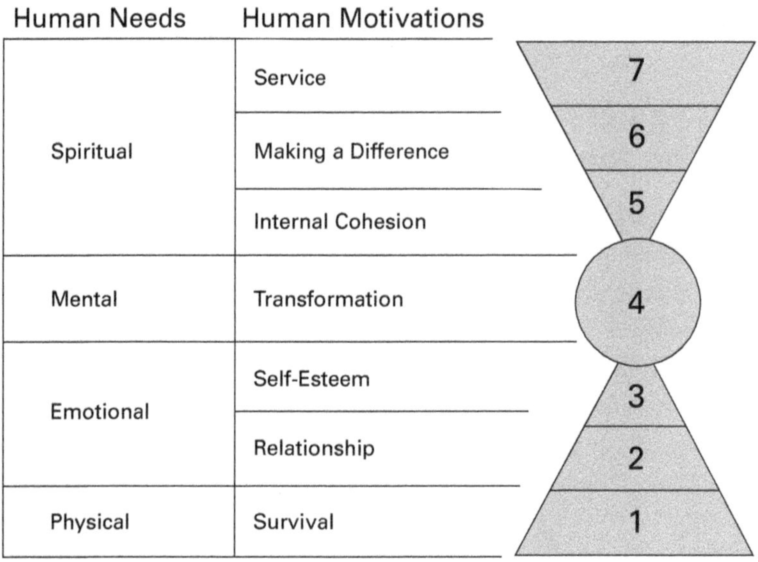

| Human Needs | Human Motivations | |
|---|---|---|
| Spiritual | Service | 7 |
| | Making a Difference | 6 |
| | Internal Cohesion | 5 |
| Mental | Transformation | 4 |
| Emotional | Self-Esteem | 3 |
| | Relationship | 2 |
| Physical | Survival | 1 |

**SOURCE**: Barrett Values Centre

and it is vital that organizations make a decision based on their own circumstances, preferably after consulting with a practitioner with experience of a range of methods.

## CASE STUDY   Culture change free-style

Of course, as my factory management days showed, culture change doesn't have to be done using proprietary diagnostics. Many leaders have changed the cultures of their organizations and even countries just through the power of their own beliefs, intuition and leadership. However, in today's complex world, it is worth considering the use of valid and measurable data to steer a culture change programme.

Another entirely valid approach to culture change is for leaders to discuss and determine the values they believe are appropriate to delivering the purpose of their organization or community. On a number of occasions, I have facilitated boardroom discussions to establish corporate purpose, vision and values. I remember one MD being delighted that his team of directors had agreed a set of six values that would guide behaviours in their business. He suggested that all we needed to do next was to tell the workforce what they were.

I counselled against a traditional cascade process of *telling* staff, on the basis that you cannot tell people what their values should be with any reliable effect. The best that can be done in this situation is for the directors to engage with staff; to share the values that are important to them; to see how they resonate with the wider organization; and what they mean in the context of each function. We facilitated a workshop to do just that and representatives from each function were asked to consider the directors' values and identify six behaviours under each heading that would help them to be more effective in their work. These behaviours were adopted as team charters and contributed significantly to culture change.

One example I often share from this assignment was the different interpretation of the value *integrity* that came from the sales and engineering functions of this manufacturing business. In sales, one of the behaviours identified was greeted by a loud applause from the rest of the business. The sales representative confidently stood up to announce that integrity in sales was about 'not promising the customer anything the business couldn't confidently deliver'. This was clearly a step in the right direction, especially from the perspective of the production department where people had spent most of their history scurrying around in order to deliver the sometimes outlandish promises made by the sales team to their customers.

Meanwhile, in engineering, they described integrity as being about making sure projects were rigorously planned. The example they gave was making sure that, when an engineer's time was put on the project Gantt chart, it was checked to ensure that such an engineer existed, wasn't engaged in other work and wasn't on holiday. Strangely the company had experienced several projects over-running due to such simple errors in the planning process.

# Culture and purpose

There are many ways to determine an ideal culture for the future of an organization or community. We could simply ask people, 'What would you like it to be like around here?' Another very different question might be, 'What does it need to be like here in order for you to be more productive?' Note that these two questions could produce very different answers.

For me, a far better question would be, 'What does it need to be like around here to deliver your stated purpose?' Of course, this is not helpful unless there *is* a stated purpose. This is why I recommend leaders spend time and effort determining purpose thoroughly and from the full range of stakeholder perspectives.

There is however a difficulty in this approach. You see, *purpose* probably provides insufficient clarity on what needs to happen by when. It only tells us what we're here to do. This is why it is vitally important to translate purpose into a compelling vision that clearly indicates what the organization will be doing and will have achieved by a given time horizon. The sooner this needs to happen, the more urgent the change becomes. Urgent change usually requires a different character of operation than a more measured evolution.

So, no matter what diagnostics or change management techniques are being used, I typically deploy the power of a compelling vision to steer a group or organization in culture change. I will encourage the CEO or other leader to talk passionately about the purpose and *especially* about their vision for a certain important time horizon. I will encourage them to take account of all stakeholder perspectives and especially the primary purpose of the organization. This is usually the provision of a defined service to a particular customer base by the workforce (including the wider supply chain).

Once a leader has made the picture clear, I ask the team to put themselves at this time horizon and picture in their minds what this looks like. In this way, they create their own powerful vision, a co-created sense of future. Now they are ready to diagnose or describe their target culture using diagnostics or some other creative method.

## Leadership and its impact on culture

Leaders have a significant impact on the culture of an organization. The character of those in the boardroom naturally filters down to the rest of the organization, whether this is deliberate or not. There literally is no place to hide. And it doesn't stop there. Every manager and every individual has the potential to influence the way things get done. Even people with no formal leadership role can have a massive effect on culture. This can of course be positive or negative.

In one team I managed several years ago, there were two ladies who seemed to infect the wider workforce with negativity. I watched what was going on and concluded that one lady was feeding the other with bad vibes and harmful lines. The other was the one that engaged with the rest of the staff spreading whatever lines she had been fed by her friend. Together they were a manager's nightmare and, after careful consideration and discussion, we decided to split them up by offering the first lady early retirement, which she was very happy to receive. We subsequently shared with the second lady our admiration for her ability to engage others and began a dialogue that resulted in her promotion to supervisor. She didn't let us down and turned out to be one of our best supervisors, having a positive impact on the rest of the team.

In the *Harvard Business Review* in 2000, Daniel Goleman, consultant with the Hay/McBer Group, described six key leadership styles:

- coercive;
- authoritative;
- affiliative;
- democratic;
- pacesetting;
- coaching.

He also describes the impact these five styles have on performance in the following categories:

- flexibility;
- responsibility;
- standards;
- rewards;
- clarity;
- commitment.

The styles and categories can be found in the full article which is available online at tinyurl.com/nmgfske.

The point I wish to make here is that, while the various leadership styles have their uses in different contexts (Goleman likens them to a set of golf clubs), they each have a measurable effect on the 'climate' or culture and on performance. Interestingly, the coercive and pacesetting styles overall have a negative impact on performance whereas the others tend to have positive impact to varying degrees.

Changing leaders at any level changes culture, as does actively changing the style, behaviour or character of a particular leader. This is why the proven methods of culture change, as described above, involve measuring current culture, establishing a target culture and measuring the style or values of leaders. This allows leaders to reflect on whether they are moving the culture in the right direction and to consciously commit to behavioural change for the benefit of the organization.

This form of leadership development usually takes place in the coaching arena. Leaders need time and space to examine how they see themselves and how others see them. Then they can begin to change behaviours that may be deeply engrained. My experience is that most leaders really welcome this opportunity and I have worked with people at all levels from CEO to the shop floor who have risen well to the challenge of consciously changing what they do and how they do it.

# The boundaries of culture

As discussed at the start of this chapter, Kotter and Heskett's seminal work on culture change, *Corporate Culture and Performance* (1992), identifies that culture has a massive impact on performance. Phrased positively, a constructive culture significantly and positively impacts the bottom line. Phrased negatively, but usefully, a defensive culture places some devastating boundaries on performance.

In the spirit of inspiring performance *beyond boundaries* (the subtitle of this book), I'd like to explore some of these boundaries below, referencing some of the norms and values from the Human Synergistics and Barrett methodologies respectfully with my own take on these to evidence the boundaries leaders may unwittingly be placing around performance. Note that Human Synergistics classifies 12 cultural norms and Barrett references over 100 hundred values. So what follows is just a handful of Human Synergistics norms with my thoughts and a brief extract from one of Richard Barrett's papers.

## Cultural styles

Human Synergistics identifies the following 12 cultural norms that represent the norms and behavioural expectations in the organization:

- Constructive norms:
  - Achievement;
  - Self-Actualizing;
  - Humanistic–Encouraging;
  - Affiliative.
- Passive/defensive norms:
  - Approval;
  - Conventional;
  - Dependent;
  - Avoidance.

- Aggressive/defensive norms:
  - Oppositional;
  - Power;
  - Competitive;
  - Perfectionistic.

Full definitions of these norms are available freely at the Human Synergistics website.

The research and associated theory indicates that Constructive norms should always be highest (above the 50th percentile) and Defensive norms lower and below the 50th percentile. That said, it must be noted that this is context-specific, demanding a need for varying degrees of Defensive norms but always below the 50th percentile and always tempered with a highly Constructive norm. For example, in an aggressive market where efficiency matters, there may need to be reasonably stiff challenge (opposition) to new ideas that divert efforts along unhelpful tangents. And clearly some professions require higher levels of perfectionism than others. But let's take a handful of hypothetical scenarios (based on my experience) to show how easily boundaries can arise in connection with some of the defined norm.

## Avoidance

Perhaps the most obviously limiting boundary from the listed norms, the *Avoidance* norm is about the expectation to avoid dealing with problems or confronting difficult scenarios. In one organization undergoing significant national change, there were more problems than managers felt able to deal with. Subsequently, problems that absolutely needed to be resolved were being put to the bottom of manager's pending-trays, thus causing detriment to achievement. This example shows a culture where the managers were expected to shift responsibilities and avoid conflict. It was also reflected in personal behaviour of the managers, which showed up in their diagnosed personal style. It was also reflected in the culture where avoidance had become an organizational norm.

## Achievement

Not surprisingly, in the same organization, *Achievement* norms were un-desirably low. The relationship between Avoidance norms and Achievement norms is an obvious one and action taken to reduce Avoidance will probably lead to greater Achievement. However, there are other actions that can remove boundaries from Achievement expectations and many of them have been already discussed in this book. For example, having a clear and compelling purpose, an inspiring vision and open and encouraging engagement will all ensure that there is an expectation for Achievement, as will clear goals, targets and results that measure progress to the vision (as we'll explore in the next chapter).

## Perfectionistic

I want to talk about this because it is not such an obvious barrier to performance but it can be a hugely damaging one. Expecting perfection in its extreme form is about attending to detail in an unreasonable way, causing members to work long hours, sacrifice of family and social life and (of great concern to the business) failure to attend to more important things such as strategy, commercial relationships and personal development.

There is nothing wrong with attention to detail if that is what is required for a quality service or product or to attend responsibly to the company finances. In fact, in diagnosis, this would show as high Achievement norms. The challenge is to find the right level of detail to attend to and to make sure other important things don't suffer as a consequence. It is easy to imagine how, in an aggressive organization, people will hide in the detail and use this as an excuse for under-achievement. As practitioners we can often tell whether a high degree of Perfectionistic norm on the part of an individual is adversely affecting performance by noticing the degree of other norms, such as low Achievement, and Conventional or high Avoidance expectations.

## Power

This is such an interesting boundary and it needs to be closely examined to be understood. Let's first agree that expecting organizational power is potentially a good thing. It is, by nature, a source of energy and energy is what drives absolutely everything in our universe. But Power norms as measured by this instrument refer to members being expected to take charge and 'control' others, and make decision autocratically. Clearly there are times when this is useful and a degree of this type of power can be helpful, especially in tough times. But while the overuse of Power expectation can bring increased performance, it often breeds compliance and low performance and is short-lived. In extreme cases, if the norms result in people feeling bullied or threatened to perform, they may do so for a while, until they've had enough and consequently seek employment elsewhere. Power norms can therefore bring high attrition, long-term sickness and claims for constructive dismissal.

## Competitive

Another often misunderstood norm, Competitive in this instrument is about the expectation that people in the same team or organization compete against each other and win. It is not about expecting competition in the marketplace. Internal competition overplayed can cause people to withhold information or resources from their colleagues, for example, to win that coveted 'salesperson of the year' award or personal bonus. It is widely held that teams can seriously outperform groups of individuals. But you don't get teamwork by over-encouraging members to compete with each other.

A good example of how someone can misunderstand the organizational norms and consequently adversely modify their personal style was regarding a leader (and keen sportsman) in a local authority whom I coached as part of a culture change programme. His personal style was naturally Competitive. But he had withheld his competitive tendency in response to the views of colleagues who were fundamentally anti-competition. In the coaching arena, we discussed his style and talked about his love of football for a while. I then asked, in the context of his job, who or what the competition was. He quickly cited a long list of social ills such as unemployment, poverty, crime and so on. Realizing that this was a valid competition for him at work, he became inspired once more to *compete* in a way that would be highly appropriate to the needs of the organization.

## Self-Actualizing

I usually interpret this for clients as being about the expectation that members will experience high job satisfaction and a sense of personal meaning. Organizations with high Self-Actualizing norms are ones where the goals and values of the organization and the individual are aligned. In terms of values, this is where I particularly like the word *character* as it works at both levels.

The key question is whether the values of the organization are aligned to those of the people who work there. If there is synergy between the two sets of values, there is an inherent motivation to perform. Similarly if there is synergy of direction as suggested in purpose, vision and objectives, then people will invest extraordinary levels of discretionary energy in delivering them. The sad thing is that people often don't get the opportunity to check this out. And when they do, many organizations play small. They diminish their higher purpose and cause less Self-Actualizing through an over-focus on something like sales or profit. Such matters are important but rarely *as important* to the individual as the service being provided.

An example of where we were able to reinforce a Self-Actualizing norm was when we worked with a global clinical trial team of approaching 50 people from around the world. Their attention was so focused on the plan and budget that they had almost forgotten the amazing power of the product on trial: the power to save patient lives and improve quality of patient life.

Providing space for the scientists to convey this and thereby what their organization really stood for was powerful. It took about half an hour but caused a visible and palpable shift in motivation for the whole team.

I have just quoted a few brief examples above of the kind of cultural styles that the Human Synergistics method can draw attention to. We've only examined half of the set of 12 norms but I think we've explored enough to make the point that cultural norms can be the cause of serious performance limitations. This is why this method is so powerful as a cultural measurement and management tool that can facilitate performance improvement.

# Values and the boundary of cultural entropy

Barrett's Cultural Transformation Tools (CTT), mentioned on page 125, allow people to diagnose the culture through the selection of the values they see being lived out in the current culture, the ones they personally hold dear and the ones they see necessary to deliver a specified better future. Most of the values in the system are positive but some are deliberately negative. These are detrimental to the performance of the population under examination. Such negativity in the organization is referred to as *cultural entropy* and the following is a short extract from an excellent paper, 'High Performance: It's all about entropy', which is freely available at the Barrett website.

## Cultural Entropy (CE)

Cultural entropy is comprised of three elements:

- Factors that slow the organization down and prevent rapid decision-making – bureaucracy, hierarchy, confusion, fire-fighting, and rigidity.
- Factors that cause friction between employees – internal competition, blame, manipulation, rivalry, and intimidation.
- Factors that prevent employees from working effectively – control, caution, micro-management, short-term focus, job-insecurity, risk-aversion, and territorialism.

The Cultural Values Assessment (CVA) of the Barrett Values Centre enables organizations to measure the level of cultural entropy, the degree of values alignment, and an indication of the level of mission alignment in an organizational culture.

Cultural entropy in an organization is calculated by finding the proportion of votes for potentially limiting values that employees pick in answer to the question about how their organization currently operates. The level of cultural entropy usually falls in the range 5–45 per cent. We have found from our experience of measuring the cultures of more than 6,000 organizations that when cultural entropy reaches the upper end of this range bankruptcy, implosion or aggressive takeovers that strip the assets of an organization frequently occur.

SOURCE: www.valuescentre.com

From this powerful narrative, it is easy to see how cultural entropy is another way of describing the unwanted cultural boundaries organizations place around performance.

**CASE STUDY**    Cultural entropy and being sensitive and informed about local ways

One of our clients is a global chemical company that acquired a plant producing an ingredient for a pharmaceutical product. This was a 24/7 process that converted the raw material into a purified substance which was then transported for final processing elsewhere.

The plant had the potential to be highly profitable but was located on a remote island where the local culture was very strong and very different from that of the new parent company. It was even different from the prevailing culture on the nearest mainland, a factor that was quite unanticipated by the parent company. It was also critically incompatible with the expectations of the plant's new owners to fulfil its commercial potential.

The local, almost pre-industrial culture was influenced significantly by local townships and a crofting (small farm) community. One of many challenges was an unswerving commitment to observe holy days that made it difficult to staff the plant at these times. There was a strong sense of hierarchy in the community away from the workplace that trumped the management hierarchy at the plant, making workplace discipline difficult. Prior to takeover the management style was similarly old-fashioned, autocratic and very different from that of the more modern parent company.

The general manager was inherited by the parent company. Although quite new to the business, he was seen by the staff to be very closely associated with the previous owner–manager and the autocratic culture that characterized the plant at that time. Together they had engineered the sale of the plant to the new owners. However, due to the new technology issues, the general manager struggled to achieve the significant plant performance expectations necessary to deliver growth opportunities. The cultural challenges associated with the staff were also prevalent in the senior team, preventing them from getting fully aligned to the new corporate expectations.

As well as performance below expectations, difficulties were highlighted in an employee opinion survey. Tensions between management and the workforce were apparent. There were also many breaches of procedure including some that put production, the actual plant and even people's lives at risk.

My colleagues worked closely with the general manager to investigate the challenge and to support him through coaching and leadership facilitation. Barrett's CTT methodology was used to collect data on the current cultural challenges and to establish a target culture for successful operation. Significant cultural entropy (over 40 per cent) was identified (see how bad this is in reference to the extract from Richard Barrett's paper above). Leadership and management development were provided to all managers and supervisors and there was also a plant-wide team development intervention. All of this was conducted in a manner that would specifically support the required cultural change.

Another key move that supported the transition was the appointment of a new production manager, reporting to the general manager. This new appointment was made on the basis of experience, interpersonal ability and cultural compatibility. In a way he served as a bridge between the various cultural differences.

As a result of this intervention, life at the plant has improved greatly. Relationships have improved and productivity has increased. A greater sense of community within the plant has resulted in teams working purposefully out of choice to develop the quality of collaboration between departments. This is resulting in fewer disruptive incidents, greatly reduced reworking, less employee absence and little wastage. Targets are now being met as a matter of course. At the time of writing, the last quarter's production was as much as the whole of the previous year.

The senior management team is now a cohesive unit which is actively engaged in developing the quality of leadership experienced within the plant. The plant's business unit management has now stepped down the level of time and attention expended on the plant in recent months to concentrate their efforts on more urgent issues elsewhere. Confidence has increased so much that the parent company has planned for further capital investment as part of its 20-year strategy.

# All may not be what it seems

A common trap that many companies seem to fall into is to make the definition of their corporate character nothing more than a game of words. I have had first-hand experience of companies where their nicely crafted values statements and images are proudly posted in reception and elsewhere but where there has been little engagement with the people who work there or even with the managers. I was speaking at a management masterclass in a pharmaceutical company where this was the case. I made reference to the values I had seen in reception and the audience admitted collectively that they did not even know these were the corporate values. They thought they were just 'inspirational posters'.

**CASE STUDY**  Enron

Interestingly, Enron, whose leaders went to jail and which went bankrupt from fraud had the values *integrity, communication, respect* and *excellence* displayed in their lobby. Of course there was a big difference between these nice-sounding words and what was really respected at Enron as the following extract from an article in *The Economist* shows:

> The twister hits: Nothing about Enron's demise was surprising; nor is what must be done
>
> WITH each fresh turn in the Enron tale, one conclusion gets plainer. America's biggest bankruptcy was not a result merely of commercial misfortune or personal crookedness. The collapse was possible only because of flaws in the way that American capitalism has worked over the past decade. These flaws were widely known, and much discussed. But as America's economy and stockmarket boomed, few had an interest in fixing them. Presumably that will now change.
>
> America's love affair with equities played a part in Enron's failure. The pay of senior executives and board members hangs on the performance of a company's shares – their reward for good performance aligned their interests with those of shareholders, supposedly. In practice, the alignment of interests is imperfect.
>
> Equity-related pay schemes tempt managers to seek to boost the share price in the short term, giving them the chance to cash out their stakes, to the detriment of the company and its shareholders in the long run. Enron's

*managers made wide use of 'special purpose entities' (SPEs), vehicles that shifted losses and debts off the company's balance sheet. The company's directors should have asked tough questions about the practice, but they did not. After all, a lot of personal wealth was at stake, for Enron's creative accounting suggested to investors that the company was more profitable and less leveraged than it really was. That kept Enron's share price up. The interests of 'insiders' were thus at odds with those of outside shareholders. If managers and directors were not allowed swiftly to sell the shares they were given, then interests would be better aligned. Last year, executives sold stacks of shares even as Enron got into trouble.*

*Employees at lower levels fared less well. Many lost chunks of their retirement funds, which were invested in Enron shares: an absurd risk for supposedly prudential savings schemes. Congress may now legislate to cap the proportion of a plan that may be invested in an employer's shares.*

*The Economist* (print edition), New York, 17 January 2002

# History

As with any culture, the *way things are done* in an organization is significantly dependent on the history. We talked about biology and cell life earlier and made the point that even single cells keep a record of their character in their DNA and that this is a product of many generations. Humans are programmed by their parents and they, in turn, pass down ways of doing things to their children. No wonder then, in complex organizations, that the culture is massively affected by the corporate history. This is further exacerbated by the complexity of corporate growth through mergers and acquisitions and the practices of subcontractors and partnerships. Culture is complex and history needs to be understood in order to make the best of all possible futures.

One useful technique for understanding the history of a culture is to identify the written and especially the 'unwritten rules' that affect behaviour and that have emerged over time. Deciphering 'why we are where we are' enables an effective strategy for change and is at the heart of the culture change methods used by the Foretel Group (**www.peopleandculture.co.uk**).

Sadly there is a tendency, primarily due to the ego of leaders, to discredit what went before or the way things get done in other parts of the organization. This practice is frequently unwise. It is especially disheartening for staff to hear how bad things were in the past, especially if it was a past they were a part of. Far better for leaders to honour and respect the past while acknowledging that the future demands new ways. The key is to move forward by building on and adding to existing strengths and eliminating what no longer works.

## CASE STUDY    Honouring the past, artefacts and language

You will recall from earlier that in the 1990s I managed a small factory that refurbished and tested electricity meters. Shortly after being appointed, the very first meter station manager died. I instinctively chose to fly his son over from the United States to open a new extension to the factory. He unveiled a brass plaque which we'd had engraved to commemorate his father, remembering him as the founder of the factory and honouring his work and that of his colleagues. I didn't realize it at the time but I was later told by our staff how powerful that simple gesture was and how it inspired them to work hard to keep the factory going through tough times.

Some of the worst aspects of the culture were actually embedded in the very artefacts and language of the factory. For example, when I took over, there was pornography posted on the walls by the mainly male workers. Then there were the rooms where people met. First there was 'the mess' where people ate and the 'bollocking room' next to the foreman's office where people went for 'performance management'.

As part of creating a more positive place to work, I posted new signs on the doors to these rooms. They became 'Talk Shop One' and 'Talk Shop Two' respectively. Not only was I changing the language (obliviously at that time) but I was also changing the artefacts of the organization. I also changed the artefacts by taking down the pornography and replacing it with framed pictures of smiling staff, taken on an outdoor experiential team building event I had organized.

In Talk Shop One we further enhanced the positive culture by installing some display cabinets with the history of metering shown with some old meters that had previously been gathering dust in a corner of the warehouse. This simple gesture made a bold statement that electricity meters were interesting and that the staff who had worked on them over the years had an important role to play in the electricity industry.

## *Further evidence of the power of heritage, imagery and evolving language*

One of my clients is the managing director of a company that fabricates the ducting that is used on nuclear power stations. In the boardroom of the same company hangs a picture of the first premises that the company had – a bicycle shop. My client is very proud of this heritage and cites it in the fabulous rapport he has with his staff, their families and the local community.

Interestingly, the same company is also deliberately changing artefacts looking forward through imagery. It is in the midst of a culture change programme, prompted by a desire to take advantage of growth opportunities. My client has chosen to brand the change programme Right First Time. To anchor this, his managers have held focus groups with staff to enquire what 'right first time' means in the context of each work team. A marketing team was then given the task to turn the thoughts of the staff into powerful imagery to be displayed in their respective workplaces.

There are many more examples that further evidence the power of language in culture change (as hinted in my meter station case study above regarding the transition from 'the mess' and 'the bollocking room'). For example, we've all witnessed the evolving language of staff in catering and other service industries where they have been trained to show respect, good manners and generally care for customers. In the early days, changes to a more customer-centric behaviour had to be systematically trained in to those providing the service. But once it became the *way things are done*, it no longer required such strong leadership. Remember, once behaviours are embedded in the subconscious or in the DNA, they no longer need to be consciously applied. Having said that, it is wise to encourage mindfulness in customer service to prevent lapses into unhelpful ways.

### Activity: Check the language

Think back to the last time you felt good about the service provided at a restaurant or shop. What sort of language was being used? How did that make you feel? And how did it affect the atmosphere of the place?

How could you begin a new language trend at your place of work that initiates or supports a desired culture change?

# The culture of a learning organization

In Chapter 3 on engagement, we talked about how a purposeful organization should usefully and systematically become a *learning organization*, taking time to make sure that people collaborate about how they go about their work, especially regarding topics that are important, such as those mentioned in the vision. We said that even the act of sharing provides learning, that the learning increases when it is combined and is especially valuable when it is reapplied and sustained in context of the work in hand.

Sadly, too many people consider a learning organization to be one that simply keeps track of its knowledge, making it available to others via databases. While good knowledge management is essential to the learning organization, this isn't the hardest part. As with most change programmes, the difficult part is changing the culture. Here are just a few cultural changes that are essential if an organization is to become a true learning organization:

- **Purposeful:** I unashamedly place this as my number one value for a learning organization. People should be totally aligned and committed to the purposes of the organization.
- **Curious:** People should be actively curious to learn better ways of delivering the purpose of the organization.
- **Open:** People must be prepared to share knowledge openly with others in the best interests of the organization.
- **Selfless:** People should be prepared to subjugate their personal agendas and egos beneath those of the organization in terms of knowledge and learning.
- **Challenging:** People should be prepared to challenge and be challenged about the espoused best practices and work together to establish the new best way to do something.
- **Supporting:** People should become advocates of better ways of working, role-modelling what is best for the organization.

Some of these values or characteristics don't come naturally and therefore have to be actively developed.

Starting with being *purposeful* we all know how easy it is to be caught up in playing our personal part in the company's activities. People need opportunity and reminders to keep the big picture in mind.

When the going gets tough, it is hard to break off from the urgent challenges of the day to investigate better ways of doing things. Purposeful learning organizations encourage *curiosity* by staging learning opportunities and sponsoring professional development. They systematically watch what is going on in their marketplace and encourage new ways of working that keep them ahead of the competition.

Some people are more *open* than others and those who are naturally more reserved will need encouragement to share insights. Putting time in the calendar for knowledge sharing is one way of doing this, as is the provision of social media specifically for collaboration. But such systems should not be a substitute for frequent informal chats and an open-door policy where constructive dialogue is the norm.

People can get very precious when they have authored a particular way of doing something and may take it personally when others find potentially better ways of doing things. Leaders need to reinforce that the discovery of new ways shouldn't be insulting to those associated with the old. This isn't always an easy shift to make.

Cultivating such a spirit of *selflessness* paves the way for constructive *challenging* which is much easier to secure when people are selfless in serving the purpose.

Finally, a culture of *support* and encouragement for learning and sharing is required for a productive learning organization. Lapsing into old ways of criticism, blame and silo operation will cause the spirit of purposeful learning to fade rapidly.

## *Using structure to manage culture*

In Chapter 4 on structure, we looked at the importance of putting structure into the way we do things. This applies not only to the obvious ways we structure our processes and have systems for management information and knowledge. We can also use structure and logic in the way we manage the character of our operation at any level. The diagnostics we described above, such as Human Synergistics and Barrett Values Centre, clearly provide structure and clarity to the behaviours manifest in an organization. I remember working with one head of IT and wondering whether he would *get* the culture thing. I discovered to the contrary. Once he could see the data, it all became clear.

Organizations who define their corporate values and behaviours systematically put structure around character. They are thereby saying that 'to fit in around here' and to contribute positively, these are the things that need to matter and here are some behaviours you can take as examples. Corporate values provide structure at the highest level and, as described above, I like to work with teams of people in an organization to turn the values into team charters that define what the values mean in the context of each team's work.

The same applies to us at a personal level. We can check how we fit into a set of values by asking what they mean to us. We can also start from a clean sheet of paper and work out our own values and use these to help us manage our behaviours.

---

### Activity: Personal values exercise

Think about what is important to you and make a note of these as personal values. As an example, my personal values are *spirit, vitality, family, adventure, service* and *compassion*. In my smartphone I carry notes for each year and, as I think of things I need to do, I ask which value they support and in which year they will happen. This forms my life plan and it is inspiring to see how the future begins to clarify for me. Incidentally, this is also a way of growing my vision and ensuring it grows in line with my values.

Against each of your values, list the key beliefs, behaviours, actions, goals, or activities (according to your preference) that bring the values alive for you.

You may also wish to compare your personal values with those of your organization. How aligned do you think you are?

---

## Measuring progress towards the cultural vision

Like any activity that is important, there is merit in measuring progress along the journey. If you've used a diagnostic to help you plan your cultural future, you will probably want to measure progress along the way. Don't be disappointed if, a year into your programme, the target hasn't been met. The important thing is whether you are making progress. Also, test the character of your organization by asking people whether things are changing and in what way. Even if you haven't used a diagnostic, that's no excuse not to test your progress.

If your organization has a set of corporate values, perhaps you can test the progress towards their delivery by surveying the extent to which they are being lived. If you have specific behaviours, then use these for more granular measurement. Better still, if each team has established its charter, then measure against that. Finally, if people have made personal commitments in their performance objectives to do something to support the values, then measure that too. At Primeast, each year, every member of staff commits to three of our values and a specific behaviour for each that they would like to attend to in the coming year.

## Corporate philosophy: Statements of belief

Usually when we talk about corporate culture, we speak in terms of values and behaviours and a great deal of effort goes into establishing corporate values and managing the ensuing behaviours. But we do well to remember that our values are a function of what we believe.

Leaders can win (or lose) the hearts and minds of their people through powerful statements of belief. It is often our beliefs that cause us to make a stand for something. As we shall examine closer in Chapter 8 (on talent), this happened to me when the beliefs of others were flying around large corporations in the 1990s. In a nutshell, some people were expressing a belief that: 'talent is scarce, you'd better get your share, pay it well, develop it and hang on to it'. As a result, organizations were identifying (and some still are) elite streams of high-potential people, naming them *talent* and focusing significant budget on their development. Now don't get me wrong, I absolutely believe in developing people according to their potential but I don't believe in creating elitist, divisive strategies where some people are labelled as *talent* and others, therefore, as *not*.

I found myself repeatedly making this statement of belief:

> Organizations reach prime performance when they recognize, value, develop and use the talents of **all** their people in the delivery of their objectives.

I also warned business leaders:

> Neglect the 90 per cent at your peril for they're the ones grafting at the sharp end right alongside your customers.

I didn't know it at the time but I was making a statement of belief. This (first) statement has become known as our philosophy of *talent liberation* which runs as a thread through the programmes we deliver around the world. It stems from an unshakable belief that everyone, without exception, has amazing talent to offer the world, especially when they discover their vocation, and that leaders in organizations have a duty to recognize it, work out how it adds value, encourage its development and make good use of it. We know this philosophy works and can deliver massive performance improvements.

The point is this: if something is as important to an organization as talent is to me, then leaders do well to understand how it supports the purpose and vision of their operation and articulate this belief in the form of a philosophy statement. I've seen good leaders do this formally and informally on many subjects that are important to them such as health, safety, environment, quality, customer service, diversity and corporate social responsibility.

Now test how effective your own organization is when it comes to character.

# 10 questions on **character**

*To what extent...*

...does your organization have a strategy for managing culture in a purposeful way?

...has the current culture been measured to understand the character of your organization in a quantifiable way?

...has an ideal culture been targeted in consultation with stakeholders to consciously deliver the purpose and vision of the business?

...does your organization have a set of values or other criteria that describe the intended culture, that are made available to all stakeholders?

...have all stakeholders been given the opportunity to engage with these values in order to work out what they mean in terms of behaviours in the work that they do?

...have teams been given the chance to commit to shared behaviours in the form of a team charter that supports the organization's values and from which they can regularly hold each other to account?

...are people given the opportunity to review the organization's values and commit to new behaviours to support these values on a regular basis, as part of performance development?

...have people been given the opportunity to diagnose or otherwise state their personal values and hold these alongside those of the organization to test and encourage their alignment?

...has your organization explored the key threads of its vision and established a clear and guiding philosophy for aligning these threads (eg customer service, quality, safety, corporate social responsibility, talent management etc)?

...specifically, has your organization chosen to be a learning organization and paid deliberate attention to the characteristics of such an operation?

## Score

| | |
|---|---|
| **0** not at all | **6** reasonably well |
| **2** a little | **8** very well |
| **4** moderately | **10** completely |

What do your scores tell you? Make notes on the implications and actions that spring to mind.

You can find further resources to support your thinking on this topic at **www.primeast.com/purposefulorganisation.**

## Further reading

We've affirmed the relationship between the character of an organization and the values that are lived out by its people every day. We've also referenced the work of values guru Richard Barrett. How appropriate that David has selected a book that gives a how-to guide on living our values, with an introduction by Barrett himself.

## The 31 practices: Release the power of your organization's VALUES every day, Alan Williams and Alison Whybrow

This book opens with a dedication from Richard Barrett – 'we dedicate this book to the alchemy of relationships, curiosity and serendipity' – who goes on to describe the text as an 'encyclopaedia of understanding about what it takes to build the neural pathways of an organization'. At the heart of its 31 chapters, the book is essentially about authenticity; and about the 'how' of what we do at work, in support of all the normal goal-setting and performance-management tools and techniques already embedded in the organization.

As Barrett implies in the quote above, it is also very much a reference book: the chapters are bite-sized, which makes this an easy pick up/put down tome. Furthermore, each chapter concludes with a 'want to know more?' panel, offering further reading.

So, what about these 31 practices? Well, the concept of developing 31 values-based practices that can be adopted and practised by your employees – one for each day of the month – reflects the recent seismic shifts in the world of work; partially resulting from the growth in technology as an enabler to trading and operational effectiveness, partially from the increasing sophistication in consumer understanding; and partially from the fact that an organization's stakeholders increasingly control the perception of that entity, not the organization itself (for example, for customers the least senior people have the greatest influence in forming perceptions about the entity).

If you accept all of that, then enduring organizational success is firmly embedded in its core values. Values, deeply held beliefs that reflect what is important to us and what motivates us, define how organizations are perceived and experienced by their stakeholders. They are a 'behavioural and decision-making compass' (Rosanna Fiske, quoted by the authors). The purpose of the 31 practices is to enable people in organizations to reconnect with what is at the core, to promote authenticity and consistently high, positive performance at work and to facilitate individual wellbeing.

After a comprehensive introduction, the authors move on to a discussion about purpose: they argue that unless there is a compelling purpose (the 'what'), the values (the 'how') are pretty much redundant. Selecting the most appropriate organizational purpose means that entities can ride out periods of turbulence in a way that less-grounded organizations cannot. Interestingly, the examples given (pages 65–66) by the authors of organizational purpose focus on employee, rather than on customer; the logic being that an energized and focused employee will naturally look after and delight the customer.

There follow a number of sections that cover the development and implementation of values in support of the purpose. These are practical in nature, giving the practitioner–reader the opportunity to take away tools for deployment in the organizational context. They draw on the work done by Barrett's Values Centre on the seven levels of organizational consciousness. And they look at the measurement and refinement of the values as they transition from concepts into the 31 practices.

Part 3 of the book looks at the underlying principles that give the 31 practices their robustness – these are discussed under the three headers of heart, mind and body; the emotional (which deals with emotions, inspiration and happiness), the mind's inner landscape (mindfulness, resilience and storytelling) and the physical (practice, strengths and discipline). This section of the book is incredibly powerful, personalized and instructive. It focuses on the individual as the key unit of effect in the delivery of organizational excellence, and it is a precursor to Part 4's attention on the broader context of the organization.

Part 4 of the book deals with some big topics – complexity, change, wisdom, neuroscience, choice and leadership. These are covered with useful summaries on the latest thinking for each topic, made accessible and practical.

In Part 5, the authors provide additional case studies to show how the development and application of the 31 practices can benefit organizations. Furthermore they demonstrate that the approach can be individualized for personal development and performance.

This is a great reference book for those seeking to bring some meaning and order to the ever-changing world of work. As a framework for fundamental organizational change; as a 'how-to' guide for someone wishing to bring order into their life; as a reminder of what's possible in our complex world – this is a must-read.

# Results to track purposeful progress

## 06

> *However beautiful the strategy,*
> *you should occasionally look at the results.*
>
> **WINSTON CHURCHILL**

# An affirmation

Before going into detail, I want to begin by concisely affirming in my own words why results are so important in the context of a purposeful organization:

> A purposeful organization understands exactly what it is there for through the eyes of all its key stakeholder groups. It works hard to find synergy between these perspectives and to translate them into a clear, comprehensive and compelling vision at the most important time horizons. To test its progress towards this vision, the organization will measure key results that correspond to the most important features of its vision. In a fractal manner, this will happen at every level of the vision from the strategic to the personal with results being measured in an appropriate level of granularity that is meaningful to those responsible for the work. In short, if we want to know what to measure, we need only to examine our vision.

# Purpose-driven or results-driven?

There is a key philosophical question to be answered at this stage in the book. The question is this:

> What is it that drives performance in our organization?

Think back to how many times you've heard each of these two phrases: *purpose-driven* and *results-driven*. It may be to do with the circles I move in but I reckon I hear 10 times as many references to results-driven as I do to purpose-driven. This excludes of course dialogue with my close colleagues and better known clients who tend to speak a similar language to me anyway.

I have seen too many executives wracked with pain and trapped in misery in organizations that proclaim a singular focus on results and which glorify their results-driven culture. I also know of excellent leaders who have left such organizations, especially when short-term financial results have stood in the way of more sustainable, purposeful progress. The CIPD paper *Purpose, the Golden Thread*, referenced in Chapter 1, clearly identifies the dangers of this and reinforces the need for a more purposeful focus.

Everything we have said thus far is about how purpose should absolutely drive everything in our organization. Our purpose should be very clear, well understood, inspiring and balanced to take account of all stakeholder perspectives. Spending time understanding our purpose and tuning it in this way makes everything else we do clearer and more aligned.

There are so many dangers associated with a results-driven mindset and with results-driven organizations. Consider for a moment the subtitle of this book: *How to inspire performance beyond boundaries*. It is easy to see how targets and results are likely to place boundaries around performance which may or may not be desirable. Depending on the character of our organization, a target will be something we are supposed to hit, almost hit, slightly over-deliver on and in rare cases smash to pieces. Whatever the perspective, targets have a tendency to define and hence place boundaries above and below performance expectations.

Target-driven results (which most measured results are) tend to be transactional. At the personal level, if you pay me £100 I expect to give you value for your investment, a level of performance that represents a fair return. If you desire a greater return, you may have to pay me more. Of course, not everyone has this transactional, even mercenary attitude. Some people will simply do their best whatever their remuneration and whatever the target.

Then there is the old saying *What gets measured gets done*. Targets focus the mind and guide our actions. This can of course be a good thing but not if it takes our eye off our purpose.

Being purpose-driven doesn't mean we don't have targets and results or that they don't matter. But psychologically we remain conscious that our purpose is our reason for being, our reason for doing the work we do. Purpose is what gets us out of bed in the morning. Being purpose-driven causes us to lift our eyes above the horizon of our targets to a greater quest. It drives us to be creative, to think more widely than the current best way and to explore new opportunities to serve our customer and the world better. This just happens to be good for our organization as well, especially if we have taken time to harmonize stakeholder expectations, as affirmed in Chapter 1.

Being purpose-driven also gives validity to our targets. If we believe that our services are good news for our customers and the wider world, then we will naturally want to be able to bring more of what we do into play. We want to make a maximum contribution to the world we live in. Putting our work into such terms of reference changes the deal for everyone involved. Serving the world more and better becomes a heart-felt duty rather than a rational commercial objective.

So let me be absolutely clear. Results matter, but they should serve our purpose not the other way round.

# A 10-step guide: Targeting and achieving powerful results

If we accept the above premise that our organization, complete with the teams, people and partnerships that make it work, should be fundamentally purpose-driven, there emerges a step-by-step logic to the establishment of helpful measures which check the performance of our organization. Note that, while there is some logic to the sequence of these steps, this is an iterative rather than linear process. So, for example, while Step 6 involves thinking about *how* to share results, it would be wise to consider alignment and the accompanying story before doing so:

1 Purpose
2 Vision
3 Outcomes
4 Targets
5 Representation
6 Sharing
7 Alignment
8 Story
9 Response
10 Success

## Step 1: Purpose – make sure purpose is well understood, balanced and harmonized

In summarizing the lessons from Chapter 1, now with an eye to measurement, we need to make sure our purpose is clear and compelling, that it takes full account of all stakeholder perspectives and that tensions between stake-holder views have been discussed, harmonized and, better still, synergized.

My dictionary tells me that to synergize means 'to act co-operatively or in combination, especially to mutual benefit'. So, to me, while harmony is about removing discord and ensuring that stakeholder perspectives sit well alongside each other, synergy takes things a step further. As well as perspectives sitting well alongside each other, smart leaders will look for ways for one stakeholder purpose to actively support or promote another.

For example, take the potential conflict between making a profit, being efficient, and investing in customer service. If the relationship between customer service and profit is well understood, it is possible to see how sensible customer service targets will work in the best interest of all shareholders. Similarly with a subject close to our hearts at Primeast, learning and development is all too often regarded as a necessary expense in order to give people satisfactory training. However, if the organization knows and measures the return on investment in training, it can be managed with synergy to the shareholder perspective on the corporate purpose.

Similar logic can be applied between all stakeholder perspectives and time spent by leaders and their organizational architects 'synergizing' will have a knock-on effect on the vision of the organization and its efficient operation.

**CASE STUDY**     Finding synergy between seemingly conflicting purposes of two stakeholders

A good example of synergized purpose can be seen in the relationship between the governance needs and employee needs for one of our clients.

*UK Asset Resolution Limited (UKAR) is the holding company established to bring together the government-owned businesses of Bradford & Bingley plc (B&B) and NRAM plc.*

*Together, the combined organization supports around 467,000 customers with £61.2 billion of loans, with some 2,150 colleagues based at its main sites in West Yorkshire and the north east of England. UK Financial Investments Limited (UKFI) manages HM Treasury's 100 per cent shareholding in UKAR Limited.*

*UKAR has been established to facilitate the orderly management of the closed mortgage books of both B&B and NRAM to maximize value for UK taxpayers...*

*The executive team of UKAR manages both organizations, focusing on this common objective, while ensuring that both companies continue to treat customers fairly, deliver consistently high levels of service and support those customers who are facing financial difficulty.*

*In addition, from 8 October 2013, UKAR Corporate Services (UKARcs) became responsible for the day-to-day administration of the Government's Help To Buy Mortgage Guarantee Scheme on behalf of HM Treasury. This new subsidiary business, UKARcs, operates entirely separately from UKAR's core function of servicing the loan books of B&B and NRAM.*

**SOURCE:** UKAR website, **www.ukar.co.uk**

In a nutshell, UKAR's core business mandate is to recoup debt from two former mortgage banks. It cannot make new loans. So it is essentially a business with a strategy to decline, to recoup the customer debt for the benefit of the UK taxpayer.

At first sight, you would think that this purpose would clash significantly with the interests of employees, especially with regard to their development and career growth. However, the leadership team at UKAR, supported by their HR and talent management professionals' have held these two stakeholder perspectives side by side and examined the synergy between them. They now have vibrant talent management and learning and development strategies that equip employees not just for the internal business needs but also to make employees highly employable in the external market in readiness for the day when they must leave the core business. Far from being seen as a waste of taxpayers' money, this strategy is highly regarded as being essential to staff retention and succession, without which the core business could not function efficiently. This is a great example of finding synergy between stakeholder purposes that are apparently in conflict.

## Step 2: Vision – translate the purpose into a compelling vision

Having found compelling purposes for each stakeholder perspective and synergy between them, this combined purpose must be translated into a compelling vision. My recommendation is to spend quality time on purpose before moving to vision. My logic is simply that working at a deep and creative level with purpose will prompt the compelling vision to naturally arise. There is therefore a sensible logic to conducting these two stages during one workshop. This process is also iterative in that, as the vision emerges, the leadership team may wish to revisit the purpose for fine tuning.

As the vision emerges, it is worth checking back to the purpose statements or stakeholder charter to make sure nothing has been missed. If there is anything that is present in purpose which is not brought to life in the vision or anything present in the vision which is not related in any way to purpose, there should be a conscious effort to 'join the dots'.

So in the following hypothetical 'care home' case, note how just one stakeholder purpose translates into a powerful vision.

**MINI CASE STUDY**    Care home

**Purpose:** to provide a joyful, quality of life experience to a growing number of elderly people in France.

**Vision:** by 2020 we will be successfully operating six care homes modelled on our popular operation in Marseilles. This will provide joyful, quality-of-life care to a total of 300 full-time residents and 50 respite guests. We will have detailed plans in place for a further six such homes in France in the subsequent decade.

Note how in the above example the purpose is succinct and timeless. It will remain current, presumably until the leadership determines that it has reached a size of operation where further increase in scale would be detrimental to one or more stakeholder group. The vision, however, is time-stamped and completely measurable.

If a vision arises that does not describe clearly the time, quality, quantity and other measures (including financial where appropriate), this should prompt dialogue to put figures and information in place if these are deemed important to the leadership team and stakeholders. Of course there is nothing fundamentally wrong with an attitude of letting things evolve in a more natural way – as long as everyone buys into it. However, such an approach does present challenges. For example, imagine if our care home vision was less specific. How could the marketers work at a pace that fitted to the capability of operations to scale up?

Some organizations like to have visions for multiple time horizons and it may be the case that some horizons are less well defined that others. Typically, it may be easier to be specific in the near or medium term than might be the case for the long term. With regard to measurement and alignment, while the long-term vision may be inspirational, the medium-term vision may be more measurable.

For example, I once worked with a group of college students in Malawi to apply this concept to their chosen topic which was the eradication of HIV-related deaths in Africa. While this aspirational vision was incredibly inspiring, it did not help the hypothetical planning process. Instead we had to ask, *with this purpose and long-term objective in mind,* what progress will we make at a time horizon that is imaginable and meaningful to us?

The class came up with the target of halving the number of deaths within a five-year time horizon. It is easy to see how this could be translated into annual targets that take account of trends and known advances in tackling the various factors that contribute to such tragic loss of life.

## Step 3: Outcomes – determine outcomes to measure from analysis of the vision

This translation of vision into specific targets that can be measured and reported as results needs to happen right across the breadth of the vision in a *balanced* way, turning the intuitive creation of vision into the discipline of strategy. According to Kaplan and Norton, developers of *The Balanced Scorecard* (1996):

> The formulation of strategy is an art. The description of strategy, however, should not be an art. If we can describe strategy in a more disciplined way, we increase the likelihood of successful implementation. With a Balanced Scorecard that tells the story of the strategy, we now have a reliable foundation.
>
> Kaplan and Norton (2011)

This idea of a balanced scorecard has served organizations well for almost 20 years (see Figure 6.1). And clearly the four categories proposed by Kaplan and Norton (financial, customer, learning and growth, internal business) make sure our measurement is broader than the more obvious criterion of finance.

However, we should also take account of recent developments in thinking such as a more sophisticated use of analytics as suggested by Mark Graham Brown in his 2007 book *Beyond the Balanced Scorecard* and by Marshall W Meyer whose 2003 book *Rethinking Performance Measurement* examines the tensions between long-term aims and current measures and the difficulties of combining dissimilar measures into useful indicators.

We might also examine the use of new software offerings that enable key results to be measured and combined in true fractal manner as hinted in our earlier discussions on the fractal nature of our organization's structure. One such system is that offered by OrgVue and used to good effect in the National Health Service in the UK, according to the head of human resources at one of our NHS Trusts recently. If this sort of system interests you, just type OrgVue into YouTube to access some concise and informative videos on the subject.

Moving beyond these important considerations, I'd like to propose some new thinking into the measurement arena that stems from the whole notion

**FIGURE 6.1**   Balanced scorecard framework

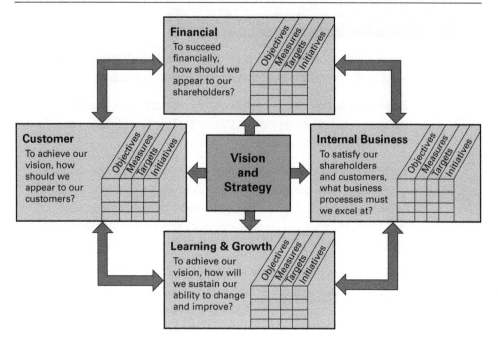

Kaplan & Norton *The Balanced Scorecard.*
Harvard Business School Press: 9. Original from HBR Jan/Feb 1996, p.76.

**SOURCE:** adapted from Kaplan and Norton (1996)

of being *purposeful.* At this stage my thinking is largely hypothetical but I include it in this book as a prompt to further thinking and an intuitive belief that there will be progressive and purposeful organizations already measuring performance using similar logic. If your organization is one of them, please let me know so we can learn from your experience.

I will call this method *purposeful outcomes analysis.*

My thinking is this. If we accept that purpose is the key driver and that it manifests in a measurable way in our vision, then clearly the vision provides clues about what to measure. This seems a fitting place for creativity and expansive thinking to get the best from such an important part of our operation. So here are some things that could be done, shown as an exercise for a leadership team that has already spent time clarifying its purpose and vision. I have expressed it in a format that can be facilitated in a workshop, probably the same one that had already revisited the organization's purpose and vision. But the logic could also be translated to other methods.

**Activity: Purposeful outcomes analysis for a leadership team workshop**

1 **Name obvious outcomes:** Systematically work through the vision and identify all the obvious outcomes we might want to measure.

2 **Brainstorm further outcomes:** Discover many more outcomes we could measure without judging them at this stage. This could be done on a flip chart or using sticky notes.

3 **Look for stakeholder synergy:** Prompt further creativity by considering what outcomes might represent progress for multiple stakeholders. For example, measuring the level and proportion of repeat business might indicate quality of product, customer service and uniqueness of offering etc.

4 **Find consequential outcomes:** From each potential measurable outcome, identify further consequential outcomes. For example, in the business of learning and development, it is easy to measure learner satisfaction at the end of a workshop. However, a more consequential outcome would be the measurable action taken by the learner back at the workplace. And a further consequential outcome would take account of not only what the learner has done but also what else has happened due to the ripple effect of their action.

5 **Plot relationships and dependencies:** When there is a wide range of outcomes representing measurement options and derived from the above steps, systematically examine the relationships and dependencies between the outcomes. Coloured string, tape or mind-mapping software could conceivably be used for this purpose.

6 **Prioritize options:** By now we will have a lot of data on the wall and it is time to do some prioritization. For such an analysis with a leadership team, I like to use sticky dots. Simply give everyone a number of sticky dots to post on the wall chart according to whatever criteria are important to the group. For example, you may wish people to vote on the following:

   – How challenging is this outcome? So if we don't measure it, there is a strong chance it won't happen. Something that is easy and likely to happen anyway probably doesn't need to be measured.

   – How important is this outcome to the organization? The more important something is, the more likely we will want to measure it.

— How easy is this outcome to measure? While ease of measurement alone isn't a good reason for measurement, combined with importance it becomes a helpful contributory factor.

7 **Examine the data:** By stepping back and looking at the data on the wall, the leadership team will have a good sense of what needs to be measured.

8 **Agree target outcomes:** Discuss and agree on a draft set of outcomes for measurement and check back to the vision and the purpose, with the concept of a balanced scorecard in mind. Is your set of measurements logical, rational, practical and balanced? Will they tell a compelling narrative for your organization's progress towards its vision?

## Step 4: Targets – determine how to measure desired outcomes

Different types of outcomes demand different types of targets. For example:

- **Numeric:** such as turnover, profit, numbers of customers, non-compliances (to quality systems), accidents, product or service output.
- **Ratios and proportions:** such as debtors to creditors, proportions of business in customer segments.
- **Milestones:** significant events that mark progress in a project or other journey.
- **Highlights:** similar to milestones but any event that generates confidence in our progress.
- **Exceptions:** results outside agreed tolerances for a project or particular strategy.
- **Indicators of progress:** such as RAG (red, amber and green) systems that say whether a strategy or workstream is on track.
- **Change:** for example, growth in any of the above, expressed as a percentage increase or decrease. As well as simple indicators, specific diagnostics might be able to measure important shifts in a measurable and accessible manner. We discussed the diagnostics

(Barrett, Human Synergistics, GlobeSmart etc) for measuring cultural shifts and tensions in the previous chapter. There is a wide range of diagnostics for other important measures such as employee opinion, engagement, customer service, innovation and so on.

What others do you use or know of?

## Step 5: Representation – determine the best way to represent the results

The obvious way to show our measures is in the form of tables and lists. But pouring over results set out this way is neither inspiring nor memorable. Using suitable charts, diagrams and other graphics will help bring numerical results to life. And for milestones, highlights and exceptions a picture will save words and bring the subject to life. Many corporate diagnostics come with excellent charts to represent what would otherwise be complex data. Certainly the culture change diagnostics mentioned above and in the previous chapter incorporate diagrams which, once understood by the audience, convey complex information easily and memorably.

## Step 6: Sharing – plan to communicate the results in a timely manner to the right audience

Now we know what and how to measure, we need to determine the frequency of measurement and publication and the audience. Typically, strategic management teams may need management information on a monthly basis, tabled at management meetings. But some data for operational purposes might be needed more frequently at say weekly, daily or even on a real-time basis. Imagine driving a car and getting hourly reports on your speed. That could be tricky.

Some information needs to be delivered at the right time, without being tied to a regular frequency. For instance, highlight and exception reporting in project management disciplines such as PRINCE2 require reporting as soon as reportable events have occurred or, in the case of exceptions, even as soon as it is forecast to happen. Philosophies such as these suggest project steering groups should only meet when there are decisions to be made, not on a monthly basis for the sake of it. So, a project board might meet to sign off the completion of a project phase and approve a subsequent phase for initiation.

Data from diagnostics such as employee opinion or culture may be one-off but if they are important, consideration should be given to annual or biannual measurement.

The audience for sharing results is also important. Too many organizations report performance to management meetings and neglect to share them with other stakeholder groups. And if they do, there is also the danger that they will recycle the information in too similar a way. Those responsible for sharing results should consider each stakeholder group separately and ask what should be shared, at what level, in what way and when.

## Step 7: Alignment – ensure results are aligned up, down, across and outside the organization

This is really a slant on the previous step about determining what to share, with whom and in what manner.

If we want our organization to be efficiently aligned to our purpose we will need to make sure that the results we measure and the associated outcomes make sense at different levels and between functions.

Earlier in this book we introduced the concept of fractals, suggesting that what happens at one level in life will resemble what we see when we zoom in to a subset of that whole. So, in terms of outcomes, each department and team in an organization needs a clear line-of-sight between what they do and what the next level up does and how this affects the big picture.

So, for example, we might expect the corporate management report to include high-level health and safety information such as numbers of reportable accidents and near misses, details of serious and potentially serious events and so on. Whereas the health and safety department will have much more sophisticated data across the whole organization and any one operational manager will have details of all the events they are responsible for. These three different sets of information should correspond and make sense to their respective audiences.

In my experience, organizations are pretty good at reporting up and down the management hierarchy. They are less good at reporting between functions, teams and individuals. There are good reasons for this. Senior managers will know what they need to report to their senior management meeting and will seek that information from their direct reports together with more detail if they might need to discuss issues at the management meetings. This tends to drive a cascading style of measurement that works to a point. However, it takes a more sophisticated management stance to consider what to report to other departments. From my experience this happens less well. The exception to this is where organizations have robust interconnected systems that map the whole operation, allow inputs from numerous contributors and make sense of the data from a range of perspectives. With advances in management information systems, this approach is evolving quickly (see my reference to OrgVue software systems on page 156).

With so many internal demands on management information, it is easy to forget the outside world. But there are several external stakeholder groups to which we need to communicate our results. For a start, every significant milestone and highlight report should be considered for external publication in one form or another. Our shareholders need reminding what our organization is all about and inspiring to continue their investment. The reason for communicating highlights to all our customers is obvious as is the need for certain customer-specific feedback, whether or not this is a contractual obligation. Communities like to know what we're up to. This might be to allay suspicions that we might be doing something they wouldn't approve of and also to affirm the many benefits we bring by way of employment and other community opportunities.

In this age of social media, there is scope for a more sophisticated and fluid form of highlight reporting where many players in the organization can cause a *purposeful buzz* around the work they do. This is a massive opportunity but needs careful planning that takes account of the marketing and motivational opportunities alongside risk management and confidentiality implications.

## Step 8: Story – consciously tell the story

In the preceding steps, I've focused mainly on data, whether these are numbers or confirmation of events. I'd now like to look at the art of consciously turning results into a story.

At its most basic level, the story is an explanation that makes sense of our results. This would be the case in most management commentaries where the head of business might describe a challenging period with external pressures and a courageous performance in the face of adversity. At its best, a good story will touch the hearts of stakeholders and reinforce their commitment to our journey. And a good story doesn't necessarily mean everything is perfect. Quite the contrary.

I recently hosted a video interview with a chief executive of a business for the organization's intranet. We had just undertaken a culture change survey using Human Synergistics methods. The picture of the current data confirmed most suspicions that there was a predominantly aggressive–defensive culture featuring significant opposition, perfectionistic tendencies and authoritarian leadership. We also measured the target culture for the company's new vision and confirmed a significant gap to be traversed.

The chief executive was nevertheless inspiring in his interview. He did not hide from or show regret for the current culture. Instead he told an inspiring story of the challenges the company had faced during the recent recession and how significant growth with limited resources had been achieved through an 'all hands to the pump' task-focused mentality. He made no apologies for the toll this had placed on his managers and staff but flagged that the company was entering a new phase where growth expectations could only be delivered with a more constructive leadership style and culture. He also explained how this would be achieved through empowerment, teamwork, coaching, mentoring and personal development.

We have to remember that each audience needs to hear the corporate story in different ways. Done authentically this is not deceitful, it is simply considerate. It is not about telling untruths or delivering spin. It is about being honest, realistic and taking the needs of our audiences into account.

I have likened this to describing a forthcoming holiday to three generations who might be travelling together. Grandma isn't in the least bit interested in the in-car entertainment. Nor do the kids want to know about the tea-shops en route. Even after the event, we will be selective about which holiday photos we share with different people, unless of course we seek to bore them all to tears. Consciously telling the same story in different ways for different audiences is a key leadership skill and a core competence for our communications professionals.

## Step 9: Response – consciously respond to results

The penultimate step in this 10-step process builds on the consciousness we referred to in Step 8. Investing time in telling the story that is indicated by our results turns our corporate journey into a great adventure. And the thing about great adventures is they rarely go according to plan. In fact, the more challenging the objective, I would suggest, the more chance that the journey will not go to plan. Remember, results are the measurement of outcomes that manifest on our journey to the vision and in service of our purpose. The outcomes they represent are opportunities to check our progress and take decisive action. This should be done carefully as the following case study dramatically shows.

**CASE STUDY**     *Touching the Void* – consciously responding to
unexpected results

This is the story of two friends who set out to climb a mountain almost 30 years ago.

In 1998, climber Joe Simpson wrote *Touching the Void*, which tells the story of his ordeal two years before when he was attempting to climb the west face of Siula Grande in Peru with his friend Simon Yates. The two men were attempting this mountain Alpine-style, carrying their own equipment and without setting out ropes for a clear and quick return.

They reached the 6,344m peak successfully but, on the way down, the two men both suffered falls, with Joe tumbling first into a crevasse and then onto a ledge where he shattered his knee. At this point Simon plans for the two men to lower each other down the mountain using the 300ft rope that held them together. They survive an avalanche and continue to the point where Joe is left hanging in mid-air.

Unable to continue, Simon reviews his options and makes the tough decision to cut the rope his friend is hanging on. He is sure his friend has died and is also convinced that he too will not survive the mountain.

Joe survives the fall into the crevasse (the void) and discovers the cut rope. He is stranded on a rock ledge. He cannot go up and fears going down. After a night of intense deliberation he chooses to go down and does eventually find a way out onto the mountain, guided by a beam of light emerging from a potential exit.

Simon meanwhile journeys down the mountain and sees the terrain where Joe must have fallen and assumes the worst. He also ponders his actions and how others might judge him. He considers looking for Joe but concludes he does not have the rope or strength to make any difference whatsoever.

Joe begins his descent of the mountain, initially following Simon's footsteps and all the way encouraged by a *voice in his head*. Eventually he is reunited with Simon and they exchange stories without blame.

The story has now been made into a film and Simon has also written about it, in a way that is consistent with Joe's account.

The reason I choose to relay a brief account of this story here in this chapter on results is to make the connection between unintended outcomes (as highlighted by our organization's results) and decision-making. It is too easy to measure our organization's activities and forget the fact that, just like Joe and Simon, we are on a journey that is a function of our plans, together with what happens as we travel.

The measurements we make of our operations are simply a representation of the progress we are making on our journey. What matters alongside the data is the story of our journey. This is why I encourage results to be portrayed simply and in an understandable form complete with charts and diagrams and especially with an accompanying narrative that brings the story to life. Our organization's journey will be full of unexpected twists and turns. The data will not always be straightforward. It needs to be put into context and importantly, acted upon.

As well as difficulties such as the falls experienced by Joe and Simon, there will be opportunities highlighted by our corporate data in the same way that Joe saw a glimmer of light within the void which suggested a possible exit route.

Our results will and should change our vision for the future and, in turn modify our expectations and targets going forward.

The story of *Touching the Void* is a captivating adventure and it is made so more by what went wrong and needed to be overcome than it was by the accomplishment of the climb. It is easy in the context of our work and life to treat disappointing results as an irritation or even as failure. But it is our considered response to unplanned situations, rather than knee-jerk reactions, that define our courageous journey.

In his book *The Hero's Journey* (2003), Joseph Campbell describes the journey we take when we are acting with purposeful integrity. His work encourages us to be absolutely purposeful and to respond rather than react to the challenges of our journey. This is great further reading for anyone exploring the psychology of responding to circumstances rather than being a victim of them.

## Step 10: Success – become acquainted with success and integrate it into our results discipline

In the next chapter I explore the profound difference between results and success. While results are logical, tangible measures of our progress towards our vision, I propose that success is an outcome that has significant meaning for those involved and which manifests as a feeling.

We shall explore the difference between personal success and collective success. We will examine how, in busy times, we might not take time to even notice how successful we have been.

Simply asking someone what success means to them, or engaging with a team to enquire what matters to them as people will be insightful. From the perspective of *results*, there is a golden opportunity to blur the boundaries between results and success. In doing so we will make our results more inspirational to our people, thus providing ignition to their talents and the ambitions we want them to bring into play for the collective good.

The more we measure that which makes our people feel good, the more our results will serve our purpose. It's a bit like the relationship between structure and character, where we emphasize the need to put structure around the character of our organization by having values and behaviours and team charters. Having the right behaviours means our structures and processes will be adhered to. It is very similar to the yin and yang of Chinese philosophy (see Figure 6.2). These two aspects of life aren't shown as a circle divided by a straight line but in a manner that suggests dynamic interplay. There is even a fragment of each element represented as a contrasting dot firmly planted within the other element. We could summarize that success is to results what character is to the structure and process that makes sense of our organization.

**FIGURE 6.2**    Yin and yang

To help you with your implementation of the 10 steps, a diagrammatic summary with all the key points highlighted has been provided in Figure 6.3.

Now check the effectiveness of your organization's results.

**FIGURE 6.3**  A 10-step guide to achieving results

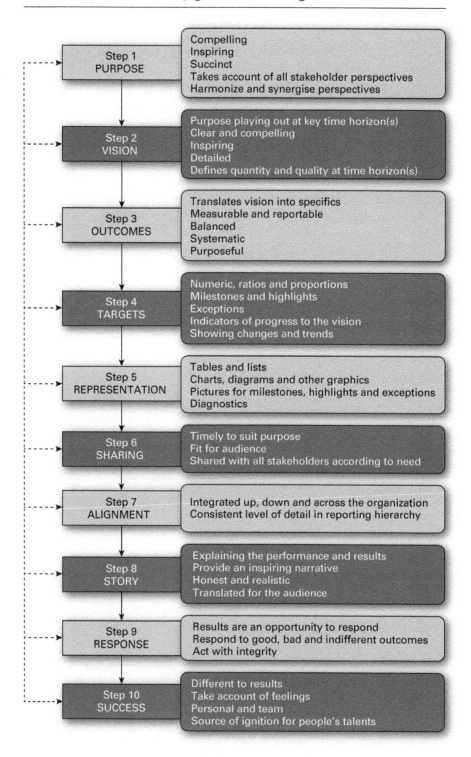

# 10 questions on **results**

*To what extent...*

...at the highest level of the organization has the vision been translated into a balanced scorecard of results that track progress towards the vision in a logical, yet energizing manner, thereby testing the effectiveness of the organization's purpose?

...is there a balanced scorecard of results in place for every subset and team within the organization?

...are results tracked at suitable regular intervals and by significant exception?

...are results kept at a suitably high level thereby avoiding unnecessary detail and complication?

...are charts and diagrams used in such a way as to make results attractive and easy to understand?

...has a commentary placed alongside results made the results interesting and memorable?

...is there adequate discussion about results with appropriately considered responses and commitments to actions that are deemed necessary?

...are results publicized widely within and beyond the organization, in an attractive manner and one that makes clear connection to the purpose and vision of the organization?

...does everyone in the organization have their own set of targets which are tracked at regular intervals?

...does everyone know how their day-to-day activities produce the desired results in support of the achievement of the organization's purpose and vision?

**Score**

| | | |
|---|---|---|
| **0** not at all | **4** moderately | **8** very well |
| **2** a little | **6** reasonably well | **10** completely |

What do your scores tell you? Make notes on the implications and actions that spring to mind.

You can find further resources to support your thinking on this topic at **www.primeast.com/purposefulorganisation.**

# Further reading

David's choice of book on the subject of results is a reminder that people are at the very heart of our organizations and the work we do to align them to the corporate purpose must also be evidence-based and measurable.

## *Transformative HR*, John Boudreau and Ravin Jesuthasan

This is a book that ostensibly has a very clear mission: to champion the cause of evidence-based HR management. There is, however, a 'sub-plot' which relates to the need for HR professionals to be able to operate with their colleagues from other functions on a level playing field; one on which they can display the full spectrum of their talents.

The authors lead the reader through a well-argued thesis based on the assertion that the HR function is still evolving; from the personnel department to task-focused HR, the function is now in the process of shifting its orbit around the centrality of human capital. These authors believe that the emphasis is on decision-making, with a far greater logic and analytical rigour than heretofore.

In truth, this book is really a sequel: in 2007, John Boudreau co-authored *Beyond HR*, in which he introduced the concept of the new science of human capital. Now, with a new co-author, he has laid out the tools by which HR professionals can surely operate with credibility equal to that of other functional executives. As the authors assert in this book, 'the idea that the measures should be focused on the business hardly seems extraordinary, but a great deal of the conversation on HR metrics is not focused on improving the business so much as justifying what HR is doing'.

The book comes in three parts: the first third lays out the central themes and explains why and how they should be applied. This section is logically presented, with five principles outlined (logic-driven analysis, segmentation, risk leverage, integration and optimization) and then developed to support the foundation-stone that HR decision-making should be rigorously determined through insight and analysis rather than simply with raw, barely interrogated data.

Central to the five principles is the need to decide what the vision is for HR and how it is going to support the delivery of the business objectives. From this seemingly obvious starting point, the development and delivery of human-metrics insight can commence. The authors use examples from supply-chain management to show how existing organizational skills can be deployed within HR. And this is a recurring theme of the book: marketing, risk management and finance also provide tools and techniques that can be exploited in the pursuit of more robust HR decision-making.

The authors devote a chapter to each of the five principles, supported with detailed case studies; and each chapter concludes with a paragraph headed 'the one thing you should take away' which is a helpful reader-aid. Chapter 4 is of particular value, since it deals with the ways in which HR can be more integrated within the organization and how synergies between different HR activities benefit HR's overall contribution to business performance.

The second third of the book contains six detailed case studies to demonstrate how evidence-based HR change has made significant impacts in large organizations. These reinforce the work outlined in the first part of the book and enable the authors to show that theory and practice can be combined to deliver robust change.

The final third contains closing thoughts – with a particularly useful summary of leadership characteristics for the function – and well-annotated appendices and references.

The messages that come through are that HR should be viewed and managed as a science rather than as an art. Furthermore, HR decisions need to be constructed within the context of customer-based outcomes rather than on any framework created from within the function. There is room for intuition and gut-feel. These experience-based decision-making tools are certainly valid. But the organization and exploitation of relevant data not only gives a more robust decision-making platform; it also enables more effective presentation of the resulting decisions to colleagues and stakeholders.

This book has both a philosophical and a pragmatic value. It paints a vision of HR's future role as well as providing a number of practical approaches. The case-study examples demonstrate this strongly, showing how the principles in the first third of the book can be deployed in practice to add business value.

# The secret of success

## 07

In separateness lies the world's great misery.
In compassion lies the world's true strength.

**BUDDHA**

# Success is personal

There is a widely held notion of success: that it's personal. The Buddha quote comes from a different point of view: that what matters is what's shared.

Think about success from those two, apparently polarized vantage points, and something profound arises. It's not that one train of thinking is correct and another incorrect. It's just that by understanding them we can take the notion of success to a new level that will inspire a team or corporate performance beyond boundaries – much more than the sum of its parts and more sustainable than any success we can achieve on our own. This insight not only fuels high-performing teams but it gives the organizational architect a further justification to build the purposeful organization.

The way I believe it works is this. At the very core of who we are, we are connected. We are connected to the human race, to life on this planet, to creation itself. Different traditions tell this story in different ways but they all tell the same story. However, mainly to ensure our survival, most of us currently experience life as an individual, as a person. So there is no wonder that we have a strong personal sense of success influenced by our context. However, when we connect with others in the same or similar context and discover that our shared and long-term ambitions are best achieved in co-operation with them, there is also no wonder that a deep and shared sense of success and of shared consciousness arises which is even more powerful than our own.

With these thoughts in mind, allow me to lead you on a journey first into the notion of personal success and from there into the even more profound and exciting world that emerges when we discover the inspiration of a felt sense of shared success, experienced collectively as a team, organization or wider community.

# The perceived wisdom of the world until now

Most books in the self-help section suggest that success is highly personal.

Robert Kiyosaki wrote *Rich Dad, Poor Dad* with Sharon Lechter in 2000. Their book principally explains how to secure financial independence as a springboard to being able to live life according to our personal desires and ability to contribute to our world as we feel called.

There is a part of me that applauds the message held within the chapters of their book. I do not doubt that financial independence offers significant opportunity to contribute to this world in ways that most people can only dream of. And yes, there are many stories of people who have become financially independent from the most unlikely starting places and who went on to do amazing things.

But rather than seeing financial independence as a primary or even necessary goal, I prefer people to ask the following questions instead:

- What resources, skills, talents, and abilities am I blessed with – right now?

- What's going on around me that I really, really care about – right now?

- What excuse do I have for not pointing all that I am and all that I have at that which I care most about, in the most effective manner and in collaboration with others who care in a similar way?

Towards the end of this chapter, you will discover that these questions, which I have personalized with my own words, have been influenced by and adapted from the thinking of Laurence Boldt as described his book *Zen and the Art of Making a Living* (1999).

Financial independence may be one of the resources we have at our disposal right now but for most of us it isn't. We have families to feed and bills to pay. It may be a useful goal to support our life purpose, in which case let's add it to the to-do list. But let's also not get carried away. Many people lead remarkable lives, purposeful lives, without coming even close to financial independence. It all depends what we were *born to do* which is a function of who we are within our perceived contexts. That is what life and success are all about.

The basketball coach John Wooden – the 'Wizard of Westwood' – was one of the world's most successful sports coaches. He was quoted as saying: 'Success is peace of mind which is a direct result of self-satisfaction in knowing you did your best to become the best you are capable of becoming.' He amplifies that definition in his Pyramid of Success reproduced on the next page. Note that one of the building blocks in his pyramid is *poise* which he describes as, 'just being yourself, being at ease in any situation, never fighting yourself'.

I absolutely concur with Wooden's affirmation that we must be authentically ourselves. This is the starting point for a successful life. Note also that Wooden's Pyramid of Success also emphasizes the need for team spirit as one of the building blocks.

But I believe that we can go a step still further with inspiration from the Buddha as quoted above.

So with the philosophical scene thus set, let's start right at the beginning....

**FIGURE 7.1** John Wooden's Pyramid of Success

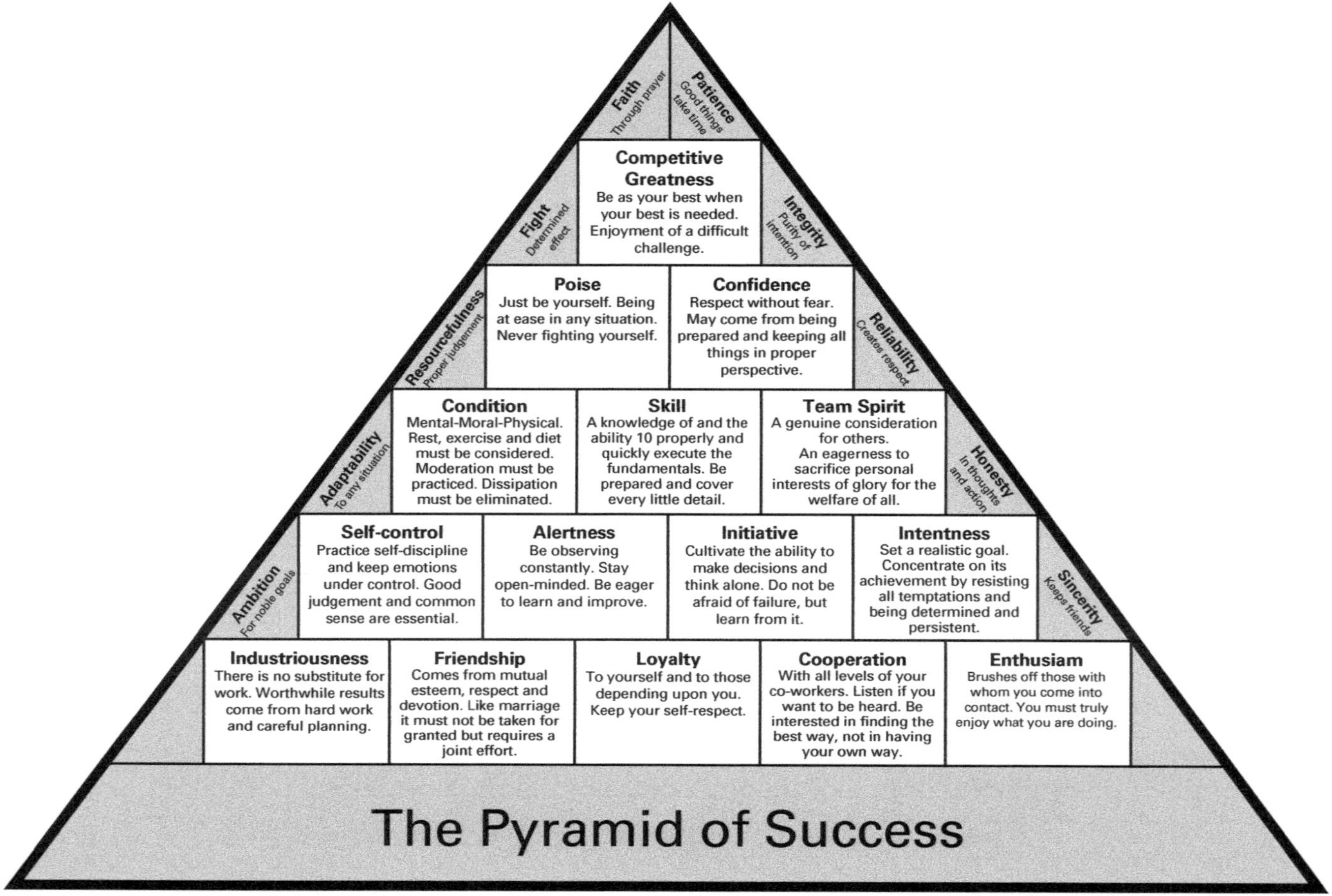

The Pyramid of Success

**Faith** — Through prayer

**Patience** — Good things take time

**Integrity** — Purity of intention

**Reliability** — Creates respect

**Honesty** — In thoughts and action

**Sincerity** — Keeps friends

**Fight** — Determined effort

**Competitive Greatness** — Be as your best when your best is needed. Enjoyment of a difficult challenge.

**Poise** — Just be yourself. Being at ease in any situation. Never fighting yourself.

**Confidence** — Respect without fear. May come from being prepared and keeping all things in proper perspective.

**Resourcefulness** — Proper judgment

**Condition** — Mental-Moral-Physical. Rest, exercise and diet must be considered. Moderation must be practiced. Dissipation must be eliminated.

**Skill** — A knowledge of and the ability to properly and quickly execute the fundamentals. Be prepared and cover every little detail.

**Team Spirit** — A genuine consideration for others. An eagerness to sacrifice personal interests of glory for the welfare of all.

**Intentness** — Set a realistic goal. Concentrate on its achievement by resisting all temptations and being determined and persistent.

**Adaptability** — To any situation

**Self-control** — Practice self-discipline and keep emotions under control. Good judgement and common sense are essential.

**Alertness** — Be observing constantly. Stay open-minded. Be eager to learn and improve.

**Initiative** — Cultivate the ability to make decisions and think alone. Do not be afraid of failure, but learn from it.

**Ambition** — For noble goals

**Industriousness** — There is no substitute for work. Worthwhile results come from hard work and careful planning.

**Friendship** — Comes from mutual esteem, respect and devotion. Like marriage it must not be taken for granted but requires a joint effort.

**Loyalty** — To yourself and to those depending upon you. Keep your self-respect.

**Cooperation** — With all levels of your co-workers. Listen if you want to be heard. Be interested in finding the best way, not in having your own way.

**Enthusiasm** — Brushes off those with whom you come into contact. You must truly enjoy what you are doing.

---

**Opening activity: My successful day**

If you are reading this chapter towards the end of your day, think back to the events that have led to this moment. If it is morning for you right now, recall the events of yesterday. Without any judgement or deep analysis, write down as many successes, small or large from this day that has just passed.

Now look ahead: what will make the coming day equally or more successful?

Finally, imagine lying on your bed on the last day of your life. What has made your life successful?

Without further judgement, read the remainder of this chapter. You may wish to revisit this page and your notes once you have completed your reading.

---

# What is success?

Despite having its routes in delivering an outcome, good or bad, the word *success* is defined today in my dictionary as 'the accomplishment of an aim or purpose'. So to truly understand the nature of success for this book, it seems we have to go right back to where we started and reflect once more on the nature of *purpose*.

In the opening chapter we talked about two aspects of purpose. First as a noun, purpose is *the reason for which something is done or created or for which something* or *someone exists*. Secondly it is a 'mass noun' – *a person's sense of resolve or determination*.

So, if purpose is both a reason for being and a sense of resolve *and* success is the fulfilment of purpose then it makes sense to suggest that **success is both an outcome and a sense or feeling**. This seems to work.

This insight is more important than we think, as is the difference between *results* (which we explored in the previous chapter) and *success*. You see, a result is a very necessary, rational, logical measure of our progress to a defined outcome or vision. At their utmost, results confirm the complete delivery of the vision. But they are not the full outcome itself. Nor do results necessarily convey any *felt* sense of the achievement. Success, on the other hand encapsulates the whole experience and the accompanying feeling we get when we achieve something purposeful.

So there is a significant challenge in all this. It seems to me that it will be very hard to feel truly *successful* if we have no *sense of purpose*. Equally, we will never fully experience success unless a conscious connection is made between the achievement of an outcome and the original purpose that began the chain of events leading up to it. This in turn leads to a further important insight. Let me illustrate this by asking a series of questions:

- Have you ever had a day, a month or even a year where you got so busy that you didn't feel as though you had time to draw breath?
- At the end of that period, did you struggle to identify what you even did with your time?
- Did you wonder what 'that' was all about?
- Did you get a sense that you just might be heading in the wrong direction?

I guess we've all been there. The point I'm making is this:

*We need to be systematic about success. Success requires time and space, time and space to clarify our purpose and time and space to acknowledge its delivery.*

Without this systematic approach to success, we simply lose or forget our sense of purpose. We lose our direction. We lose the meaning of our life. We lose our inspiration and our motivation to perform.

On the other hand, conscious connection to purpose and the systematic celebration of its delivery brings with it the opportunity for renewal, re-connection and enhancement of motivation.

There are numerous opportunities to celebrate success but we won't do this unless we have taken the time to identify them and to make them systematic. A methodical approach to the identification and celebration of success reinforces purpose, creates a sense of flow, builds momentum and inspires more of the same.

## *Personal success is derived from personal purpose*

In our opening chapter, we hinted that purpose is the force behind life, all of life and especially *our* life. I propose that success is the feeling we get as we play out our purpose. If purpose is the life force, success is the accompanying satisfaction or joy that makes it all worthwhile.

Discovering our personal purpose in life is inspirational. It's also really hard to do. The truth is that we have as many purposes as there are contexts in which we serve. So it makes sense to scan these perspectives and then check for commonality that gives an overarching sense of who we are.

One way to explore our personal purpose is to view it from the perspective of *our* stakeholders: our families, friends, colleagues, manager and others. The way *we* see our purpose will vary as our context changes and as we think about the needs of our various others. This is one reason our purpose is so hard to pin down.

Being in tune with our purpose in numerous contexts enables us to notice common threads or themes that run throughout. Being conscious of these threads is key to being self-aware. For example, in almost everything I do, I find myself obsessed with supporting others to be more purposeful, to do well in their chosen endeavours. So I take great delight in others' achievements. This is what success means to me. It plays out with my family, friends, colleagues and clients. This insight gives me my sense of self and steers me down the path of being a facilitator and a coach. This sense of success is derived from my personal belief that the world would naturally be a better place if everyone discovered and lived their purpose.

Being in tune with our purpose in numerous contexts also serves to keep our success in balance. Success in one context at the expense of another is not helpful. For example, if we neglect our family or health in favour of our work, as well as losing our families and becoming ill, ultimately our work suffers as well.

So in order to tune in to what success means to each of us, let's revisit our sense of purpose across our various contexts.

## Activity: Determining our purpose as seen by our stakeholders

Mentally scan your various contexts: family, friends, leisure, health, work – you choose the headings.

Make a note of your personal key stakeholders. Then make a note of how you see your purpose as it affects them. Incidentally, don't forget that for some categories, you could well be the primary stakeholder. Your perspective counts too.

Now, take the opportunity to have a chat with some of your stakeholders. Ask them how they see your purpose, first in general terms and then as it affects them directly, and make notes.

What is it about what they have said that particularly inspires or excites you?

# Our success at work

As this book is about designing the purposeful organization, I'd now like to focus on our purpose and corresponding sense of success in the organizational context. What are we here to do and what do we find compelling about this? How can we discover a passion in our work that will inspire us to spend most of our time doing it with enthusiasm? Maybe there is a clue in the words of Steve Jobs who affirmed, 'The only way to do your best work is by following your heart. Do what you love, and love what you do.'

**CASE STUDY**    The teacher

I was speaking alongside my co-director Russell Evans at a conference in Ghana when we broached the subject of success with our audience. After an earlier conversation (under the heading 'results') about exam passes and attendance rates, one teacher stood boldly and exclaimed, 'Success for me is when little Johnny comes back to school after he's left and says, "hey teacher, thanks for my education, I'm a motor mechanic now (or lawyer..)"'. Clearly this lady had a strong sense of purpose focused on preparing children for their working lives.

I guess many teachers will share a similar sense of purpose. But they may not. For some teachers, success may be to do with growing their personal knowledge of a subject and sharing it with others. For some it may be about giving children the support and sense of belonging that help them become confident young people. For some it may simply be something they're good at and which is also a way of earning a living to support another purpose or cause in their lives.

Returning briefly to our teacher in Ghana, I reflected many times after the conference as to why education authorities do not systematically invite alumni back to share their post-educational progress. It would clearly be a great motivator for the teachers and inspirational for the children still at school who are choosing their career paths. Imagine my delight when I discussed this with my wife Frances, a careers adviser at a grammar school, and she confirmed that she had recently done just that. I enquired further and discovered that such programmes are now referred to in non-statutory guidance to schools by the Department for Education in the UK.

On this topic, note how, if the school makes such events systematic and regular, they are effectively embedding the new practice in *structure* as suggested in

Chapter 4 and making it sustainable as suggested by the ELAS process in Chapter 3 on *engagement*. Note also how this good practice can be placed on a natural spiral of growth similar to that defined by the Fibonacci progression (see page 69) by subjecting it to regular review and improvement. The benefit could be grown even further still by sowing seeds to other schools through career practitioners' forums.

The key thing is this: people in the workplace will absolutely establish their own sense of purpose derived from who they are in the context of the workplace as they perceive it. So, while we might seek to inspire them to support the purpose of the organization, we won't know how their sense of purpose is evolving or shifting unless we are in dialogue with them.

For example, if we treat people badly in our organization we will certainly damage their sense of purpose at work. In the worst cases, it might become something like: 'to do as little as possible and still get paid; or to sit out this reorganization and get my redundancy payment'.

On the other hand, if we emphasize a higher purpose in the work they do, we are likely to inspire them to think of success in a different way. A few chapters ago I mentioned the African revenue authority. Let's ponder for a moment the world of the tax collector, so often demonized by the wider population, especially in a poor country. If tax collectors see their job as taking money from people who cannot afford it, they are unlikely to be inspired to go the extra mile. But if they see themselves as builders of a great nation, they may achieve a real sense of success when they see schools, hospitals and roads being built. Or perhaps success will be when they have conversations with entrepreneurs and recognize their contribution to a growing economy.

So while success may be regarded as a very personal thing, we can greatly influence some sense of shared success through the design of a purposeful organization. We have an opportunity, perhaps even a duty, to state the purpose of our organization in the most inspiring way we can. We need to look for the greatness in what we do and be happy to emphasize this, for it could stimulate a shared sense of purpose, together with ensuing feelings of success and meaning for the people who deliver it.

Our personal purpose in our work situation is the key driver for our personal sense of success in that context. By inference, understanding what success means to us, is a good way of establishing a sense of purpose.

For some people *purpose* might be too big a concept to access easily, especially in dialogue with their manager. In striking up conversation, some people may be more comfortable talking about *success* or some related (but perhaps more attractive) subject such as what excites them or simply what they enjoy most about their work. A key challenge for a leader is to find out what success means to each person delivering, receiving or having anything to do with the service being provided and the right language to access this. For in this knowledge lies the secret to positive motivation. People with a strong personal sense of success often accomplish a great deal.

**CASE STUDY**    Personal success in leadership
Lord Coe (Sebastian Coe)

My co-director and specialist in leadership Sarah Cave is passionate about how, when we connect authentically to our sense of success, we can do amazing things. Her favourite case study in this respect is of Lord Coe and his leadership of the London Olympics in 2012. This is Sarah's take on his success story.

The London Olympics 2012 is undoubtedly one of the shining success stories of recent years, but what does that mean?

The Games were organized by a huge group of people but the face of the Games and the man accredited with their great success was Lord Coe. There have been many interviews with him, all of which try and distil from him what he considered successful Games to be before the event and then what he reflected on as success afterwards.

It is interesting to look at two facets of success which Lord Coe cites in various articles and interviews:

1  **Olympic legacy for young people:** The most powerful and inspiring measure of success which Lord Coe had before the Games was the sporting legacy it would create for the young people of Great Britain. It's worth remembering that he has frequently pointed out that conversations with his own children had inspired his focus on legacy for young people. His vision was to inspire a generation of sportsmen and women for the future. His belief was that that sport is for everyone and not just those with the ability to be the future Olympians.

   Pupils of 24,000 schools in the UK signed up for the sports education programme Lord Coe was promoting. They were offered 175,000 free tickets to the Games. This provided them with the opportunity to see the world's best athletes competing in the most prestigious sporting event in the world. What a fabulous source of inspiration! In addition 93 national Olympic federations made their pre-Games training bases in this country. The facilities were improved before their arrival and are now open to local schoolchildren. Finally, 15,000 of the volunteers who took part in the opening and closing ceremonies were aged 18–20.

So does this mean success in this category has been achieved? Absolutely. There has been significant improvement. Many youngsters have been inspired to try out new sports and many have continued with them. Young people certainly have greater access to improved sports facilities across the UK. Time will tell if this legacy is real and lasting but the general feeling in the UK seems to be positive.

2  **Getting it right for the competitors:** The Olympic Games competition was not designed as a spectacle for the general public, but as a place for athletes to compete against their peers and to prove that they are the best at their chosen sport. So as he is an Olympic gold medallist it is no surprise that a key success factor for Lord Coe was to get it right for the competitors. He was quoted as saying:

*In the end nothing can quite compare with winning your first Olympic gold medal. I'll always see the Games through the eyes of the competitor, and for me it's absolutely vital that I deliver something for the athletes that allows them to compete at the highest level at the defining moment in their life. We have to make sure that we leave no stone unturned. We have to provide them with venues that work, transportation that works, an Olympic village that gives them the right environment. So, for me it will always be about the athletes, but I know there's lot more that I have to get right.*

In testing how Lord Coe's personal sense of purpose translated into success for the Olympic venture, it seems fitting to listen to the athletes' opinion of the games in order to make this judgement. Here are some quotes:

*The volunteers were so great. Everything was so good. The crowd was good and also during our match against GB they were screaming for everybody and it was great. Everything was perfect.*
                    Dutch hockey gold medallist Kim Lammers

*It was a perfect experience... everything was taken care of.*
       Dutch gymnast Epke Zonderland (gold medal in the men's horizontal bar)

*It was amazing, London did it well.*
                    Jill Boon (Belgian hockey player)

*The Games were awesome. The people were so good to us. All the volunteers were so friendly and gave us a lot of support. I have to say to Britain – you guys did a great job.*

Tumua Anae (US water polo team and gold medal winners)

From these powerful quotes and the broader press coverage during and immediately after the Olympics, it is clear that these Games were a positive experience for the competitors. From the food and facilities of the Olympic village to the transport around the capital, the volunteers who helped and escorted the athletes to the crowds who came to cheer them on, it all added up to the perfect chance for athletes to perform at their best.

# Providing structures for success

Leaders create the conditions in which the organization can define and then deliver its purpose. So they have a responsibility to align personal success with corporate success. As discussed above, this requires leaders to have an honest, high-integrity dialogue with their people. Rather than leaving such discussions to chance, leaders and the organizational architects that support them can provide structure to facilitate this need. For example, there could be a prompt in the performance development process that encourages leaders to reference the purpose of the organization and ask their people what success means to them. Similarly, people might be encouraged to say what success means to them on their personal profile. Maybe the communications strategy could systematically focus on what success means to the organization's people, one at a time, in the staff newsletter, journal or intranet. Any structure that systematically explores and shares the success factors of those who work in the organization is likely to boost their personal and collective sense of purpose.

## Linking success to personal values

In Chapter 5 on character, we talked about diagnosing and creating a culture that would support corporate success. One of the mechanisms for doing this is to take stock of the values people hold dear as individuals using a technique such as a Barrett Values Assessment. Discovering the values held by our people will give us some indication of where they might perceive success to lie.

## Facilitating success

Facilitating success is different from but closely associated with facilitating performance. The important thing to bear in mind is that success is both an outcome and a feeling. And, unless teams are given the opportunity to explore collective success, these feelings will be predominantly personal. So, a leader needs dialogue with individuals to understand what success means to them. Only then can they work out what to do with this valuable insight. The Ghanaian teacher case study discussed on page 178 is a good example of how personal success factors can be systematically used for the collective good.

I have several clients in science and engineering and many of their people take enormous pride in the projects they work on and deliver. There are so many ways to facilitate a feeling of success for such people. For one person, it may be entering their project for an award, for another it may be talking about the work they do in front of an appropriate audience. For yet another, it may be the opportunity to network with like-minded people at a conference to share stories of success informally. In the main, organizations will organize such experiences in an ad hoc manner. But for a spiral of growth based on success, why not make such activities regular and systematic? Why not make it something the corporate communications team is responsible for delivering in a purposeful manner?

Personal perspectives on success might also influence how we set up the work itself. For some people, success might be about seeing a project through from start to finish, whereas others like variety and the opportunity to contribute their skills to a wide range of initiatives.

## Celebrating success

Some of the suggestions described above begin to touch on celebration. Organizations and their people have choices about how success might be celebrated. Again it's about working out how to do this in a way that suits those involved. There are obvious opportunities such as the completion of a piece of work. But what about key milestones or times when people overcome significant difficulties? How can the organization celebrate its heroes in ways that will be well received?

I recently coached a project manager as part of a culture change programme. His leadership style profile showed a lack of achievement as perceived by his colleagues. The truth was that this manager was delivering all his project expectations. But because neither he nor the organization was celebrating project successes, few people were aware of the good work he was doing. Celebrating project successes is not only important for the people involved, it also gives confidence to the project sponsors and to the organization at large. This is one of the reasons that 'highlight reports' feature as essential in most project management disciplines such as PRINCE2.

---

**CASE STUDIES** Celebrating personal success on the supermarket floor

---

When I was researching the training programme, Progressive Strategies for Talent Management, for the Chartered Institute of Development (CIPD) in the UK, I interviewed the people director of one of the UK's major supermarket chains. He told me the story of Jackie, whose sense of success was connecting with the community on the supermarket floor. As a result, Jackie got involved in several community initiatives, mainly to do with fund-raising. One day, Jackie became interested in some work in Romania helping children with autism. To celebrate Jackie's personal successes, her employer gave her a week's paid leave which, not surprisingly, she used to visit Romania.

Another interview that I conducted was with the chief executive of a global transport business. He told me about his organization's 'life-long learning' programme. In this programme, any member of staff that has a skill or knowledge in anything at all (even and especially things unrelated to the business), can be given the facilities to teach others what they know. It could be teaching people a foreign language in readiness for their holidays. However, the chief executive's biggest pride was telling of a supervisor who had a flair for IT. He actually went on to teach IT at a technical college which meant him leaving the company. This didn't stop his chief executive from taking great delight that the company had helped this man to find out what success felt like and to discover a new purpose in his life.

## Activity 1: What is success to you and to others?

Think about your own work. Make notes about what success means to you in this context. Think also about how your successes are acknowledged or celebrated.

Then, repeat for someone else you know. You may wish to ask them personally. What thoughts arise for you from this activity? What could you do about it?

## Activity 2

If you enjoyed the above activity and want to deepen your thinking still further, choose two people who do the same or similar jobs on the front line of your business operations. Find a time to have an easy conversation with each of them. Ask them about their work, what they like about it and what they don't. Don't dwell on the latter. Explore what they like a bit deeper and find the right moment to ask them what success means to them in the context of what they do. They may well ask you what you mean and you may have to find the right way or a different way of asking the question. Questions like, 'what gets you out of bed?' or 'what would a good year look like?' or 'what makes your work special?' may do the trick.

Make some notes, especially about the similarities and differences between these two people.

# A purposeful shift in consciousness

OK, so by now I'm trusting that we are agreed that exploring personal purpose at work is a good thing, as is an ongoing attempt to engage people with the purpose of the organization in the hope we can inspire them with this. The last activity may even have got you thinking about the notion of shared purpose. So, perhaps it's time for a thought experiment that might just shift our sense of success from the personal to the collective.

To do this, I want to briefly revisit the biology lessons explored in previous chapters. You will recall that each one of us is actually a community of trillions of cells and each cell is a life form in its own right. Yet our consciousness in the most part is at the human level. In other words, we think mainly in terms of 'me' and 'my success', giving little if any attention to the particular wellbeing of our cells.

It is also widely accepted that human consciousness and sense of self evolves and is continuing to evolve. It evolves personally as we grow up and it evolves collectively as a species with the passing of time and the enhancement of shared wisdom. When we are young we are most certainly 'dependent' on others for our survival, especially our parents or guardians. As we grow we strive for a sense of 'independence'. Our consciousness focuses on our personal needs and feelings. But there is a stage beyond this which we know as 'interdependence'. In its simplest sense, this is a mature and adult recognition that we are interconnected, that our feelings generally and our sense of success in particular is connected to others. As we grow emotionally, we can even sense the feelings of other people. We begin to feel their pain and their joy. We call this empathy.

As empathetic people we feel each other's sense of success. We celebrate with and for them. I would suggest that, the more emotionally connected we are to others, the more conscious we become at the collective level and, as a natural consequence, the less attached we become to our own sense of success. We begin to want success more for each other than we do for ourselves. A team with high empathy can therefore be regarded in some respects as a highly evolved team. But this doesn't often happen by chance. For the best chance of creating a high-performing team or organization, the conscious development of a shared sense of success is vital. The steps below are a suggested sequence for rapidly achieving something that might otherwise take years of team experience.

## Team activity: 10 steps to shared success

1 Assemble a work team and give everyone the opportunity to explore their personal purpose in its broadest sense, first alone and then in pairs or threes. Use this chapter for ideas about how to do this.

2 Discuss what is known about the purpose of the organization and this team within it.

3 Ask team members to describe their personal role and purpose specifically in the context of this work.

4  Ask them how they feel about this and then get them to create a set of statements (on separate sticky notes) that describe what success at work means to them personally.

5  Ask team members to share their personal success statements by posting them to a wall.

6  Look for common themes in this collective output. This can be done by reviewing the notes on the wall and clustering them to form an 'affinity diagram'.

7  Ask the team to give each cluster a heading they can all buy into as a set of team success factors. Remember that some factors will naturally resonate more with some people than others. But don't reject success factors unless there is an overwhelming sense of them being unimportant to most people.

8  Discuss and determine how best to celebrate the agreed success factors on a regular and ongoing basis.

9  Create a SMART action plan to do this.

10 As a test, check that the previously understood purpose and vision for the team is still valid. Could it be enhanced in the light of this new work? As suggested at the end of the previous chapter, is there any scope to reframe some of the results this team measures on a regular basis in order to integrate this evolving sense of success?

Remember that, while doing this once could be inspiring and performance enhancing, doing it regularly will put success on a virtual spiral of growth (cue quick glance once more to the cover of this book). It will also close the gap between results and success on a progressive basis.

# Successful teams

I used to say that a successful team is one that delivers its shared vision and one that delivers each member's stated sense of success. However, based on my more recent reasoning above, I'm now inclined to think that:

*A successful team is one that has a shared felt sense of success which takes account of, but which is more powerful than, the personal successes of all its members.*

A similar statement could be made regarding a successful organization, or even a successful community, nation or planet. But I'll leave the consequences of that ultimate train of thought for another book.

---

**Shared success**

From your own experience, what do you think about shared success? Make some notes.

---

**CASE STUDY**    An unforeseen team purpose

Going back to the 1990s and to the change programmes associated with electricity privatization that I was involve in, one shared team success that arose in an unplanned way sticks in my mind. We had a project called Meter Operator Project, affectionately known as 'MOP'. The main aim of MOP was to put in place systems that would record and process metering data, including readings and details of the contractual relationships between the parties involved.

The project team looked at various options for delivering the aims of the project and decided that the best way to do this was to collaborate with two other electricity companies who, incidentally, would ultimately become competitors. The value of collaborating on system requirements outweighed the competitive edge that could be gained by going it alone.

Working as a three-company consortium, the project delivered a powerful system that quickly became the envy of other companies. As a result, three further companies made requests to purchase the system from the original consortium. Consequently, it became apparent that this project had the capability not only to deliver its stated aims, but also to be the only project in the privatization pro-gramme to be profitable. This strong sense of success quickly became a new team motivator and I really believe it helped the delivery of a tough project in many ways.

Note, however, that this particular sense of team success arose naturally rather than through any premeditated process. From which I conclude that a wise leader will both allow a shared sense of success to evolve as well as being systematic about fast-tracking the process.

## Success and contentment

As I have explored the idea of success in dialogue with others I have discovered a word I don't personally use that often (but perhaps I should) and that word is *contentment*. For some people, contentment is a key personal value and aspiration. As such it is worthy of mention.

Contentment is a powerful concept that seems to have fallen out of favour for many in a world of work that is constantly striving for higher performance and greater contribution. Yet contentment is something that is vitally important to many people who work in our organizations. It is a word that resonates with them and provides a strong foundation to who they are. It became important for me to explore contentment as a form of personal success that leaders need to understand in order to achieve their objectives and for the organizational architects who are trying to align the hearts and minds of people to the purpose of the organization.

The Oxford dictionary defines *contentment* as a 'state of happiness and satisfaction' and confirms its roots in late Middle English (denoting the payment of a claim, from the French *contentement* and Latin *contentus*. Interestingly the Greek equivalent is *autarkes*, meaning 'sufficient for one's self, strong enough to need no aid or support'.

Contentment is not about being lazy, unambitious or without purpose. In fact I know of many people who have lost their sense of purpose and who are anything but content. I also know several purposeful and committed people who work hard for things they believe in and yet have a wonderful air of serenity and contentment at the same time.

As the dictionary definitions suggest, contentment conveys an independence from material gains or 'extras' surplus to perceived needs. But the power of contentment seems to lie in a sense of happiness and satisfaction, qualities that will mean very different things to different people. It depends on what is going on in people's lives and their ability to serve those situations. Some people will be pulled in many directions: home, family, community involvement or profession and will rightly want to contribute in proportion to the needs of the moment. For others, their life really is their work and they will do whatever it takes to make their maximum contribution. If we are to design a high-performing and purposeful organization, we have to understand the diversity of drivers within our workforce and how to work with it.

In most organizations, there is a mix of people with very different perspectives and agendas. There may be very bright, knowledgeable people with young families who want to participate as parents and work part-time while their children are young. These people may sit alongside others who work long hours, are always available and will willingly work through the night when the job needs it. The challenge is to design the purposeful organization in such a way that this is possible without unnecessary tension.

## Reward and recognition

The solution to this challenge lies, once again, in that all-important word *purposeful*. Just as we said in the very first chapter that we need to understand and harmonize the purposes of various stakeholder groups at the strategic level, we similarly need to harmonize the purposes of teams and individuals within stakeholder groups. This calls for challenging, open and honest dialogue on such matters as performance, recognition and reward. In this respect, it is worth remembering that organizations are built on performance, not on attendance or activities. So, one person might deliver amazing value to the organization in a few hours that someone else working long hours fails to achieve. At the same time, there is clearly a value to the organization for people who can work flexibly in terms of time and geography, according to need. A purposeful organization will take these factors into account when it comes to designing reward and recognition strategies.

This book does not seek to promote any single reward strategy but organizations do need an approach, right for their context, which people feel is fair and compelling. This may be through policies that reward performance based principally on the deliberations of colleagues, such as that preferred by WL Gore, manufacturers of the famous Gore-Tex fabrics. Alternatively, the organization might adopt flatter reward structures within bands of job-type, based on a belief that individual performance and pay is less important than that of the team and the organization as a whole. Neither is right or wrong, it's all to do with the values and beliefs of the organization as discussed in Chapter 5.

Incidentally, the WL Gore case study is one of 10 that feature in a report by Sung and Ashton that was funded by the Department of Trade and Industry (DTI) in the UK and brings together 'high performance work practices' (HPWPs). It concludes a survey of 294 companies facilitated by the CIPD.

The following is another case study I have personally encountered which draws attention to the wide perspectives and needs of employees – with particular focus on young people.

**CASE STUDY**    Convergys and the millennials – the concept of 'success' is changing, rapidly

In April 2014 I facilitated a 'Talent Forum', a small group of human resource professionals in the north east of England. This is something we do quarterly and each time we meet we share the talent management challenges we each face and explore one in depth using an Action Learning Set method.

On this occasion the challenge was posed by Convergys, an impressive global customer contact business. The question was, 'how to engage the millennials'. The local head of business and the head of human resources explained that it was essential to employ young people to meet the growth expectations of the business but retaining the youngest employees, now known as the 'millennials', was increasingly difficult. Attrition is costly and an impediment to operations so the topic is a priority.

These young people live in a different world to the one we 'baby-boomers' grew up in and to some extent still inhabit. The millennials were born in a digital age, permanently connected by their smartphones to friends, social life, interests and information. Their interests are what they are and are unlikely to be set aside for work unless their work *is* their interest.

Many young people have different life and work expectations. Property is less accessible to them and often less important. They could well be less motivated by the big house and car that incentivized their parents. They are inclined to travel more and live life as an adventure rather than settle down with a family. Many have interests away from work that are much more important to them than work itself. It's easy to see how difficult employee retention is and the talent forum members concluded that the answer to improving the situation resides in this oft overlooked condition for a purposeful organization, *success*, and how people of different ages view it.

Having listened to our talent forum members and given this matter further thought, here are my personal tips for engaging the millennials which, to be honest, will apply to the engagement of any workforce. What works for the millennials could well be a breath of fresh air for others at work who would relish a more modern experience. Of course, I realize that the tips that follow must absolutely be reconciled with the needs of the job. And by the way, much of what follows is drawn from best practice I have personally witnessed in *successful* workplaces over recent decades.

1  **Discard the need to judge others by our own standards.** We may have a so-called 'work ethic' that places work as more important than other things. But not everyone does. Some people have relatives to care for, interests to pursue, involvement with community or charity organizations. They may have all manner of appointments to keep and will be massively demotivated if they're not allowed to do so.

2  **Implement as much flexible working as operations allow.** With mobile data, many people can work anywhere any time. I recently coached a manager who had lost his wife and often needed to collect his children from school. However, once they were in bed, he would get back to work at his home. He didn't make a big thing of this so many colleagues assumed the worst.

3  **Encourage trust and openness.** Leading on from the previous two tips, leaders have a role to play in encouraging these two values. Simply accepting that people are different and helping everyone to understand that creates a more tolerant and productive workplace.

4  **Train leaders to facilitate diversity.** Progressive leadership doesn't happen by accident. Leaders need time to explore the rationale for tolerance, openness and encouragement.

5  **Bring personal success out into the open and celebrate it.** Another leadership role is to find out what success means to each of their people and to share this within the context of teams and wider. As a consequence, action can be taken to celebrate personal success in an appropriate way.

6  **Accept differences in performance and reward them appropriately.** Clearly in a more tolerant and diverse workforce there will be differences in performance. The person who flexes to suit the business and works long hours when needed may well be adding more value than someone on a short week who leaves at 3 o'clock sharp to pick up their children. The challenge is to respect everyone and reward them fairly, whatever this means.

7  **Work out how to align people to the purpose of the organization.** This book contains hundreds of gems on how to do this, from having a compelling purpose, a vision to die for, engagement strategies and so on. If we can make work vitally important to people that is ideal. But for some this will never happen – so read on.

8  **Respect those for whom work is an enabler for other things.** This really is the 'elephant in the room' topic. For some people, work is the most meaningful thing in their lives. For others it is an enabler for other things that they see as

being far more important. As long as they are contributing well and feeling good about what they do, that could well be fine. The leader's role is to manage the differences.

9   **Satisfy people's wants and needs.** Apart from the business purpose and money there are many reasons people enjoy coming to work. The manager's job is to find out and facilitate as many conditions for their satisfaction as they reasonably can. Here are just a dozen needs that might be catered for:
    - financial security;
    - experience;
    - learning;
    - social contact;
    - friendship;
    - being part of a team (work, community or sports);
    - pleasant or inspiring surroundings;
    - good food;
    - fun;
    - personal coaching;
    - exercise;
    - respect.

10  **Consider a values assessment.** In our previous chapter we spoke of the need to manage culture and the merits of a values assessment. In situations where a specific group of people need to be engaged, it is worth taking stock of the values they hold dear and those they perceive as prevailing in the organization. This data enables the organizational architect to systematically manage the culture in a way that is more attractive to those we are seeking to motivate and retain.

There are many more. Don't take my word for it: brainstorm a hundred reasons to come to work with your colleagues and friends.

There needs to be an interest in the whole person. Having someone to talk to who is able to coach or mentor around work, career and life in general is of immense value to many people. This could be their manager but it could equally be provided through mentoring, coaching or buddying.

## *Alignment to the organization's purpose*

The above discussions on contentment and flexibility are not an excuse for misalignment. People may have other priorities in their lives. But, in order to do a good job, to be of value, there must be sufficient alignment with the purpose and values of the organization to maintain an acceptable focus on service.

Even if we adopt some of the strategies suggested above for retaining the millennials (and others), we still need to shift their focus progressively to service when they are working. In any work team, there will be those for whom service is a priority and something they enjoy. This is another good reason for the manager to know what success means to all their people. If there are no conversations about success, people just won't think about it. But if there is sufficient conversation, it enables the culture to shift in the following way. Here is the sequence that manifests. It is a useful blue print for managers:

1 Have regular conversations with people about what success means to them. These can be one-to-one or in groups. Check out the team activity on page 186.

2 Pay attention to emerging success factors that are aligned to the purpose and values of the organization.

3 Follow the energy of these topics. Ask to hear more. Show an interest.

4 Notice where more than one person share similar ideas about what success means.

5 Connect people to others so they can build on each other's ideas.

6 Look for ways to enhance and celebrate these success factors. Task them to do the same.

7 Celebrate the successes that align to the purpose and values in an appropriately meaningful way.

8 Build processes and systems into the organization that embed and sustain this flow of energy.

---

**CASE STUDY**    Tapping into personal success in the health service

---

My family has had recent mixed experiences with the National Health Service (NHS) in the UK. My wife and I have had three of our elderly parents receiving end-of-life care in hospital. Our feeling was sadly that patient care had slipped down the priority list. The things that were done well were things that were essential and mechanistic, such as giving the correct medication (the things that were being measured). The things that we thought had slipped were to do with compassion and personal attention.

This is by no means unique and I know of others who have had similar experiences. It is further reflected in the findings of *A Review of the NHS Hospitals Complaints System: Putting Patients Back in the Picture – Final Report* (2013) by the Rt Hon Ann Clwyd and Professor Tricia Hart. Compassion was one of the five key points raised in the report, identifying that, 'patients said they had not been treated with the compassion they deserved'. Dignity and care was a second point, the report identifying that, 'patients said they felt neglected and not listened to'. The other three key points were lack of information, staff attitudes and resources.

Bear in mind that we are just emerging from a recession where there have been funding challenges in the NHS and an increasing amount of work to be done. There is no doubt that efficiency has been a priority. There is no wonder that value for money has been high on the list. But when financial efficiency is significantly more important than core human values like care and compassion, things start to go wrong.

So imagine if an NHS manager could find nurses for whom success was making lives for people in hospital as comfortable and loving as possible (and there are many that do). If they attended to this conversation and found ways to embed good practices and celebrate them, it could potentially help the situation enormously.

### Postscript

Co-incidentally, just after writing the words above in June 2014, I met Alf Turner, Director of Organizational Transformation at Royal Surrey County Hospital, a dual-strength hospital serving a population of 320,000 for general hospital services and 1.2 million for cancer services. He described patient care as the core purpose for the hospital. This is further emphasized in the aspirational vision of 'delivering the best patient care, anywhere'. All three of the hospital's values ensure that the core purpose is reflected in behaviours. These values are:

- safe and efficient care;
- respect for people;
- continuous improvement.

To ensure that the purpose, vision and values are translated into departmental and personal objectives, the hospital uses a strategy deployment process based on the OrgVue system that we discussed in the previous chapter on results as a possible step beyond the balanced scorecard (see page 156). The objective of the strategy deployment process is to ensure that the individual and team objectives throughout the hospital are aligned to deliver the overall trust strategy of the best care anywhere. This is reinforced by a performance contract which is signed off between the individual and the organization.

The strategy deployment process is shown in the diagram in Figure 7.2 as the two layers of the triangle (under strategies) that support and enable the delivery of vision, mission, goals and values. I was encouraged by Alf's commitment to a strategy for patient care and by the time this book is published, I will have interviewed him to camera with the intention of bringing his strategy alive for you online.

**FIGURE 7.2**  Royal Surrey County Hospital: Strategy deployment process

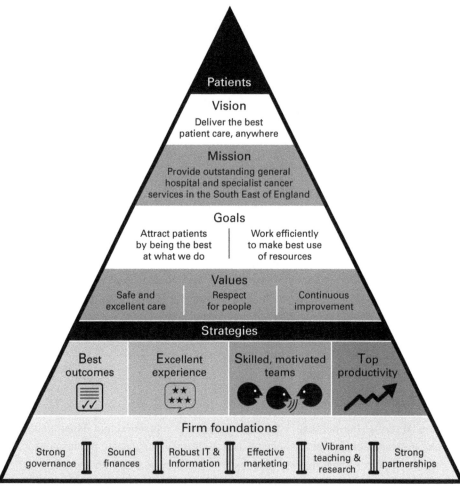

**SOURCE:** Royal Surrey County Hospital

## Creating a spiral of success growth

The discussions above are examples of closing the success loop. The manager identifies what success means and facilitates an opportunity for their team to celebrate success and encourage more of the same. A virtuous cycle results.

But, despite their benefits, I would encourage organizational architects to be less than satisfied with virtuous cycles. I want to go back to what we said about natural growth. Life isn't satisfied with doing the same good things in an endless cycle, its natural inclination is to grow. This is what the Fibonacci progression and spirals are all about. Life is cyclical and in growth at the same time. Life follows cycles but with every cycle, the impact builds and builds. Thus the cycle ceases to be a circle and instead becomes a spiral. As we near the close of this chapter, pause to take another look at the front cover...

What must you do to ensure that the great things that are happening in your organization, often associated with personal success for some or many of your people, are systematically placed into a spiral trajectory that makes them more and more impactful for everyone's benefit?

# Success and talent

This is a great opportunity now to begin to shift your attention to the next chapter which examines the eighth and final condition for designing purposeful organizations.

I truly believe that there is a strong link between talent and success. In fact I'd go further and state that: *success is the feeling we get when we apply our natural and most powerful talents (and other resources) to something we care deeply about in an effective manner.*

I have been precise in my articulation of the above statement. This is because the statement can become a system, should we choose to make it so.

To put the statement into a logical order:

**1** We need to know what our natural and most powerful talents are.

**2** We need to take stock about what we care deeply about.

**3** We need to check that there is scope to apply our talents to the thing we care about.

**4** We need to work out how to apply our talents in the most effective way.

My hypothesis is that if we, as organizational architects, can systematically facilitate opportunities for this to happen in our organizations, then we will have inspired and motivated people to really care about our shared purpose and bring the best of who they are in order to play their unique part in its delivery.

More of how to do this in the next chapter as we explore the art of *talent liberation*.

---

## Activity: Success and social media

So, as we come towards the end of this chapter, before we reflect with my usual 10 questions and consider David's recommendation for further reading, I'd like to consider the massive impact social media is having on our organizations. I know many organizations avoid social media because of the potential risk of the wrong things being said and the damage that can be caused. But what if we had a clear company policy for everyone to share success stories via social media? What if every employee was encouraged to think about their greatest success of the week (or even day) and post it to social media? What if, every time a customer or a member of the public had something nice to say about our organization or one of the team they were encouraged to follow our organization and post their feedback on the social media page? What storm of success might we create?

Consider the story of Nike as posted by Digital Marketing advisers, Convince & Convert:

> *Nike celebrates Instagram milestones by thanking its community*
>
> *It all started with a hashtag – two years ago, the ceremonial first fan photo with a #Nike tag on Instagram. Fast forward to the present, and Nike has amassed more than one million followers and more than six million photos with the tag #Nike on Instagram.*

You can read more at the Convince & Convert website, or find a plethora of social media success stories on the Digital Insights blog, or simply search the Internet for 'celebrating success on social media'. You'll not be short of some amazing success stories.

And what about our personal lives? Knowing what success means in all aspects of our lives and making a conscious effort to take stock each day is a great way to remind ourselves of our purpose. It also cultivates an attitude of gratitude. Sharing this authentically with others also lets them discover who we are. We may not want to do this on social media, but it's a thought.

Now test how success is being made use of in your organization.

# 10 questions on **success**

*To what extent...*

...have key stakeholders in the organization been asked what success means for them? ☐

...have stakeholders' perspectives on success been compared with the organization's purposes to check for implications? ☐

...is personal success explored at performance review or some other regular time with all employees? ☐

...is personal success considered during job design? ☐

...are there mechanisms built into the structures of the organization to facilitate, recognize and celebrate personal success? ☐

...are leaders and managers trained to identify personal success and leverage this to improve purposeful performance? ☐

...are organizational successes recorded and publicized in such a way that acknowledges those involved and their personal sense of success? ☐

...are personal success factors shared within the organization, such as in personal profiles that are made visible internally? ☐

...are personal success factors shared within teams, translated into team successes and celebrated systematically? ☐

...do teams in turn share success stories systematically with the wider organization? ☐

## Score

**0** not at all  **4** moderately  **6** reasonably well
**2** a little  **8** very well  **10** completely

What do your scores tell you? Make notes on the implications and actions that spring to mind.

You can find further resources to support your thinking on this topic at **www.primeast.com/purposefulorganisation**.

# Further reading

David's choice of book on the subject of success resonates particularly with me. It is a book I read just after training to manage culture change in the electricity industry. The powerful questions posed by Boldt caused me to leave my 27-year career in that industry and move to a consulting role so I could serve any organization that sought to be more purposeful. Great choice, David!

By the way, I often re-ask myself the questions prompted by and adapted from Boldt using my own words (as I did at the start of this chapter):

1 What resources, skills, talents, and abilities am I blessed with – right now?

2 What's going on around me that I really, really care about – right now?

3 What excuse do I have for not pointing all that I am and all that I have at that which I care most about, in the most effective manner and in collaboration with others who care in a similar way?

Remember that these are my words and an interpretation of Boldt. I encourage you to read his book to see how the master puts it. Over to you, David.

## Zen and the Art of Making a Living: A practical guide to creative career design, Laurence G Boldt

Choosing to review a book like *Zen and the Art of Making a Living* is an act of bravery, if not bravado: it is such a Big Book in every sense. I hope, therefore, that I can capture just a little of its essence in this 900-word review without diminishing its value and gravitas.

In a world where sound-bites and wikis cater for our every information need, why would anyone want to read a large, challenging and discomfort-inducing tome (this last adjective refers to the disquiet that comes from having the basic tenets of modern life challenged)? The answer is that this book makes you think; will make you feel slightly uncomfortable and will probably change your perspective on the world (of work particularly, if not the whole entity).

The book's essence is about being true to yourself: it is about finding yourself and creating your own future; defining the success measures as you go. The explanation of the title is that – as the author explains – Zen is the spirit of the everyday; the integration of the spiritual and the material. The book divides into five main sections – lenses, if you like: in each, the author reviews life as Art, as a Quest, a Game, a Battle and a Voyage of discovery. The starting point is that we must get an honest and comprehensive understanding of ourselves, to discover our own unique talents and gifts. Boldt explains his belief that our lives are constrained by restricted thinking and a focus on the potential downsides and negatives: the things that limit our thinking are denial, availability (of options, resources and other things that might limit us), approval of others and lack of self-confidence.

Generation Y and the post-millennials are at the forefront of a significant shift in the way we conceptualize work: there is a discernible shift in attitude towards greater balance in our lives, wherein success is measured with a more personal and balanced yardstick. This almost feels like a social movement, but one without political action committees, paid lobbyists or national/international organization. While throughout the 20th century work was viewed principally as a means to an end – be it survival, security, status or power – today it is increasingly being valued on its own terms, and more and more people are coming to expect that their experience of work should include some meaning. The criteria for success now include meaning, challenge, self-expression and joy. In this respect, the book – written in the late 20th century – harks back to the social/organizational behaviourist writings of the 1960s and early 1970s and looks forward to the century we are now in.

Some may see this text as rather revolutionary; one which says that doing the conventional and the expected might not be in the best interests of the individual. Indeed, Boldt asserts: 'The implicit goal of virtually all education for many years now has been to equip students with the skills and attitudes that will make them more valuable as workers for those whose agenda they will spend their lives serving. It has not been to help students discover their own purposes and construct and realize goals based on these.' Since Zen is about being present and conscious to what we are and do, its application in the world of work is to be conscious about the choices available to us and in the way that we conduct our work. This is about determining what success looks like for us all as individuals; being aware of this and acting upon it. And it implies not having our agenda set solely by those who employ us.

The author reviews the usual list of factors governing the shift in fundamental job and working practices and the impact on people's attitudes to work and employment. The debilitating impact of technology, consumerism and reliance on bureaucratic state mechanisms all have a blunting effect on our personal drive. On our way to developing a new paradigm of work, the author encourages us to take a Jungian perspective wherein our psychology has elements of 'being' and 'doing' (feminine and masculine traits). And our understanding of our self and our environment also draws from opinion (sense), science (dialectic) and illumination (intuition). In his opening chapters, Boldt makes a strong connection between work and the dissatisfaction one feels in one's personal life; and this does beg the question of what success really means for each of us. The message is not to ignore who we are and what we could be: rather, to get our heads up and view the larger landscape of the world and be more expansive in our thinking. Work should be an expression of self not a chore or economic exigency.

The author talks about the four facets of being at work: we need to see ourselves as the Hero (seeking and choosing the right road through the power of decision-making), the Magician (using the power of showmanship and imagination), the Warrior (single-mindedness and tenacious creativity) and the Scholar (potent personal growth, life-long learning and wisdom). Each of these themes is developed into useful narratives for the reader – put into the context of careers and life-plans. The sections dealing with each of the four facets are supported with practical checklists and to-do exercises which leave readers with an obligation to take action for themselves.

This is an expansive, wide-ranging life-manual that uses history, mythology, the arts world and philosophy to contextualize the choices that we all have about how to lead our life. With a liberal use of quotes from people as diverse as Tolstoy, Abraham Lincoln and Confucius, it does not step back from aggressively promoting single-minded pursuit of personal self-realization within a framework of social conscience and communitarianism.

Be bold: pick up this book and prepare to change your perspective on all the things that drive your life.

# Liberating our talents

ignition progressive strategies
alignment WAR FOR TALENT develop
value USE constellations
purpose 8-step programme
TALENT LIBERATION
collaboration ● talent
recognise
PURPOSEFUL TALENT

> *I fear not the man who has practised ten thousand kicks once, but I fear the man who has practised one kick ten thousand times.*
>
> **BRUCE LEE**

# Defining talent

Before I get into the thick of a topic that I find so compelling, let's begin with some simple definitions that I believe to be crucial for reasons that will become apparent. Too often these words are used interchangeably but they actually have very different meanings. Everyone in the workplace needs to know what they mean when they use these words. These definitions are my own and I believe they very simply highlight the differences and show how they complement each other in the quest for enhanced performance:

- **Competence** is the ability to do a task to a satisfactory and defined level – without significant error.
- **Talent** is something we are naturally good at – as a result of nature or nurture (usually during our childhood).
- **Strength** is a talent that we have developed to such an extent that adds significant value for ourselves and others.

So in summary, if we can ensure we are competent in skills necessary to prevent loss or damage or to ensure completeness of role, and be strong in areas where we have natural talent and can add most value, we will enhance our performance significantly.

# The war for talent and our obsession with competence

In the 1990s there was allegedly a *War for Talent* (Michaels *et al*, 2001). It was asserted that talent was scarce and that organizations had better get their share or (rather) more than their share, develop it, retain it and put it to good use. A whole new industry of 'talent management' was developed with most large organizations appointing talent managers to establish and implement talent strategies.

While I absolutely believe that organizations should secure the right people to do the right things in the right way with enthusiasm; and that people should be developed in proportion to their potential; I also believe that everyone has talent. Therefore the practice of labelling 10 per cent of our people as *talent* only serves to estrange the other 90 per cent.

There was another obsession in the 1990s that was sound in concept but which was simply taken too far. This was our obsession with competence. Through various psychometrics, we discovered that we could measure the skills of people at work. We also discovered that we could measure the skills required to do a particular job. Thus by holding the personal skill profile against the job profile we could establish the fit between individual and role. This all sounds great and in many ways it is. However, alongside all this, we were learning through the research of the Gallup Organization and others that success results primarily from playing to our strengths.

Don't get me wrong, I absolutely understand that competence is essential in so many activities and disciplines. I wouldn't want an incompetent surgeon sewing me back together after an operation. But I would also want her to have strengths in her particular specialism. We also wouldn't want to see any incompetence where there is a risk to life and limb, to the environment or to expensive material or financial assets. The trouble was that the world of work became obsessed with competence and the consequences were that talent and strength in their broadest sense were neglected.

Human resource professionals implemented competency frameworks and the very act of doing so prompted managers to pay attention to lack of competence and direct their learning and development budgets to putting it right. By enquiring from the platform with conference audiences, I deduced that on average somewhere between 80 and 90 per cent of learning and development budgets get spent on fixing weaknesses.

After all, why would we develop someone who is already good at something? Well, I'll tell you in a nutshell why we should. As affirmed by Gallup and others, people perform to the best of their ability when they play to their strengths. Excellence has its root in strength and excellence is what provides competitive edge.

Think of it like a racing speedboat. Competence is about having a boat that doesn't sink and will get you to where you're going. Strength is having a streamlined shape, an awesome motor that will take you there as fast as possible and, of course, a world-class sportsperson to make the whole thing out-perform the competition.

## Progressive strategies for talent management

A few years ago, knowing of my passion for talent and playing to strengths, the Chartered Institute of Personnel and Development (CIPD) in the UK asked me to put on a programme for HR Directors called Progressive Strategies for Talent Management. The idea was to take talent-thinking a stage further and encourage organizations to establish talent-centred cultures that embraced the talent of everyone.

In preparation for this programme, I interviewed the people-professionals and CEOs from a number of organizations that I thought would be progressive in their thinking. I went to Google, Asda, the First Group, Tata, Aimey, Tube Lines, Deutsche Bank and others in the private sector and also to the UK Cabinet Office, universities and consultancies.

I discovered that these professionals, without exception, believed that everyone in their organizations had talent and that the secret of high performance was to recognize it, value it, develop it and put it to good use in the delivery of their organizations' objectives.

# Talent liberation

At Primeast, we began to refer to this philosophy as *talent liberation*. I remember being quite animated at one conference and saying 'talent doesn't need to be managed, it just needs to be liberated'. Of course, such liberation does indeed require a management strategy, it doesn't happen by chance. But I think I made my point, so much so that we had tens of thousands of drinks mats printed with the words:

> **Talent liberation:** Organizations reach prime performance when they recognize, value, develop and use the unique talents of all their people in the delivery of their objectives.

It wasn't long before we were running programmes that did just that. Typically we would engage with groups of leaders in a workshop for two or three days and give them the opportunity to co-create a powerful and purposeful sense of future and work out how to play to their strengths in its delivery. In fact, in about 20 years now as a practitioner, I have run more programmes aimed at aligning talent to a purposeful future than anything else.

I didn't realize it at first, but the sequence of words *recognize, value, develop* and *use* was a remarkable insight. I first arrived at the sequence after listening to a compelling talk by one of the key players in the 'strengths movement', Marcus Buckingham, at a CIPD conference. Referencing the Gallup research, Buckingham made a compelling case for organizations to play to the strengths of their people. He affirmed that this research wasn't new and admitted to being bemused as to why organizations weren't implementing strategies to play to their strengths in greater numbers.

After that conference, I returned to my office and pondered this question deeply. I had previously conducted the personal strengths diagnostic, 'strengthsfinder', derived from the Gallup research. I took out my strengthsfinder profile and then it dawned on me. I had a good insight into my own strengths but I realized that since that insight, nothing had changed. I began to ask other questions such as 'What do I need to do differently?' But, the big question that unlocked my learning was, 'how do my strengths add value to the work we do?' I began to make connections between my strengths and the value of our business at Primeast. At that point I reasoned there was a sequence that needed to happen and happen in the right order: *recognize, value, develop, use.*

## Recognize

First, we have to *recognize* our natural talents, appropriate to the context being considered. So in the workplace, it's about knowing what we're naturally good at regarding the work we do. While there are some great diagnostics that will give us some clues, I also believe we should authentically own our talents. This means describing them in words that mean something to us, words we can relate to, the sort of words we would happily put on our curriculum vitae or biography. It is worth noting here that if these talents are already adding value in the work we do, they are likely also to be our strengths as defined earlier in this chapter.

## Value

Secondly, we need to do some analysis to work out how these strengths add *value* to our organization. In the workshops we run, I often ask for a volunteer to have one of their talents valued. I am always staggered, as are the talent-owners, by the value we identify in about 10 minutes. For example, one manager of industrial services identified 'problem-solving' as the talent he wanted valuing. I asked him to think of a time he had used it to good effect. He described a telephone call from a customer indicating that there was a problem with a project. Rather than make do with a phone call, he went out to see the customer on site.

Together they solved the problem and, in the process, they identified some other things the customer required. When I asked him how much time he had invested in solving the problem and spending the time with this customer, the manager estimated it was just a few hours. When I asked him to estimate the value of doing this, he came up with a significant sum, drawing the conclusion that his talent for problem-solving was immensely valuable, much more so than he had previously considered. We did actually calculate a figure, as I always attempt to do in these circumstances.

Asked what else he concluded, the manager affirmed that doing the brief calculation had made him more determined than ever to spend time with his customers, using every problem as an opportunity to provide better service.

Over the years, I have had the fortune to hear many such stories, some in workshops and some in coaching sessions. People are usually amazed and encouraged when they realize how much value they can add when they play to their strengths.

## *Develop*

For reasons described above, it is very rare that we will invest in the conscious *development* of talents that are already strengths. We are so used to focusing on our weaknesses and might even consider development in our areas of strengths to be an indulgence. I would suggest that it is not an indulgence. Rather we have a duty to ourselves and others to identify our strengths and develop them as much as we can in order to add more value.

This doesn't always mean going on a training course. Though of course it might. In his 2009 book *Outliers: The story of success*, Malcolm Gladwell popularized a theory previously highlighted in a 1993 psychology paper. The theory is that it takes 10,000 hours of practice to become a master at anything. I would also concur with others such as Buckingham, Clifton and Coyle that there should first be signs of a natural talent to be tapped in to. Otherwise, the person is unlikely to make sufficient initial progress to keep them motivated to do their practice. The best form of development in my view is to discover what we're good at, what excellence looks like in this respect and to practise hard to achieve it.

I enjoy writing, speaking, facilitating and coaching. Fortunately I get to use these strengths significantly in the work I do. But it doesn't end there. I take every opportunity to write and to write in ways I don't necessarily find easy. For example, a few years ago, I was asked to write the life story of a friend who had made a success of his life in the world of business and regional development. As I'm not a trained ghost writer, I didn't feel I could accept payment for this work so I did it in lieu of a donation to charity. The personal development benefit to me was that I got to practise my writing skills at the same time. I also write articles, sometimes on my own and sometimes with colleagues, and a couple of years ago I started to write poetry at least once a month.

Similarly with speaking, time permitting, I will happily speak just about anywhere to any audience on the subjects that I feel passionate about. This is not just in my professional capacity, but also on other subjects I care about. In addition, to take me outside my comfort zone, to a space of learning, I often review the papers in the studio of a local BBC radio station. The same is true of facilitation and coaching where I will gladly offer my services freely in situations outside my professional arena where I feel I can make a difference.

## Use

In most cases, when people have taken the time to recognize, value and develop their talents, they will naturally put them to good *use*. Furthermore, the better they become in their areas of strength, the more people notice and ask them to do more. It's a virtuous cycle of continual improvement. It is in fact a playing out of ELAS as discussed in Chapter 3 on engagement. As we *engage* our talents, we *learn* to be better at what we do. We are thereby encouraged to *apply* our talents and *sustain* the benefits by being conscientious, embedding them in our work routines and sharing our talents with others.

It really is very simple: when we know how we add value, we simply do more of the same and do it better and better.

## Making space for talent liberation

One of the biggest barriers to talent liberation (and thereby a boundary to performance) is lack of time. Other things get in the way. And the better we get at playing to our strengths, the more frustrated we will become when this happens.

The first thing is to notice when we don't have time to do the important things, such as playing to our strengths. Then we need to identify what gets in the way and do something about it. Do you remember the case study in Chapter 1 about Steve Connolly who recognized that 80 per cent of his time was spent in solving problems with his direct reports, leaving only 20 per cent for key commercial relationships and strategy (his strengths)? Note how he absolutely resolved to get more time to *use* his strengths. In fact he more than doubled the scope to do this by securing 50 per cent of his time. No wonder he significantly grew the business. Incidentally he subsequently received a number of rapid promotions to become the COO of this global business.

# Purposeful talent: a question of ignition

Daniel Coyle's *Talent Code* (2010) is one of my all-time favourite books. It provided me with numerous insights, such as the scientific explanation as to why practice makes perfect in the talent arena. In short, as we practise, we strengthen the neurones in our brains and insulate them by wrapping them with a substance called myelin to prevent energy leakage. In fact, in another of his books, Coyle is actually quoted as saying:

> Practice doesn't make perfect. Practice makes myelin, and myelin makes perfect.
>
> Daniel Coyle (2012)

But, for me, the most thought-provoking concept in Coyle's *Talent Code* is that of *talent ignition*.

Coyle makes the point that everyone has talent but not everyone becomes world-class. Something has to happen to make someone put in those 10,000 hours of practice that will make them a master at what they do. Something has to provide the spark. This is what Coyle calls *talent ignition*.

I had placed *purpose* in pivotal place in the eight conditions (the core chapters of this book) for a successful enterprise right at the start of my consultancy journey. It was always my anchor in that it made good sense that the design of a successful organization should be focused on one thing: its purpose. It wasn't until I read Coyle's narrative on talent ignition that I realized that *purpose, vision* and *success* could all be the source of talent ignition and thereby the means to *inspire performance beyond boundaries*.

All the thoughts in Chapters 1, 2 and 7 of this book (to do with *purpose, vision* and *success*) provide clues to the ignition of talent and they go hand in hand. In *Zen and the Art of Making a Living*, Laurence Boldt suggests that the way to have a successful career is to ask three questions. I gave my personal, expanded slant on these questions in the previous chapter on 'success' and below is a more succinct version:

A. What skills and other resources do you have?

B. What do you care about?

C. What's stopping you from pointing A at B?

What we care about is a spark that can ignite our talent. This may be manifest in a powerful purpose that we have bought in to, a vision of a better future, or some idea of what success means to us (whatever gets us out of bed in a morning).

Of course other things might also provide the spark to our talent. It may be an inspirational leader or role model or a team we feel part of. In which case, the *engagement* chapter in this book could give us clues.

When we know where our spark comes from, we should make sure we access it often. If it is a cause we feel strongly about, perhaps reading about the cause on a regular basis will work. Or better still, going there. This reminds me of the passion I have for Africa, and in particular for the Open Arms Infant Home in Malawi. A few years ago, I had been raising funds for Open Arms through speaking ventures. After a while, I determined I would go to Malawi and visit the home. There were two reasons for doing this. First, I wanted to see how the money I was raising was being spent. Second, I suspected that a visit to the home would strengthen my resolve to be involved. I was correct in my assumption and my visit not only strengthened my connection to Open Arms but also to the wonderful country of Malawi, rightly known as 'the warm heart of Africa'. It's a story for another time but since my visit, I started doing work there and Primeast now has an office in the Malawi capital city, Lilongwe, which principally serves the United Nations and other agencies in their efforts to support and encourage growth for and with the people of that region.

---

### Activity: What ignites your talent?

Make a note of your top four talents. Write a short description of each talent, how it adds value, how you will develop it and how you use it. Now make a note of what inspires you in all this. Maybe it's the purpose and vision of your organization. Maybe it's your idea of success or perhaps it's an individual or a team. Whatever the case, write a short statement about what ignites your talent.

## Talent constellations

In working in the field of talent for about a decade now, I have discovered something powerful about the way that talents work: there is often an important connection between our talents in the form of a flow, a loop or a constellation. Here is my personal talent constellation as applied to what I do for a living:

1 **Learning:** usually prompted by my field-work I research books and videos to discover more.

2 **Writing:** I make connections from my learning and take the time to articulate my own thinking.

3 **Coaching:** I will draw on my learning as I coach clients.

4   **Facilitating**: where the learning can benefit a group I will draw on it in group facilitation.

5   **Speaking**: having learnt something, written it down and applied it, I am keen to share my insights with others.

On the left of Figure 8.1 is my attempt at drawing this constellation, my talents and their interconnection. The connecting theme is 'learning' and there is at least a hint of ELAS, as discussed in Chapter 3.

**FIGURE 8.1**   Talent constellation

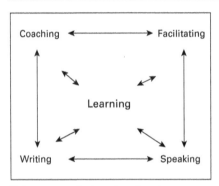

Talent constellation showing the relationships between the talents

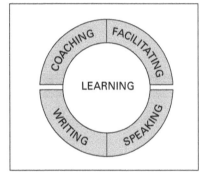

An alternative view which may better represent your talents, their interconnections and balance

On the right of Figure 8.1 however is a second drawing derived from my initial 'constellation'. Once I have understood the relationships between my various talents, I can represent it in any way that makes sense for me.

**Activity: What does your talent constellation look like?**

It may not be linear or a loop, but take a sheet of paper and draw your constellation. What does this tell you?

For me, I absolutely know that my talents have to be in some kind of balance. If I spent my time learning without doing something it would, in my view, be pointless. And without doing something, my talks and writing would be full of empty words.

# Talent alignment: creating a purposeful talent-centred culture

Getting one person to align their talent to a compelling future is amazing. Getting a whole team or organization to align their diverse talents to a compelling future, to me, is simply out of this world.

Talent alignment is always work in progress. In my experience, people can make significant progress in just a few months. And it may take years to achieve collective mastery. It is always a journey and an exciting one at that.

## Where to start with talent alignment?

In a traditional hierarchy, the best place to start would be at the top and work down. Of course, in practice, it rarely happens like that. The truth is you can start anywhere. In global corporations we often find that it will be a senior leader who, for some reason, wants to begin a talent-focused initiative. Perhaps they have heard or read something or have been comparing notes with a friend in another organization.

While it is always wise to check out what else is going on, there is rarely a problem with a leader taking the initiative to pilot their ideas in their part of the organization. But caution is advised, just in case there is a clash of a wider philosophy or strategy.

Once we know it is safe to do so, I would recommend the implementation of the following 8-step strategy. It is the same strategy I teach to HR directors on my Progressive Talent Management programmes. Below, I offer the steps in summary form and then I will discuss each one in more detail:

1 **Direction:** consider the direction of the business or part of the business – make sure you fully understand its purpose and vision as discussed in Chapters 1 and 2.

2 **Philosophy:** in the light of this direction, work out what you believe about talent that will support its delivery. I spoke more about philosophy in Chapter 5 when we discussed *character*. In particular, state whether you believe everyone has talent and what balance should be achieved between securing competence and supporting people playing to their strengths.

3 **Process:** test all the people-related processes against your new philosophy. Do they work or not? In a pilot, there may need to be compromise in the light of corporate processes.

4 **Plan:** as a result of testing existing processes against the newly affirmed philosophy, establish a plan of action that will (a) bring alignment of process; and (b) bring cultural alignment by including the remaining steps in this sequence.

5 **Communicate:** now there is a plan, it can be communicated confidently. Communicating before having a reasonable plan only causes confusion.

6 **Leadership:** the cultural change really kicks in when leaders begin to recognize, value, develop and use their own strengths and subsequently those of others.

7 **Teamwork:** the talent-centred culture goes a step further when all teams have had the opportunity to engage with a compelling and co-created future and to work out how to play to their strengths in its delivery.

8 **Review:** like all good processes, there should be review at the completion of each stage and probably on an annual basis.

For each of the above steps, I offer a bit more granularity below.

## Step 1: Direction

As discussed above, direction, especially a sense of purpose and a shared vision, is a major source of talent ignition. Also, the direction of the business will affect the philosophy greatly as well as the actual talents required to deliver it. This is another reason why Chapter 2 is so important. Without a good look ahead, how can we possibly know what is required in terms of talent?

For the architect of the purposeful organization or the talent manager, talking 'direction' with the senior leaders of the organization also shows concern for the things that matter. This is not about implementing talent management because it is fashionable. It is about doing so because it is essential for the efficient delivery of purpose. Having these conversations with leaders also warms them up to exploring philosophy which might otherwise seem like navel-gazing.

## Step 2: Philosophy

Having just engaged with the purpose and direction of the organization, it becomes inspiring to discuss thoughts on the talent that will deliver it. I am sometimes asked to interview leaders in order to support this dialogue but I may well choose to avoid words like *philosophy* which wouldn't be in the corporate lexicon.

Having just spoken about the direction of the organization, it is a natural next step to ask the leader about the implications their stated direction will have for talent. They may wish to specifically talk about new talent needs and how this might affect recruitment. They may affirm that existing people will need new skills or mastery of existing skills. They may be concerned with the loss of key people and the need to retain them or establish robust succession plans. At some point, if it doesn't arise naturally, there may need to be a prompt to find out whether the leader believes everyone has talent and the implications of this. I actually haven't yet spoken to a leader of any substance who didn't believe that everyone has talent. Similarly, in exploring the subject of competence, most leaders acknowledge the need to prevent costly mistakes but also stress how vital it is to play to strengths. Capturing these affirmations is essential.

Video-recording such interviews is priceless. Even better is getting the views of all members of the senior leadership team and editing them into a single compelling montage that will anchor the talent strategy.

## Step 3: Process

Auditing the talent processes of the organization, what they say and how they are used seems like a big task. But invariably senior leaders or people-professionals will know these at headline level and will identify where they support the philosophy and where they don't. Nevertheless, reference to the appropriate documents is worthwhile and will provide the evidence for putting together a plan. Key policies to look at will include those that make up the talent pipeline: anything to do with recruitment, appointment, induction or on-boarding, learning and development, performance appraisal and management, reward, succession, career planning etc, right through to retirement. In addition, examine anything to do with culture, equal opportunities, teamwork and communications.

## Step 4: Plan

The talent policy audit will inform what will go into the talent plan or strategy from a process perspective. However, as discussed at length in this book so far, process change will not work effectively without a corresponding and supportive shift in culture. Chapter 5 on *character* affirms that culture is a significant driver of change and that culture is greatly affected by leadership and what goes on in teams. So as well as the audit, it is worth adding the remaining Steps 5–8 of our 8-step process to attend to the required culture shift.

## Step 5: Communication

This fifth of the eight steps to a progressive talent strategy is communication. First of all, this informs people and begins to pave the way for making things happen. In most cases, company-wide communication should really only begin once the plan has been formed. Communicating too early will only create problems and unhelpful noise.

As well as communicating the plan, there needs to be regular communication regarding its delivery. In this respect, it is worth creating a communications strategy that can be added to the talent plan described in Step 4. This can be very creative. For example, if you decide to embark on a programme of leadership development and team development as suggested below, why not appoint some internal journalists to investigate what happens and to celebrate the successes of those involved. This all supports the establishment of a talent-centred culture.

## Step 6: Leadership

To me, this is the most exciting of all the steps. When leaders become engaged in recognizing, valuing, developing and using their own talents in the delivery of purpose, amazing things begin to happen. Even if no formal attention were given to team development as suggested below, I absolutely believe that every leader who understands the power of talent liberation will naturally want to apply the process immediately to their team.

However, when we initially work with leaders we ask them *not* to do this. The reason is this: if they focus on liberating other people's talents there is a real danger they will neglect their own. To become good role models and great encouragers of team talent (when the time is right) they first really need to know what it feels like and experience first-hand the benefits of playing to their own strengths.

For this reason I like to provide leaders (ideally in the context of their leadership teams) the space and opportunity to really focus on the purpose and vision of their organization. If they thoroughly understand the power of purpose as described in this book and can establish a vision that holds all stakeholder purposes in harmony and synergy, they can then begin to point their strengths in the direction of travel. Even when leaders are working as a leadership team I encourage them as individuals to consider and share the answers to the following four questions:

1  What does the future of this organization mean to me?

2  What strengths do I personally bring to its delivery?

**3** What new commitment will I make to play to my strengths for the organization?

**4** What value will this add?

---

**Activity on purposeful leadership: Playing to my strengths**

Why not take some time out to answer the above four questions right now?

---

## Step 7: Teamwork

As described above, once leaders have experienced the benefits of playing to their own strengths, they will naturally want to involve their people. Of course, this can be done in one-on-one conversations and day-to-day dialogue where people simply get into the habit of noticing strengths in others (recognize) witnessing the value they add and encouraging further development and greater use. However, when a team gets together to share the strengths they bring, have them affirmed by their team mates, and to make a concerted effort to work out how to play as a team, amazing things can happen.

In one leadership team I worked with, there were four field managers, all allegedly doing the same job but each (as might be expected) with their unique talents. One was a super organizer and driver of performance, one had a great head for processes, one was a well-respected coach and the fourth was simply a great all-rounder. The coach sticks in my mind for the fact that almost all the senior people in the organization had spent time with her. They consequently became inspired and equipped for more senior roles. These four ladies pooled their talents and shared what they had to offer across the wider group of people that worked for them.

## Step 8: Review

Talent liberation, as I like to call it, is an amazing adventure for the organization as a whole and for each person within it. while I have been encouraging clients in the 8-step strategy described in this chapter, I also know that the journey will have many twists and turns and many unexpected challenges. For this reason, it is important to stop at appropriate times to see how the strategy is working.

In review, it is worth considering all the previous seven steps systematically. The following are examples of the types of questions you might pose:

- Have we learnt something from our talent management strategy that could inform the direction of the company?
- What have we learnt about talent that might be used to update and refresh our philosophy?
- Are our processes better aligned?
- Are we progressing the plan in an appropriate manner?
- What feedback have we had from our communications strategy and what are the implications?
- How are our leaders responding to their development and are we celebrating their successes to motivate others?
- What progress has been made in our teams?

While I have every confidence that the eight steps to talent liberation described above are sensible and I've seen them working, I'm also sure there's more that could be done. In this respect, please don't see this book as a one-way process. I'd like to know what you're doing to liberate talent in your organization. So please keep in touch, especially as you review your strategy.

# Talent collaboration: talent forum

In doing my research for CIPD and to keep me connected and up to date in the world of talent, I regularly facilitate talent forums for people in the business of playing to the strengths of their people. I guess that could include you.

Our talent forums are held regionally wherever there are about a dozen or so people-professionals or leaders who want to share talent challenges. One company will host the forum and everyone will share their biggest talent challenge. One volunteer will do this in depth from the 'hot seat' and we then use action learning methods so that each member of the forum can offer their most valuable question or comment. This is facilitated in rounds until the person in the hot seat knows what action they will take and shares it with the forum. We then all share our learning and return to our day-jobs.

The point is this: in the world of talent management, there is always a challenge to share and new things to learn. If talent is important to you and your organization, I encourage open collaboration.

Now: test how talent is being made use of in your own organization.

# 10 questions on **talent**

*To what extent...*

...has your organization articulated its philosophy on talent in a manner that will support the delivery of a purposeful future?

...has this philosophy been held alongside the people policies and processes to check their alignment to it?

...has a plan been determined that will bring the processes and culture of the organization into alignment with the talent philosophy as well as the purpose of the organization?

...has this plan been communicated widely throughout the organization?

...have leaders been trained to recognize, value, develop and use their own unique talents in the delivery of the organization's objectives?

...have leaders been trained to recognize, value, develop and use the unique talents of others in the delivery of the organization's objectives?

...have teams been given the opportunity to recognize, value, develop and use the unique talents of their members in the delivery of the team objectives?

...have people throughout the organization been given the opportunity to recognize, value, develop and use their unique talents in the context of a purposeful career?

...is the culture of the organization talent-centred?

...is a thorough review of talent strategy conducted on a regular basis and at each major milestone on the talent plan?

## Score

| | |
|---|---|
| **0** not at all | **6** reasonably well |
| **2** a little | **8** very well |
| **4** moderately | **10** completely |

What do your scores tell you? Make notes on the implications and actions that spring to mind.

You can find further resources to support your thinking on this topic at **www.primeast.com/purposefulorganisation**.

# Further reading

David's final book choice on this, the eighth condition for a purposeful organization, concurs with our view that talent has to be owned by the individual and brought willingly to the organization in support of a compelling purpose and in the context of values that foster constructive and aligned working.

## *Strategic Talent Development,* Janice Caplan

This book is the latest in a large number that tackles the subject of talent. In truth, although talent is very much at its heart, I think this is really a useful guide around the topics of organizational development and the management of change. Given that, it is practical and grounded in delivery.

Like many contemporary business authors, Caplan spends some time early on contextualizing the work environment in which strategic talent development resides. The emergence from the economic downturn, the imperative of innovation and innovative thinking, the increasing speed of change and new ways of working brought about through globalization and technology: all these factors – and more – challenge us to think differently about the way we run our business operations.

The critical trend for the corporate world is, perhaps, the continuing shortage of skills in the workplace and the difficulty of finding and hiring the right people. A phenomenon first popularized in the mid 1990s remains:

the nurturing, retention and fulfilment of talent. The journey that Caplan takes us on is one from the job-for-life era to the world of selection and self-determination.

Its introduction rightly emphasizes the tenet of 'shared values, shared visions and shared understanding'. This is not only the basis of the management thinking of our age: it also provides the cornerstone for the management of talented individuals in whom the organization is encouraged to invest. The author introduces us to her model for strategic talent management, which provides the framework for the rest of the book. Starting from the individual's perspective, the model moves through from 'future focus', 'self-managed succession', 'people databank' and 'shared management' – a progression from the individual to the corporate.

The author also talks about the conditions in which talent can thrive, and this means having to identify the boundaries within which individuals need to self-manage. Thus in addition to a substantial section about values and ethics, there is a helpful discussion about the role that employee engagement plays and the need for leaders to establish the conditions in which talent can thrive via a coaching style and distributed leadership. In a chapter on organizational values, she highlights the importance of creating a 'framework for employment', wherein role-ambiguity is minimized and openness and sharing maximized – 'one aim of your talent and engagement strategy is to join up your people processes and integrate them with business strategy so that your processes transmit consistent messages and influence consistent behaviour'.

Not surprisingly, Caplan emphasizes the point that self-improvement is largely our own responsibility and that corporate resources are there to support rather than drive individual progress. HR's role is to support line management and provide the expertise to all so that resources can be given the best possible chance of adding value. A key emerging theme throughout the book is the rolling back of the old command-and-control approach to management and the emergence of distributed responsibility. Indeed there are several points in the book where the author stresses the benefits of a human-capital-based strategic planning process rather than the traditional market-driven or top-down approach to corporate planning. Another leitmotif is the need for managers to regard their people as human capital – a pool of assets – rather than simply as 'inputs'.

The middle of the book deals with learning and career management from the perspective of the employee, and Caplan launches this section with the bold statement that 'the pace of change will be so rapid that people may have to acquire a new expertise every few years if they want to be part of the lucrative market for scarce talent'. If you believe this, then a facet of management surely has to be to ensure that the workplace becomes a learning environment, where experience is valued, captured and shared. Inherent in this is the shift from a focus on an individual's role and on organizational needs, to an emphasis on the capabilities that will ensure long-term value.

Furthermore, organizations need to manage their systems, processes and data-capture mechanisms to support learning, personal development and the identification of development opportunities for individuals. Without these structures being in place, it is unlikely that resources will be appropriately organized. The later chapters deal, therefore, with the convergence of HR processes with talent management and human-asset deployment.

This is a practical, useful and valuable book that contains some well-conceived frameworks and is altogether well presented.

# A call to action

recap
milestone
REWRITING OUR DNA productivity
compassion

## A quick recap

As we arrive together at the final chapter of this book, I am trusting that you have enjoyed your journey through these pages as much as I have enjoyed writing them.

We have explored the nature of *purpose*: that it is the anchor for all we do and that performance is dependent on harmonizing and synergizing our purpose as seen from the perspectives of our stakeholders. Crafting our purpose is at the core of inspiring business performance beyond boundaries.

We have affirmed that, while purpose tells us why we're here, *vision* tells us where we're going. Our vision is in a state of flux and held in the hearts and minds of everyone on the journey.

How we *engage* with our purpose and vision is crucial to a shared and aligned direction. We have learnt that our vision identifies what is important and gives clues to the structures we should put in place for efficient delivery. It also informs the necessary character of our operation.

We discovered that organizations, their *structures*, targets and results are fractal. What we see working at one level gives clues to what might work at another. We can even learn from billions of years of evolution in nature evidenced by millions of case studies.

We've affirmed that the *character* of operation necessary to deliver our purpose and vision is unique to us. Our current character and the one we require can be conveniently measured, as can the leadership styles of those involved. Thus the art and craft of culture change can be supported by data and method.

We've distinguished between *results* and *success*, and have identified personal and team success as fertile ground for improvement, igniting the talent and ambition of our people.

Finally, we have rewritten the rule book for *talent* management, shifting from divisive processes to an inclusive talent-centred culture, complete with a clear eight-step pathway to achieving it.

# This milestone

Speaking of pathways, your route to this day and this place has been unique. It has been different from mine and yet there will inevitably be similarities associated with our shared interest in the world of work. You and I are both involved or interested in making organizations fit for the future. We now stand at a new place for the first time. We have new knowledge, thoughts and ideas. I am wondering: *what is that one thing that resonates most for you in this book?* It may seem grandiose but we cannot share ideas and learn together in this way without the world becoming a different place.

*We are change agents. What we do matters to the many more people who work in the organizations we serve.*

The people we serve care. As they progressively connect to their purpose in a myriad of different ways, the world evolves. Engineers design, build and operate the facilities that the modern age relies on. People in life sciences and biotech industries discover new treatments to extend the duration and quality of life. Financial services people keep our money systems working to energize the world we know. And a huge humanitarian industry strives to make sure no one is left hungry, poorly, abused or otherwise disadvantaged by the modern world.

There may be much criticism and judgement of the world and of the work our fellow humans do. But I wonder what would happen if, instead of pointing the finger, we encouraged everyone to make sense of their own context, connect to others, and be consequentially purposeful and account-able to all their stakeholders.

# Consciously rewriting our DNA

As we have discovered in the occasional biology lessons offered in this book, even the cells that make up our bodies are conscious of what is going on around them and will re-write their DNA in order to thrive. They are not mere slaves to the system but conscious members of a living team. How much more important, then, that we encourage people at work to be fully awake in what they do, questioning, learning and modifying their actions with the deliberate intention to be of better service.

# Compassion and productivity at work

Anyone who has been in business for any time knows that when we act we never act alone. If we are to have any lasting success in what we do, we must absolutely take account of all our stakeholders.

Aligning our purpose in tandem with the purpose of others is good business sense. It secures co-operation and avoids conflict. It is more likely to succeed. It also makes for a more harmonious and compassionate workplace. A place of less conflict is likely to be a place of more productivity.

As my career has progressed and my experience and confidence has grown, more and more I have challenged and encouraged my clients to be more purposeful and I've seen the effect this has had on their organizations. People enjoy their work more and are more productive, largely because they can see that their leaders care enough to prepare the ground for them to work without the petty conflicts that too often get in the way of high performance.

# On reflection

So finally, in the style of the body of this book, I'd like you to conduct one last activity with me before we part company:

Ponder the following questions or, better still, discuss them with people in your close circles. On this occasion, don't bother scoring your answers, just work out what they're telling you.

**1** If your organization was truly purposeful, what difference would that make to you and others who work there?

**2** What difference would being purposeful make to your stakeholder groups?

**3** If your local community was truly purposeful, what would that be like? What difference would it make to its various subsets – to young people, those who are ill, to parents and children, the elderly, those wishing to be healthier, those with problems?

**4** If your family was truly purposeful, what would that be like? What purposes would your family serve?

**5** How would a purposeful family be different – for young and old, those at home and those far away, those doing well and those struggling with life's challenges?

**6** If your nation was truly purposeful and values driven, what would that be like? Does it matter?

**7** What purposeful questions might you pose to electoral candidates on polling day?

**8** Is a purposeful world out of reach or is there something you could be doing?

**9** What key lessons have you taken from this book?

**10** So what do you need to commit to, to serve your organization better and to play your part as an architect of a purposeful world?

# Postscript: Signing off with work to do

## Will you join me?

For me, publishing this book is the culmination of a career journey of over 40 years. Many of the concepts in this book have been learnt the hard way, through managing teams in the electricity industry. More recent learning has been the result of working with clients around the world and alongside some powerful thought leaders in leadership, teamwork, culture change and talent management. I especially include here my colleagues at Primeast, all great facilitators and each with their personal specialisms and insights. I also include those outside Primeast who have written and taught us so much in their chosen fields. Many are referenced in this book and many more are not.

### *Staying connected*

Helping organizations to be more purposeful is all work-in-progress and your involvement will greatly help me and my colleagues to be of greater service.

### *Video interviews*

I'd really like to discover how your world becomes different from today. We are blessed to live in an age where engagement beyond the published word is easier than ever before. So if you'd like to continue this journey, I invite you to contact me direct as indicated below. If you're willing to participate, I could even set up a video-recorded interview with you over the internet. You can ask me any questions that this text has stimulated for you and I will ask you about how the power of purpose is playing out in your world. Then, providing we're both happy with the recording, we'll share the best of it online so others can benefit from the continued learning.

### Professional forums

I'd also like to encourage you to engage with like-minded people face to face in small groups locally. I frequently facilitate small forums of about a dozen professionals and find this to be a helpful way of understanding current challenges and solutions in the field of purposeful leadership and talent alignment. These forums are notified on the events page of the Primeast website. There's a slight chance that one will be happening in your neighbourhood but even if there isn't, don't hesitate to contact me so I can help you set one up in your part of the world.

# Affirmation

For me, writing this book has put many things into perspective. I am now even more convinced than I was when I began writing that purpose is the driving force behind all that is and all that will be. And so, getting to grips with purpose, personal and shared, is the secret to a meaningful career and meaningful life.

# A more purposeful world?

As the years have passed, I have increasingly asked the question:

> If a sense of purpose can be nurtured in each individual, alongside respect and encouragement for the purpose of others, what difference would that make to our world?

On a cautious day I might answer that it would be no bad thing. On a bolder, more confident day, I start thinking about giving the answer 'A more purposeful world, a better world, less conflict and prosperity for all'.

Purposeful people make purposeful organizations, families, communities and nations. My work and engagement with like-minds have given me a real glimpse of what a purposeful world might look and feel like. In April 2014 I was privileged to talk about my work at the second global Spirit of Humanity Forum in Reykjavik. Five of our team from Primeast attended and we joined hundreds of other change agents who shared a quest to make the world more compassionate, purposeful and values-driven. This was the most inspiring experience of my entire life.

When the *who we are* meets the *what's going on*, a feeling arises in us which is the root source of all our thought and all our action. Whether we call this feeling *a sense of purpose* or *love* is a matter of choice. Either way, we are compelled to act because we care; we are compelled to act out of compassion.

## So, what of the future?

Here at Primeast, we will continue to coach leaders and facilitate workshops where their people can nurture their strengths and align the best of who they are to a compelling purpose. We will do this because we love doing it. We also know it adds value and provides more meaningful and enjoyable work for everyone involved.

Please do keep in touch.

Clive Wilson
**clive.wilson@primeast.com**

# REFERENCES

Barrett, R (2010) *High Performance: It's all about entropy*, available on the website http://www.valuescentre.com/uploads/2011-12-14/High%20 Performance%20-%20It%27s%20all%20about%20entropy.pdf

BBC News, 6 March 2014, 'John Lewis staff get 15% annual bonus', http://www.bbc.co.uk/news/business-26462969

Benyus, JM (2002) *Biomimicry: Innovation inspired by nature*, Harper-Collins, New York

Benyus, JM (2005) 'Biomimicry's surprising lessons from nature's engineers', TED Talk, http://www.ted.com/talks/janine_benyus_shares_nature_s_designs

Black, O (2009) The Mind Gym Philosophy on Talent, interview with Clive Wilson, https://www.youtube.com/watch?v=PTCnVzhJWGw

Boldt, LG (1999) *Zen and the Art of Making a Living: A practical guide to creative career design*, Penguin Arkana, USA

Boudreau, JW and Jesuthasan, R (2011) *Transformative HR*, Jossey-Bass, San Francisco, CA

Boudreau, JW and Ranstad, PM (2007) *Beyond HR: The new science of human capital*, Harvard Business School Press, Boston, MA

Brown, MG (2007) *Beyond the Balanced Scorecard: Improving business intelligence with analytics*, Productivity Press, London

Buckingham, M and Coffman, C (1999) *First, Break all the Rules: What the world's greatest managers do differently*, Simon & Shuster, London

Campbell, J (2003) *The Hero's Journey: Joseph Campbell on his life and work*, New World Library, New York

Caplan, J (2013) *Strategic Talent Development: Develop and engage all your people for business success*, Kogan Page, London

Chartered Institute of Personnel and Development (CIPD) (2010) *Shared Purpose: The golden thread?* available from www.cipd.co.uk/hr-resources/survey-reports/ shared-purpose-golden-thread.aspx

Clywd, A and Hart, T (2013) *A Review of the NHS Hospitals Complaints System: Putting patients back in the picture – Final Report*, available from https://www.gov.uk/government/uploads/system/uploads/attachment_data/ file/255615/NHS_complaints_accessible.pdf

Collins, JC (2001) *Good to Great*, Random House, London

Collins, JC (2005) *Built to Last: Successful habits of visionary companies*, Random House, London

Collinson, S and Jay, M (2012) *From Complexity to Simplicity: Unleash your organisation's potential*, Palgrave MacMillan, Basingstoke

Convince and Convert (2013) 'Nike celebrates Instagram milestones by thanking its community', available from http://www.convinceandconvert.com/social-media-case-studies/nike-celebrates-instagram-milestones-by-thanking-its-community/

Cooke, RA and Lafferty, JC (1987) *Organizational Culture Inventory*, Human Synergistics International, Plymouth, MI

Coyle, D (2010) *Talent Code: Greatness isn't born. It's grown*, Arrow Books, London

Coyle, D (2012) *The Little Book of Talent: 52 tips for improving skill*, Random House, London

Digital Insights, http://blog.digitalinsights.in/category/campaigns

Dotlich, DL, Cairo, PC and Rhinesmith, S (2006) *Head, Heart and Guts: How the world's best companies develop complete leaders*, Jossey-Bass, San Francisco, CA

*The Economist* (17 January 2002) 'The twister hits: Nothing about Enron's demise was surprising; nor is what must be done', available from www.economist.com/node/941205

Faust, G (2012) 'Life Cycle of Organizations', available from http://youtu.be/GMEsAO9V8xs

Foretel Group (2009) *Introduction to Culture*, white paper, www.peopleandculture.co.uk

Gallup Consulting (2007) *Employee Engagement: What's your engagement ratio?* www.gallup.com/file/strategicconsulting/121535/Employee_Engagement_Overview_Brochure.pdf

Gladwell, M (2009) *Outliers: The story of success*, Penguin, London

Goleman, D (2000) Leadership that gets results, *Harvard Business Review*, March–April 2000, pp78–90, or available from www.haygroup.com/downloads/fi/leadership_that_gets_results.pdf

Google, https://www.google.co.uk/intl/en/about/company/philosophy/

Greenleaf, RK (2002) *Servant Leadership: A journey into the nature of legitimate power and greatness*, Paulist Press, Mahwah, NJ

Grundling, E (2003) *Working GlobeSmart: Twelve people skills for doing business across borders*, Aperian Global, Nicholas Brealey, Boston, MA

Grundling, E, Hogan,T, Cvitkovich, K with Aperian Global (2011) *What is Global Leadership?: 10 key behaviors of great global leaders*, Nicholas Brealey, Boston, MA

Gupta, A and Anish, S, Insights from Complexity Theory: Understanding organizations better, *Tejaz@iimb*, Indian Institute of Management, Bangalore (retrieved 1 June 2012 via Wikipedia)

Human Synergistics, www.humansynergistics.com/uk

Jobs, S (2010) Video recordings from All Things Digital conferences (D5/D8), http://allthingsd.com/20111005/steve-jobs-appearances-at-d-the-full-sessions/

John Lewis Partnership, 'Our principles', available from www.johnlewispartnership.co.uk/about/our-principles.html

Kaplan, RS and Norton, DP (1996) *The Balanced Scorecard*, Harvard Business School Press, Boston MA

Kaplan, RS and Norton, DP (2001) *The Strategy Focussed Organization*, Harvard Business School Press, Boston, MA

Kiyosaki, RT and Lechter, SL (2000) *Rich Dad, Poor Dad: What the rich teach their kids about money – that the poor and middle class do not!* 1st edn, Business Plus, New York

Kolb, DA (1983) *Experiential Learning as the Source of Learning and Development*, Financial Times/Prentice Hall

Kotter, KP and Heskett, JL (1992) *Corporate Culture and Performance*, Free Press, New York

Lewis, M (2004) *Moneyball: The art of winning an unfair game*, Norton, New York

Lipton, BH (2005a) *The Biology of Belief: Unleashing the power of consciousness, matter and miracles*, Hay House, London

Lipton, BH (2005b) *The Wisdom of Your Cells: How your cells control your biology*, audio book, Sounds True Inc, Louisville, CO

Lipton, BH and Bhaerman, S (2011) *Spontaneous Evolution: Our positive future and a way to get there from here*, Hay House, London

Macleod, D and Clarke, N (2012) *Engaging for success: Enhancing performance through employee engagement*, Department for Business, Innovation and Skills, www.engageforsuccess.org/wp-content/uploads/2012/09/file52215.pdf

Mandelbrot, BB (1982) *The Fractal Geometry of Nature*, Freeman, New York

Marquet, LD (2013) *Turn the Ship Around! A true story of building leaders by breaking the rules*, Portfolio-Penguin, New York

Meyer, MW (2003) *Rethinking Performance Measurement: Beyond the balanced scorecard*, 1st edition, Cambridge University Press

Michaels, E, Handfield-Jones, H and Axelrod, B (2001) *War for Talent*, Harvard Business School Press, Boston, MA

Moss, B (2013) 'How to juggle three balls', video available at https://www.youtube.com/watch?v=_xye0tHas_s

Nonaka, I and Takeuchi, H (1995) *The Knowledge-creating Company: How Japanese companies create the dynamics of innovation*, Oxford University Press, USA

Oxford Dictionaries Online, www.oxforddictionaries.com

Pink, D (2010) 'Drive: The surprising truth about what motivates us', Royal Society for the Encouragement of Arts, Manufactures and Commerce, RSA Animate video, http://www.thersa.org/events/video/archive/dan-pink-drive

Simpson, J (1998) *Touching the Void*, Vintage, London

Sinek, S (2009) 'Start with why', TED Talks, http://www.ted.com/talks/simon_sinek_how_great_leaders_inspire_action

Smith, J (2013) America's most inspiring companies, *Forbes*, www.forbes.com/sites/jacquelynsmith/2013/10/01/americas-most-inspiring-companies-2013/

Sung, J and Ashton, D (n.d.) *High Performance Work Practices: Linking strategy and skills to performance outcome*, DTI/CIPD, available from tinyurl.com/nfe56ah

Wagner, R (2007) *12: The Elements of Great Managing*, 1st edn, Gallup Press, New York

Whole Foods Market, 'Our core values', www.wholefoodsmarket.com/mission-values/core-values

Wick, CW, Pollock, RVH and Jefferson, A (2010) *The Six Disciplines of Breakthrough Learning*, Wiley, Chichester

Williams, A and Whybrow, A (2013) *The 31 Practices: Release the power of your organization's VALUES every day*, LID Publishing, London

Wooden, J and Carty, J (2010) *Coach Wooden's Pyramid of Success*, Regal Books, Ventura, CA

Woods, M and Coomber, S (2013) *Beyond the Call: Why some of your team go the extra mile and others don't show*, Wiley, Chichester

# INDEX